For Valour

JOHN PERCIVAL

For Valour
The Victoria Cross:
Courage in Action

Thames Methuen
London

First published in Great Britain 1985
by Methuen London Ltd
11 New Fetter Lane, London EC4P 4EE
in association with
Thames Television International Ltd
149 Tottenham Court Road, London W1P 9LL
Copyright © 1985 John Percival

Filmset, printed and bound in Great Britain by
Hazell Watson & Viney Limited,
Member of the BPCC Group,
Aylesbury, Bucks

British Library Cataloguing in Publication Data

Percival, John
  For valour: the Victoria Cross in action.
  1. Victoria Cross—History
  I. Title
  355.1'342   CR4885
  ISBN 0-423-01690-3

Contents

List of Illustrations

Acknowledgements

Although it delves rather more deeply into some aspects of the history of the Victoria Cross and the motivations of some of the men who have won it, this book of course has its origins in the Thames Television series 'For Valour'. All television productions are the result of teamwork, and the team which put together the programmes were also, in a sense, the progenitors of the book. I would like to thank in particular Catherine Freeman, Controller of Documentaries and Features at Thames Television, for sustained faith in the project from the beginning; Roy English, the departmental manager, for patient support; Michele Dillon, who put such wit and vitality into the research; Edna Ewing, who kept the whole train on the rails; Adrian Wood, the mole of the film vaults; Miriam Cooper, who explored forgotten archives, Brian Mongini the film editor; Frank Haysom, film cameraman; and many, many others.

I am deeply indebted to the Victoria Cross and George Cross Association, their Chairman, Rear-Admiral Godfrey Place VC, CB, DSC, their energetic secretary, Didy Grahame, as well as all the members who so kindly gave me their time and co-operation. I am also grateful to the military historian, John Keegan, for his advice and assistance; to Miss Rose Coombs, for her enthusiastic support; to Mr Ron Biddle and many other kindly informants, including the authors of the various books listed in the bibliography.

Lastly I would like to place on record my thanks to Mr Kanwal Sundar Singh, whose chance remark in a London art gallery set me off in pursuit of the story of the Victoria Cross, and to my wife Lalage for putting up with my not being there for so long.

Introduction

'Courage is a quality so necessary to virtue,' said Dr Johnson, 'that we admire it even when it is associated with vice'. We may know that war is hideous and we may believe that some of those who fight bravely are evil or misguided, but we still admire courage. We admire it because we know that courage helps all of us to cope with the everyday troubles of existence, from the terrors of childhood to the inescapable fact of our own deaths. But if for any reason war becomes inevitable, courage is not just desirable, it is essential. Without courage whole armies disintegrate and flee in confusion, and lonely men die an ugly death for want of anyone brave enough to rescue them. Without courage there is no power on earth to deter an aggressor, nothing to oppose the principle that might is right.

Anyone who has even been close to the shock of battle knows that it provokes extreme reactions in people, ranging from the most abject cowardice to the utmost heroism. Every army that has ever existed has found it expedient to reward the one and punish the other. The principle of awards for courage is therefore very ancient, but the Victoria Cross is unique. It is the supreme award for valour, and no other nation has an exact equivalent to it. It is a decoration without classes or degrees, equally available to all ranks, which is awarded only for individual acts of courage 'in the presence of the enemy'.

If no woman has yet won a VC it may be because the male monopoly has so far kept women out of the British line of battle, except as occasional victims. Awards of the George Cross, the equivalent decoration for acts of courage outside the immediate field of conflict, certainly demonstrate for anyone who is in any doubt on the matter that women are at least as brave, if not braver, than men. No doubt the first female VC is only a matter of time, but up till now the history

Introduction

of the award has been the history of brave men and brave deeds.

In this book I have traced the evolution of the Cross from its inception in 1856 to the most recent award in 1982, from the Crimea to the Falklands. Where it has been possible to find first-hand evidence I have also tried to explore the nature of courage, and to ask what it is that prompts a man to acts of extreme heroism. Are brave men deficient in imagination or common sense? Are some quite unpromising individuals galvanised into bouts of gallantry by anger, by fear, or even by the lust for glory? Or is there still room for the notion of courage as altruism, as a quality which enables one individual to triumph over his own fear and risk his life for others? And if such a quality does exist does it manifest itself in other moments of a man's life, is it forecast in his childhood and evident in his later career?

These are difficult questions and there are no easy answers. A comprehensive examination of all of them would require a monumental tome of enormous proportions. It has only been possible here to tell the stories of just a few of the 1,351 men who have won the Victoria Cross, but all of those stories are in their own way remarkable, and all of them help to explain why we find it necessary to preserve an award for courage in battle or, as the legend on the cross itself has it, For Valour.

JOHN PERCIVAL
March 1985

Part I
The Origins of the Victoria Cross

1
A Little Bit of Ribbon

On 16 August 1940 Flight-Lieutenant James Nicolson took off from the RAF Station at Boscombe down in Wiltshire into a cloudless sky in a Hawker Hurricane fighter of 249 Squadron, with two other planes in his formation. The Germans were at the height of their great air offensive against Britain and the Luftwaffe were determined to bring the RAF into battle or to bomb them out of existence on the ground. The war in the air had already been costly for both sides, but British morale remained high and, despite the fact that he had never been in combat before, Flight-Lieutenant Nicolson was determined to seek out and attack any enemy aircraft he could find. Close to Southampton the Hurricanes spotted a group of JU88 bombers and prepared to go into the attack but, very much to their disappointment, a flight of Spitfires got there before them. Action when it did come was completely unexpected. The first thing that Nicolson knew about it was the tearing explosion of a salvo of cannon shells, one of which set his spare fuel tank on fire while others tore into the cockpit, wounding him in the foot and sending a jagged splinter of perspex through his left eyelid. A group of marauding Messerschmitt 109s had jumped the Hurricanes from above, and the other two British fighters were already on their way down. Badly hurt, almost unable to see because of the wound in his eyelid, and with his aircraft in flames, Nicolson felt he had no option but to bale out. But as he began to unstrap himself from the seat he spotted another German fighter, an ME110, right in his flight path. Enraged by what had happened to him and to his comrades Nicolson decided to ignore his own desperate predicament and attack the enemy plane.

The German fighter saw the danger and went into a dive, but the blazing Hurricane came screaming after him. The

3

flames from the fuel tank turned the cockpit into a furnace as Nicolson opened up with his machine-guns. He glanced down at his hands on the joystick and saw the skin peeling off them like blistered paintwork, but he kept firing until at last he saw smoke burst from the enemy plane and one wing started to droop as it plunged earthward.

Almost too late he fought his way out of his seat harness and struggled out of the cockpit. Miraculously his parachute opened. Another Messerschmitt zoomed into the attack and Nicolson feigned death to avoid being shot up, then had to come alive with a start when he realised that he was drifting out to sea. As he swung on the cords to correct the drift he found himself veering towards a string of high-tension cables, and the whole situation, as it so often does in warfare, turned to black comedy. A local defence volunteer, zealous in the pursuit of duty, fired off both barrels of his shotgun at what he bravely imagined to be a German parachutist and hit the unfortunate flight-lieutenant in the behind. A group of bystanders rushed towards the spot where he had fallen, pausing only to beat up the owner of the shotgun, and both men were carted off to hospital in the same ambulance. He was not to know it, but Nicolson had just won the only Victoria Cross to be awarded to a fighter pilot throughout the whole of World War Two.

For some days the young pilot's life was in danger but youth and good surgery were on his side. A few months later, while convalescing at the Palace Hotel, Torquay, Nicolson heard the news that he had been awarded the Victoria Cross. Like most of those who win the VC he was incredulous to start with, but when an official telegram confirmed the fact he is said to have turned to the man in the next bed and announced, 'Now I have to earn it.' As soon as his burns were sufficiently healed he insisted on going back to operational flying. Eventually, in command of a squadron of Mosquito fighter bombers in Burma, he was able to add to his reputation by winning a DFC. And although his hands never completely healed and he was offered one enviable staff job after another, he continued to seek every opportunity to get back into aerial combat. In May 1945, having wangled himself on board a Liberator bomber as

4

an unofficial observer, he was killed when the plane inexplic-
ably burst into flames and crashed into the sea.

One might have expected that his proud native land would
be anxious to express its gratitude by making proper provision
for his young widow and orphaned child. But that is not the
British way of doing things. Medals are one thing; pensions
quite another. Muriel Nicolson was left with a Victoria Cross
but no proper means of support, and she struggled for years to
bring up her son on her own. His clothes were provided by the
RAF Benevolent Fund; his school fees were paid by a free
bursary. Embittered by her own poverty and by the penury of
other war widows who found themselves in the same situation,
Mrs Nicolson eventually decided to sell the Cross. No one
should blame her for that decision, but it is ironical that an
award invested with so much idealism and so little in the way
of material benefit should in the end be worth so much money.

Flight-Lieutenant Nicolson's Victoria Cross was sold on 28
April 1983 at a London auction house for the record price of
£110,000. The medal itself is intrinsically almost worthless: a
small bronze cross, a little over three ounces in weight, cast in
a rather solid Victorian style with no pretensions to elegance.
What makes it valuable is not the cost of the materials, nor the
undoubted skill of the manufacturer, nor the beauty of the
object itself – which is questionable to say the least. The value
is in its rarity. The Victoria Cross is rare because the qualities
needed to win it are rare, because the occasions on which it
can be won are mercifully few and because it is awarded only
after the most searching enquiry into the circumstances of the
action for which it has been recommended. This particular
Cross, as the only Battle of Britain VC, is unique.

The RAF Fighter Command Museum at Hendon understandably wanted to acquire it, but there were also others at
the auction who very much wanted to buy the Cross – perhaps
out of a cynical awareness that its value can only appreciate,
or perhaps because there will always be people who wish to
associate themselves, in however small a way, with an object
which, more than all others, symbolises courage.

The Victoria Cross was born in the carnage of the Crimean
War, even though hostilities had ceased a good twelve months

The Origins of the Victoria Cross

before the first award was made. Britain and France went to war with Russia in the spring of 1854 because they feared that the Czar had designs on Turkey, using a crusade to recover the shrines of the Holy Land as an excuse for imperial expansion. The Allied Forces chose the Crimean Peninsula as their target because the great fortress at Sebastopol was a convenient jumping-off point for a Russian attack on Turkey. It was also handy for landing troops with the help of the Royal Navy, but the British were not really prepared for war. Between the ending of the Napoleonic Wars in 1815 and the beginning of the Crimean Campaign there was a period of thirty-nine years during which the Royal Navy rather neglectfully ruled the waves and the British Army was confined more or less to ceremonial duties. Officers bought their commissions and bought their promotion. Military proficiency had little to do with the matter and, for the most part, senior officers were ill-equipped for battle. Ordinary servicemen, whether in the navy or the army, were subject to the discipline of Chief Petty Officers or senior NCOs who were necessarily much more professional than their superiors. So even if officers blundered, the ordinary soldier or seaman might still acquit himself well.

The Crimean Campaign was the first war to be covered by regular correspondents, especially by reporters as perceptive and critical as William Howard Russell of *The Times*. Under his scrutiny the errors of officers, their prejudices and rigid attitudes, did not go unnoticed. He reported the disgraceful shortages of proper clothing and equipment, the ravages of cholera and typhoid fever, which caused the deaths of 20,000 men against the 3,400 killed in battle during the war. He also reported for the first time the courage and endurance of the ordinary British soldier. When the infantry stormed the heights above the Alma River, when the 93rd formed the 'thin red line' at Balaklava, when the Heavy Brigade charged the Russian cavalry and the Light Brigade the guns, Russell watched and reported what he saw to the British public.

At the time, the most esteemed award for military prowess in the British Army was the Order of the Bath, but the Bath was awarded only to senior officers. Junior officers and even NCOs might win promotion in the field – or 'brevet rank', as this kind of promotion was called. It was also possible to win

6

distinction by being mentioned in the general's dispatches, but at the outset of the war most of these honours were given to staff officers immediately under the general's eye and very rarely to the officers actually engaged in front-line action. The common soldier might expect a campaign medal, but this would be issued to every man who took part in the war, whether he had fought bravely or not. To remedy this situation the Distinguished Conduct Medal was instituted for NCOs and privates in 1854. This medal carried a pension and was highly valued, but there was a growing awareness of the need for a decoration which would be open to all, regardless of rank, and which would more fairly reflect the individual gallantry of men in the front line.

The British sense of fair play and a genuine admiration for gallant behaviour certainly played a part in the decision to institute a new award, but there may also have been an element of cynicism. Medals are a potent incentive to courage in battle, but they are also cheap.

The French, our allies in the Crimea, already had the *Légion d'Honneur* (first instituted by that supreme cynic Napoleon in 1803) and the *Médaille Militaire*. The Russians and the Austrians also had awards for gallantry regardless of rank, and it was high time that the British followed suit. In December 1854 an ex-naval officer turned Liberal MP, Captain Thomas Scobell, put a motion before the House of Commons that an 'Order of Merit' should be awarded to 'persons serving in the army or navy for distinguished and prominent personal gallantry . . . and to which every grade and individual from the highest to the lowest . . . may be admissable'.

The same idea had also occurred to the Secretary of State for War, the Duke of Newcastle. In January 1855 he wrote to the Prince Consort, reminding him of an earlier conversation. The Duke suggested 'a new decoration open to all ranks'. 'It does not seem to me right or politic,' he wrote, 'that such deeds of heroism as the war has produced should go unrewarded by any distinctive mark of honour because they are done by privates or officers below the rank of major. . . . The value attached by soldiers to a little bit of ribbon is such as to render any danger insignificant and any privation light if it can be attained.' On 29 January the Duke followed up his

The Origins of the Victoria Cross

letter by announcing the new award in a speech in the House of Lords. At about the same time an official memorandum on the subject was circulated within the War Office setting out the details of a cross to be awarded for 'a signal act of valour in the presence of the enemy'.

Events might have progressed quite quickly if Newcastle had not lost his job within a few days of this speech. But interest had been aroused. Lord Panmure, the new Secretary of State for War, corresponded with Prince Albert on the subject and the Queen herself was actively involved in the proposals. In a letter to Panmure Albert made pencil alterations to the draft warrant, which arose from his discussions with the Queen. It had already been decided that the award should carry her name, but the Civil Service's proposal was clumsy and long-winded: 'the Military Order of Victoria'. Albert put his pencil through this and suggested 'the Victoria Cross'. Throughout the document, wherever the word 'Order' with its overtones of aristocratic fraternity occurred, Albert applied his pencil. 'Treat it as a cross granted for distinguished service,' he noted, 'which will make it simple and intelligible.'

The most radical proposal put forward by the Prince Consort, however, is in some ways the most attractive feature of the award, even if it is now so rarely evoked. Where a body of men were involved in an action of great courage with no one man standing out from his fellows, the Prince proposed that a 'jury' of those involved should select representatives by ballot amongst themselves. From the first, the Victoria Cross was more democratic than any other British medal for courage in battle.

Queen Victoria took a great interest in her new award. When Panmure made it clear that he intended to publish the names of recipients in the *London Gazette* and then place them before the Commons, the Queen wrote rather frostily that 'to make such a report to Parliament by laying it on the table of the House would look like an appeal to its decision in the matter which clearly belongs solely and entirely to the discretion of the Crown'. And so it has remained, nominally at least, to this day.

The Queen also took a lively interest in the design of the Cross. When the first drawings were submitted to her, she

8

selected one closely modelled on an existing campaign medal, the Army Gold Cross from the Peninsular War. Even now, experts on heraldry still argue the toss about whether this design is a Cross Paty or a Cross Formy (it is described in the warrant as a Maltese Cross, which it plainly is not). Unaware of this heraldic nit-picking, the Queen suggested only that it should be 'a little smaller'. She also made a significant alteration to the motto, striking out 'for the brave' and substituting 'for valour', in case anyone should come to the conclusion that the only brave men in a battle were those who won the Cross.

Lord Panmure took the commission for the new medal to a firm of jewellers, Hancock's of Bruton Street, who had a high reputation for silver work. From the beginning, however, it had been decided that the new decoration would be made of base metal and the first proof which the Queen received was not at all to her taste.

> The Cross looks very well in form, but the metal is ugly; it is copper and not bronze and will look very heavy on a red coat with the Crimean Ribbon. Bronze is, properly speaking, gun-metal; this has a rich colour and is very hard; copper would wear very ill and would soon look like an old penny. Lord Panmure should have one prepared in real bronze and the Queen is inclined to think that it ought to have a greenish varnish to protect it; the raised parts would then burnish up bright and show the design and inscription.

Inspired perhaps by the Queen's remarks, someone had the happy thought that it would be fitting to take the bronze for the new medals from Russian guns captured in the Crimea. Accordingly, an engineer went off to Woolwich Barracks, where two 18-pounders were placed at his disposal, but rather than destroy the guns entirely it was decided to saw off the cascabels (the knobs on the breech end of the cannon) which would originally have served to secure restraining ropes during firing. The cascabels were duly sawn off and Hancock's produced the first batch of medals from the Crimea guns. Despite the fact that these guns were clearly of antique design and inscribed with very un-Russian characters, nobody pointed out until many years had passed that the 'VC guns'

9

were in fact Chinese, not Russian, and may or may not have been anywhere near the Crimea. After all, one foreigner is very much like another and both the Russians and the Chinese had recently been enemies of the Queen.

The Chinese gunmetal proved so hard that the dies which Hancock's used began to crack up, so it was decided to cast the medals instead, a lucky chance which resulted in higher relief and more depth in the moulding than would have been possible with a die-stamped medal. By the spring of 1856 the Order was in hand, but there followed months of dilly-dallying on the part of Panmure and the various departments concerned, while they sorted out who would be eligible for the new award. Boards of adjudication were set up by the Admiralty and the army, but they took a long time making up their minds. Some commanding officers seized upon the opportunity to bring distinction to their regiments by putting dozens of names forward to the selection boards. Others ignored the whole thing. So while the 77th Regiment put forward no fewer than thirty-eight candidates, six regiments offered none at all. Quite a few men recommended themselves, including a French naval captain and a veteran of the Peninsula War of forty years before, but Panmure declared foreigners to be ineligible and insisted that awards should be limited to the present hostilities, the Crimean Campaign. A rather parsimonious pension of £10 a year to each recipient was finally agreed upon, and the slow process of adjudication ground on for a full twelve months.

Some of those whose claims were eventually recognised were undoubtedly amongst the bravest of the brave. Others performed deeds which, if they had occurred in the First World War for instance, would hardly have rated a mention in dispatches. The first act of courage to be judged fit for the Victoria Cross was an incident on board HMS *Hecla* during the bombardment of the forts at Bomarsund in the Baltic on 21 June 1854. As the *Hecla* closed on the forts a live shell from a shore battery landed on the deck of the ship, close to a group of seamen. The young mate, a twenty-year-old Irishman named Charles Lucas, picked the shell up in his bare hands and hurled it overboard where it immediately exploded with a tremendous roar. Lucas's action saved the lives of many men. It took great coolness and presence of mind, but it is difficult to resist the feeling that he may have been saving his own skin as well as the lives of his comrades and that the action may have been prompted by the simple desire to put as much distance as possible between himself and the shell.

Consider instead the action of the regimental butcher of the 17th Lancers at Balaklava. The butcher's job was firmly behind the lines, but when the Lancers were called forward for their catastrophic charge on the Russian guns, he deserted his butcher's block, grabbed a horse and a sabre, lit up his pipe and rode with the Light Brigade. Because of a classic piece of bungling by the commander-in-chief Lord Raglan, coupled with the tetchy pride of Lord Cardigan (the brigade commander) over six hundred men from four cavalry regiments were led into a headlong charge up a narrow valley, lined on both sides by Russian guns with the main batteries straight ahead of them. The butcher was seen in the forefront of the charge, then in the thick of the fighting at the Russian battery, cutting right and left among the gunners. Eye-witnesses reported that he killed six men with his sabre at the guns and then fought his way back when the brigade withdrew, hewing down every Russian who tried to bar his way, returning to his own lines without a scratch on him and with his pipe still alight. No one put him forward for an award. History does not even record his name. (The prudent mate Lucas, on the other hand, was immediately promoted to lieutenant and later rose to the rank of rear-admiral.)

Perhaps quite rightly, blood-thirsty zeal in action did not automatically qualify men for the Victoria Cross. Awards have often gone to men like Troop Sergeant-Major Berryman, also of the 17th Lancers, who displayed great heroism by rescuing his commanding officer, Captain Webb, and carrying him back through the nightmare of shot and shell to a place of safety. British officers were always properly appreciative of the brave men who risked their own lives to rescue others, perhaps the more so if the wounded men happened to be officers.

Also highly esteemed were those who rallied a small party of men against overwhelming numbers of the enemy. The British and French were almost always heavily outnumbered in the Crimea and relied for their effectiveness partly on

The Origins of the Victoria Cross

superior discipline and higher morale. When several hundred Russians attacked a shore battery manned by a handful of Royal Navy gunners, the twenty-year-old officer in charge, Lieutenant Hewitt, refused to retire and abandon his gun when ordered to do so. 'Damned if I will', he is reported to have said. 'Fire!' With the enemy only a hundred yards away he urged his Blue Jackets to man-handle the huge 68-pounder into a position where its fire could be brought to bear. As the Russians closed in for the kill the great gun blasted them with shrapnel at point-blank range. Under heavy fire from Minié rifles, the most accurate weapons available to either side, Hewitt put his own shoulder to the cannon to help lay it again and kept firing and re-laying the gun until the enemy were forced to withdraw. Coolness in command, courage in rallying his men and keeping them at their posts, coupled with resolute action – these were the qualities which won him the Cross.

Like Lucas, Hewitt also rose high in the service, later becoming an exceptionally irascible and difficult rear-admiral. However, as a young man, he was one of the heroes who made a particular impression on Queen Victoria when the list for the first investiture was at last presented to her. The only name which she herself struck from the register was that of Private M'Gwire of the 33rd Regiment. This man had been on forward sentry duty in the British lines when two Russians stole up on him, took him prisoner and started to march him back towards their own trenches. As they picked their way over the rocky, shell-torn ground, the man covering M'Gwire was momentarily off his guard. The British soldier seized the Russian's own musket and shot him with it, then beat his companion's brains out with the butt end. The struggle took place close to the Russian positions and some of the forward enemy sentries saw what was happening and opened fire. But M'Gwire calmly relieved the dead Russians of their weapons and equipment (and very possibly went through their pockets as well) before returning to his own lines in triumph. The French promptly awarded him the *Médaille Militaire* and Lord Raglan, the British Commander-in-Chief, also thought highly of the action, but Queen Victoria was more thoughtful. If such conduct, she reasoned, were regarded by the Sovereign as praiseworthy, it 'may lead to the cruel and inhumane practice

12

of never taking prisoners, but always putting to death those who may be overpowered for fear of their rising on their captors'.

The Queen also made it plain to Lord Panmure that she herself wished to bestow her new award on as many of the recipients as possible. But the royal engagement book being somewhat full, and the Queen herself perhaps just a little forgetful, the Secretary of State had to drop a tactful reminder to Her Majesty. On 12 June 1857 the Queen replied that 26 June would be a suitable day, that a grand parade should be laid on in Hyde Park and that she would herself 'attend on horseback'.

Preparations for the great day had therefore to be made in something of a hurry. The final list of recipients was not published in the *London Gazette* until 22 June, and Hancock's had to work around the clock to engrave the names of the recipients on the Crosses. Those destined to receive the award had somehow to be found and rushed up to London, together with detachments of the units in which they had served. It says something for Victorian organisation that despite all the delays in the two years since the idea of the VC was first mooted, the parade itself was laid on in just under two weeks. Most modern administrations might be pressed to organise a parish fête in the same time. But because of the earlier delays some of the candidates for the Cross had left the services and were therefore not in uniform when they arrived for the ceremony. Nevertheless, the Queen herself was well satisfied with the arrangements. She wrote in her diary:

> The whole was conducted in full state. Several interesting circumstances combined to make this day an important one. It was in the first place the solemn inauguration of the new and honourable order of valour – also the day of Albert's new title becoming known and the first time I had ever ridden on horseback at a great review in London. . . . It was a beautiful sight and everything admirably arranged. . . . The road all along was kept clear and there was no pushing or squeezing. Constant cheering and noises of every kind, but the horses went beautifully. . . . I remained on horseback fastening the medals or rather Crosses on the recipients. . . .

Queen Victoria caused some consternation by electing to

The Origins of the Victoria Cross

stay on horseback throughout the ceremony, because a little table had been set up on a dais ready for the awards, but the sixty-two recipients proved equal to the occasion and so did Her Majesty. There is a pleasing legend that the Queen, leaning forward from the saddle like a Cossack with a lance, stabbed one of the heroes, Commander Raby, through the chest. The commander, true to the spirit in which he had won the Cross, stood unflinching while his Sovereign fastened the pin through his flesh. The other sixty-one seem to have come through the occasion uninjured. The Queen managed to pin on the whole batch in just ten minutes, which does not suggest lengthy conversations, but the whole parade went off extremely well to the rapturous applause of the public. The only sour note was struck by the correspondent for *The Times*, the same newspaper which had done so much to bring the award about.

> The greatest anxiety was manifested on the part of the people to see the Cross of Valour men as they dispersed and left the ground; and the course of almost each could be traced by the little group that followed him, anxious to get a glimpse of the Cross, with which all found more or less fault than the first. Than the Cross of Valour nothing could be more plain and homely, not to say coarse-looking. It is a very small Maltese Cross, formed from the gun metal or ordnance captured at Sebastopol. In the centre is a small crown and lion, with which latter's natural proportions of mane and tail and cutting of the cross much interferes. Below these is a small scroll (which shortens three arms of the cross and is utterly out of keeping with the upper portions) bearing the words 'For Valour'. . . . But even with all the care and skill which distinguishes Mr Hancock, the whole cross is, after all, poor-looking and mean in the extreme.

The malice of *The Times* was partly prompted by the belief, for which there is no evidence, that Prince Albert had taken a hand in the design of the Cross. The industrious German Prince never won the approval of the British upper classes and had been ridiculed a few years previously for having designed a new military hat for one of the British regiments, a matter which was felt to be beyond his competence. Where Albert's influence was of course clearly expressed was in the terms of the Royal Warrant for the Cross which has survived, with

14

some alterations, to the present day. The phraseology of the Warrant may have been legalistic and a little archaic, but the meaning was plain enough. It was a medal awarded 'to those officers or men who have served Us in the presence of the Enemy and shall then have performed some signal act of valour or devotion to their country'. Far from striking the public as something with which to 'find fault', the new award was greeted with great enthusiasm by the British people and increased steadily in popular esteem as the century progressed and the colonial wars of the Empire produced more heroes to wear it.

2
The Indian Mutiny

In May 1857, a few weeks before the first investiture of the Victoria Cross, a great spontaneous uprising swept across Northern India. Because it began among Indian soldiers serving under British command this major war has always been known, in the so-called 'mother country', as the Indian Mutiny. To the Indians it is known today, not without justification, as the First War of Independence, but to most Europeans at the time it looked like a savage and treacherous insurrection. From the strictly military point of view this is what it was. Indian sepoys turned on their officers, killing large numbers of them with their wives and children, and then went on to fight pitched battles against the troops of their imperial masters. British regiments were only thinly scattered over the sub-continent and if some native units had not stayed loyal to their British officers it is doubtful if the Mutiny could have been contained. Even so the war was remorseless and bloody, with massacres of hideous brutality on both sides and, equally on both sides, instances of great courage and endurance.

In retrospect it seems that the British officers in command were quite extraordinarily complacent when serious disturbances and acts of indiscipline began to appear in the ranks of Indian soldiers serving in Bengal. When much more serious trouble erupted at Meerut, a garrison town close to the great city of Delhi, it took the authorities completely by surprise. The Mutiny at Meerut broke out on a Sunday evening. On the previous day eighty-five sowars, or troopers, of the 3rd Native Light Cavalry had been punished for indiscipline, paraded before the garrison, stripped of their uniforms and placed in irons. Their fellow sowars were incensed but unable to prevent the punishment because of the immediate presence of 2,000

16

armed British soldiers. These men were, however, quartered some distance away from the Indian lines and on Sunday 10 May they left their rifles in the barracks while they attended church parade. The Indian troops waited until their own British officers were unarmed and off their guard, then fell on them, killing all the men and most of their wives and children. The mutineers, about 2,000 in all, then decamped in a body for Delhi, where they quickly enlisted the support of the Indian garrison. Looting, rape, arson and murder followed, but a strong body of mutineers, intent on taking firm control of the city, made a concerted attack on the Red Fort.

This magnificent fortress stands between the old city and the River Jumna. It was for many years the headquarters of the Mughal emperors and it was still, at the time of the Mutiny, a major military installation. Most importantly, it housed the arsenal where the bulk of the garrison's powder and shot lay stored. On guard on the morning of 11 May 1857 were nine British officers and NCOs and a company of Indian troops. The sepoys took the first opportunity to desert as a large body of mutineers launched an assault on the walls. In command of the little band of defenders was a cool-headed British officer named Willoughby, who ordered such guns as were available to be loaded with grape shot and aligned on the gates into the magazine courtyard. It would still have been possible to escape by using a small back gate to the river bank, but rather than let the powder fall into the hands of the mutineers the defenders agreed to blow up the magazine and themselves with it. Accordingly, they laid a powder trail from a tree in the centre of the courtyard into the main store of the magazine itself.

To begin with there was some hope that the British garrison at Meerut would come to the rescue, so Willoughby and his men put up a determined resistance. As the sepoys burst in through the gates they were met by blast after blast of grape shot which did hideous damage in the close confines of the Fort. Then, as the mutineers began to swarm over the walls with scaling ladders, the defenders picked them off with their rifles. For five hours the unequal battle went on, until only two men in the little group were left unwounded. As the sepoys

17

closed in Lieutenant Willoughby gave the order to fire the train.

The explosion was so enormous that the entire wall around the inner courtyard, some forty feet high, collapsed in an avalanche of stone upon the mob outside. According to some reports there were nearly a thousand casualties but, miraculously, four men (including Willoughby) from the defending party survived the blast and limped out of the Fort by the sally port on the banks of the Jumna. In the confusion, ragged and smoke-blackened as they were, they managed to escape from the city. One of them, Lieutenant Raynor, even managed to bring out his wife and child who had taken shelter in the magazine, and with the help of a friendly Sikh they eventually reached the British garrison in Meerut. Two others, Lieutenant Forrest and Conductor Buckley, though badly wounded, also made their way to safety. Willoughby, who had carried the burden of responsibility and given the final order to blow the magazine, was killed by mutineers in a village outside the city.

At the time, and for over forty years to come, there was no provision for posthumous awards of the Victoria Cross. The notion was still lodged in the minds of senior officers and government ministers that the VC was more in the nature of an order, a select company of valiant knights. Since no one could adorn the order when dead, no one who was dead could be selected for the order. So Lieutenant Willoughby, the hero of the Red Fort, was killed and got nothing. The survivors, Forrest, Raynor and Buckley, were each awarded the Victoria Cross. To the highest in the land, accustomed as they were to Orders like the Garter and the Bath which were extinguished with the death of their holders, there was nothing at all odd about this. To the British public, as stories of dead heroes were brought to their attention in the press, it began increasingly to seem unfair.

The case of Lieutenants Salkeld and Home excited much comment. A few months after the destruction of the magazine, Delhi was besieged by a British force under General Wilson. A small party of engineers under Home and Salkeld were sent to blow up the Kashmir gate on the morning of 14 September. Carrying gunpowder in 25-pound bags, they advanced on the gate in broad daylight under heavy fire from an opening in the

18

gate and from the walls above. Most of the engineers managed to take shelter in the ditch at the foot of the walls, but as they attempted to place the charges at the gates, they were picked off by sepoys firing through the wicket. With great sacrifice the charges were at last laid, the gate was blown and the British column charged into the city, but by this time Lieutenant Salkeld was mortally wounded. General Wilson immediately awarded the Victoria Cross to him and to his brother officer Lieutenant Home, as he was entitled to do under the terms of the Warrant. But before the award could be confirmed by the Queen, Salkeld had died of his wounds and Home had been killed in another explosion. Subsequently their Crosses were sent to their grieving families and a memorandum appeared in the *London Gazette* stating that they 'would have been recommended by Her Majesty for confirmation in that distinction had they survived'. It was not an entirely satisfactory solution, but the War Office resisted many subsequent attempts to award the Cross to dead heroes.

Even more controversy arose over the notorious case of Havelock and Son. Brigadier-General Havelock was an officer of high reputation and great courage but he was also a proud father, and his ADC shortly after the beginning of the Mutiny was his son Henry. Father and son marched together in July 1857 to the relief of the garrison at Cawnpore. Though they did not know it, Cawnpore had already fallen to the mutineers. Short of food and water and anxious for the safety of their wives and children, the British garrison sued for peace and were offered safe passage out of the town on a flotilla of river barges. As soon as the British soldiers were on board, the barges were shot to pieces and almost everyone was killed. The surviving women and children were kept alive for about a month, then murdered, mutilated and their bodies thrown down a well. The massacre at Cawnpore excited an ugly desire for revenge in the British troops and provoked an outcry back at home. It also provided the moral justification for savage reprisals against Indian soldiers and civilians whenever the opportunity arose.

Havelock's column, on its approach to Cawnpore, was only about 2,000 strong against a rebel force estimated at 13,000. The Indian troops fought courageously, but for obvious reasons they were short of trained officers and proper supplies, so the British were able to drive through the first Indian positions until the 64th Regiment was held up by a 24-pounder gun, around which the enemy had rallied. Havelock sent his son forward to order the 64th to storm the gun.

The gallant young lieutenant rode up on his horse and found the battalion flat on their stomachs while the gun fired over their heads. Seeing no other officer on horseback, young Henry Havelock spurred his own horse to the fore, waved his sword in the air and urged the 64th into the attack. He must have made a splendid target and no one can doubt his courage in leading a successful charge on the enemy gun. Unfortunately, the young lieutenant had failed in his enthusiasm to notice a senior officer of the 64th, Major Stirling, whose horse had just been shot under him. Stirling's own simultaneous efforts to rally his troops were of course less conspicuous, and he was galled to see this dashing young staff officer charging ahead of him. Insult was added to injury when Brigadier Havelock, overwhelmed with paternal pride, recommended his own son for the Victoria Cross. Sir James Outram, Havelock's senior officer, concurred and the award was in due course confirmed by the Queen. But the officers of the 64th Regiment were outraged and complained to their new commander-in-chief Sir Colin Campbell, a redoubtable soldier with a reputation for bluntness. Sir Colin had never been in favour of the Cross. Like other generals of his day he refused to support the award to senior officers on the grounds that they were eligible for the Order of the Bath. He was slow to respond to correspondence on the subject with the War Office and cavalier in his attitude to the terms of the Warrant, but he was not slow to take up the complaint of the officers of the 64th. He wrote to the Duke of Cambridge, pointing out that young staff officers 'by their reckless and flamboyant behaviour, frequently steal the glory from their regimental colleagues, whose responsibilities give them fewer opportunities to distinguish themselves'.

Lieutenant Havelock himself had tried to prevent his father from putting forward the recommendation. Now he set out to earn the award all over again, and when his father's column entered Lucknow he again displayed conspicuous courage, riding ahead of the Madras Fusiliers and urging them into the attack. On Sir James Outram's recommendation he was again put forward for the Cross, which would have made him the first man to win a VC and Bar, but when the War Office took the matter up with Sir Colin Campbell they got a chilly response. 'The Bar should not be conferred on that officer,' wrote Sir Colin, and managed to imply in his letter that Havelock should never have won the Victoria Cross in the first place and certainly had not deserved to win it again. So Havelock did not win a VC at Lucknow, but twenty-four other Crosses were awarded for actions on one day in November when Sir Colin Campbell's troops fought their way into the city, five of them in elections by their colleagues.

The most remarkable award at Lucknow, however, was not to a soldier at all, but to a civilian. When the Mutiny first erupted, soldiers and civilians alike took refuge in the Commissioner's residency, an imposing building with a large garden, convenient for digging trenches and fortifications, which offered some fragile protection to the British men, women and children inside. Among the civilians was a 36-year-old Irishman, Thomas Kavanagh, superintendent to the chief commissioner of the province. The first relieving column, which included Brigadier Havelock and son, had managed to fight its way through to the residency but was not strong enough to extricate the garrison. So Havelock's men were also besieged in the residency along with everyone else, and the combined force had to await the arrival of Sir Colin Campbell's troops before they could be relieved.

In early November Sir Colin and his men arrived and took up positions around the Alum Bagh, an old walled garden on the outskirts of the city, some four miles from the residency. Here they stayed while patrols went forward to reconnoitre a route through the jungle of narrow streets which lay between the two positions. The city was alive with mutineers. Many of the streets and alleys ended in tiny courtyards where a large body of men could be trapped and shot to pieces from the windows and roof tops above. This had happened on several occasions during Havelock's attempted relief of the residency, and it was essential that a reliable guide with good local knowledge should make the dangerous journey to Sir Colin's headquarters and lead the troops through the city. There was an Indian spy available, a man named Kunoujee Lal, who must have had considerable courage, but the trouble with spies was that they were suspected of treachery by both sides and it was thought unlikely that Sir Colin would trust him to guide a large force of troops. So Thomas Kavanagh, who spoke Hindustani fluently, volunteered to disguise himself as a native and go with Kunoujee Lal to lead the British forces to the residency.

This was an entirely voluntary business. Kavanagh knew very well that if he was captured by the rebels he would very likely be tortured, mutilated and murdered as slowly and painfully as possible. He also had a wife, who had been wounded by a mutineer's bullet, and a young son in the residency. He was effectively under military orders and had to seek permission from the senior officer to undertake the mission. At first Sir James Outram flatly refused to allow him to go. Kavanagh persisted, arguing that he would rather put his own life in danger than risk having his wife and child slaughtered like the women and children at Cawnpore. Eventually he persuaded the general that if his disguise passed muster he should be permitted to go. An hour or two later the officers of the residency were appalled to see a swashbuckling 'badmash', or native mercenary, come striding into the mess without any sign of subservience and seat himself in one of the chairs as though he owned the place. One suspects that Kavanagh, as a civilian and an Irish civilian at that, rather enjoyed this part of the proceedings. In fact the whole episode has elements of a thumping good Victorian melodrama. The officers, full of righteous indignation, tried to eject the hero in disguise and were met with stiff resistance (for Kavanagh was a big man) and a volley of Hindustani oaths. Sir James Outram, arriving in the middle of all this, was taken in as much as anyone else. Triumphantly, Kavanagh revealed his true identity. What could the helpless Sir James do but let the hero do as he wished?

There is a splendid picture at Sandhurst by the French painter Louis William Desanges, who made a speciality of painting VCs, usually engaged in some violent and thrilling action. Desanges's painting shows Kavanagh in full costume

with a noble expression on his face, being made up for the part
by a bevy of British officers. One is adjusting his turban,
another daubing his right hand with burnt cork, while Sir
James himself is putting the finishing touches to his beard.
Identification of the subject is helped by a map, clearly marked
Lucknow, in Outram's left hand. That this painting is not
entirely fictional is borne out by the story that Outram himself
added finesse to Kavanagh's make-up by smearing a mixture
of oil and burnt cork to his face. This was essential because the
sturdy Irishman had red hair, a red beard, blue eyes and
freckles.

When he set off it is recorded that his costume consisted of
a pair of tight silk trousers, a muslin shirt, a short yellow silk
jacket with a chintz mantle around his shoulders, a cummerbund around his waist and an exceedingly tight pair of slippers
on his feet. At the last moment a considerate officer thrust a
double-barrelled pistol into his cummerbund, not for his
protection, but to use upon himself if caught.

As the two men slipped out of the residency grounds their
chances of success must have looked as flimsy as Kavanagh's
shirt. The British in Lucknow were surrounded on all sides by
mutineers. The Irishman and the Indian spy had to traverse
the entire city and make their way through the crowded
suburbs beyond to the Alum Bagh – a good deal more than
four miles by the roundabout route they would have to take.
The mutineers were known to be almost as suspicious of each
other as they were of the British, and Kavanagh's disguise
could hardly have stood up to close examination. To make
matters worse, the would-be guides had to wade through a
number of canals, irrigation ditches and open sewers which
would be likely to detract from their imposing appearance.

Astonishingly, Kavanagh and his companion managed to
make their way through the enemy lines and the streets of the
city without detection. They were challenged twice but they
were able to talk their way out of trouble in the darkness.
Avoiding the crowds in the city they came by back lanes to the
Dilkoosha Park, a large tract of land on the edge of Lucknow
which now served as the camping ground of the rebel cavalry,
but when they reached this point Kunoujee Lal was obliged to
confess that he was lost. Dodging the sowar's camp fires, they

blundered through the darkness trying to find a route to the Alum Bagh. At one point they stopped to ask the way from a man who was sitting up guarding his crops. No doubt fearing the worst, the man immediately set up a hue and cry and the two spies had to make a run for it. At last they stumbled into a hut where a woman, perhaps too terrified to yell for help, pointed out the way to their destination. By this time the moon was up and the two men were both more dishevelled and more conspicuous than they had been before. When at last, some five hours after they had left the residency, they came within sight of the Alum Bagh they found an enormous body of mutineers encamped in front of the British lines. Seeking to find a way round, they bumped into a troop of sowars but were able to bluff their way past only to meet up with a more alert sentry, who called out the guard. Surrounded by bristling bayonets, Kunoujee Lal is said to have quietly disposed of the dispatch he carried while Kavanagh stuffed his into his turban and came out with some Hindustani blarney about a brother who had been killed by a British bullet and a sad errand that they now had to fulfil. Surprisingly, the sepoys believed him and let the two men pass.

The melodrama now came dangerously close to farce. In the moonlight they stumbled into a jheel, one of the swampy pools which spatter the Indian landscape in the cool months of the year. Kavanagh was tall and Kunoujee Lal was short, so Kavanagh had to hold his companion's head above water. In doing so he washed the last of the burnt cork off his hands. His beard may also have got a trifle damp and to add to his troubles his tight slippers were giving him agony, but he did not dare to remove them in case his white feet gave him away.

With dawn on the way the danger of discovery was becoming more acute with every passing moment, but Kavanagh insisted on a rest and the two men went to ground for an hour in a grove of trees. When they emerged at four in the morning they were challenged once more, but this time it was the dear familiar cry, 'Who goes there?' A platoon of Sikh soldiers, loyal to the British, were out on patrol. The two men were led into camp where Kavanagh, as befitted a white man, was hived off from his faithful companion and put to bed by the general himself. Despite a stiff brandy the Irishman was unable to sleep for excitement. He also forgot his instructions. Tucking into a hearty breakfast of bacon and eggs, toast and marmalade at eleven o'clock in the morning, he failed to recall that he was supposed to have a signal hoisted to the roof of the Alum Bagh to advise Sir James Outram of his safe arrival. Back at the residency the British officers, and his unhappy wife and child, could only fear the worst. Kavanagh finally remembered at lunchtime, but he still had to complete his mission. He had run the gauntlet of thousands of hostile troops and equally hostile civilians to reach the British forces. Now he had to guide them back to the residency.

This he accomplished with great aplomb, personally reuniting Sir James and Sir Colin under a hail of bullets at the shattered residency some six days later. The attack on Lucknow was singularly bloody. There is no reason to doubt the appropriateness of those twenty-four VCs won on 16 November in vicious close-quarter fighting, but the sight of our gallant soldiers bayoneting two thousand rebels to death in the Secundrabagh, shouting 'Remember Cawnpore' as they did so, would not win good reviews today; nor would the grisly execution of forty sepoys by being tied to the mouths of cannon and 'blown from the guns'. None of this bothered Kavanagh, who basked in the glory of what was, in Sir Colin Campbell's words, 'one of the most daring feats ever attempted'.

The recommendation of Thomas Kavanagh for the Victoria Cross put the War Office into something of a quandary. The Royal Warrant of 1856 referred only to 'officers and men' with a clear inference that these were serving sailors or soldiers in the armed services of the Crown. This had since been amended to take in military and naval personnel in the service of the East India Company. Now there had to be another alteration to include civilians, not Kavanagh alone, but a Patna magistrate named Mangles, who had rescued a wounded soldier under heavy fire. The amendment, providing for civilians 'under the orders of a general or other officer in command of troops in the field' was promulgated in December 1858 and Kavanagh's VC was finally gazetted in July of the following year, the citation noting that he performed his task 'with chivalrous gallantry and devotion'.

There was of course no VC for Kunoujee Lal, because Indian

25

The Origins of the Victoria Cross

soldiers were not eligible for the Victoria Cross. This was because of the peculiar status of the Indian Army and indeed of India itself, which was in many ways an empire in its own right and quite distinct from the rest of Her Majesty's possessions. The Indian Army had its own decorations and, despite many heroic deeds, no VCs were awarded to Indian servicemen until the First World War. But there was no element of racial prejudice in this. A black man named William Hall, an able seaman serving with a shore detachment of the Royal Navy, was one of the Lucknow twenty-four. Hall was one of the only two men left alive to serve a gun which was battering away at the mutineers' defences at point-blank range. As others fell all around him, Hall did the work of four men and his strength and courage demanded recognition, even though he was the son of a liberated black slave.

The Mutiny, with its almost medieval battles on city walls, with gates being stormed, with sieges and sorties and valiant cavalry charges, offered numerous opportunities for the kind of valour 'in the presence of the Enemy' that can win a man the Victoria Cross. There was William MacBean, for instance, who had risen from the ranks to become Adjutant of the 93rd Regiment, known today as the Argyll and Sutherland Highlanders. Wielding his claymore during the storming of Lucknow, he took part in the butchery at the Secundrabagh, then joined the assault on the Begum Bagh Palace nearby. When the walls had been breached MacBean rushed in with his bloody sword. In hand-to-hand fighting (some more timid soul presumably keeping the score) he then proceeded to kill no fewer than eleven of the enemy. When he presented MacBean with the Cross in the field, General Garratt praised his fighting prowess and called it 'a good day's work'. The giant Scot thought this to be a great exaggeration: 'Tuts', he said, 'it did'na tak me twenty minutes.'

Not all the Victoria Crosses won during the Mutiny were awarded for quite such gory deeds. There were many instances of comrades being rescued under fire, at least one heroic climb to the battlements bearing the Colour through shot and shell, and many Crosses were awarded as the result of democratic elections in the units concerned. The 182 VCs dating from the Mutiny (the same number incidentally as were won during the whole of the Second World War) served to raise the Victoria Cross in public esteem and make it truly 'highly prized and eagerly sought after'. If some of the attitudes of the British soldiers taking part were frankly racist, arrogant and even absurd, this does not detract from the courage of those who fought. Their deeds have to be seen in the context of the period. Brave men are still brave even in a questionable cause.

There is an additional irony in that not all the men who performed brave deeds did so sufficiently noticeably to be awarded the VC, and even for those who did, the award of the Cross was often the high point in an otherwise wretched life. The story of the dashing young Lieutenant Havelock had a tragic sequel to it. Part of the 64th Regiment which had been so badly upstaged by young Lieutenant Havelock remained at Cawnpore, most of the time under siege, for many months. On 28 November 1857, the same Major Stirling who had suffered the humiliation of watching another officer lead his men to glory, again led a charge against the guns. This time he was firmly to the fore, but as he reached the Indian battery Stirling was shot dead. Again the glory went to another – this time a fifteen-year-old Irish drummer boy named Thomas Flinn, who was wounded early in the action, picked himself up and pressed forward with his comrades. At the battery Flinn was seen to take on two of the enemy artillery men in hand-to-hand combat, and his courage was so impressive that he was awarded the Victoria Cross. Two days after the investiture in Karachi, where he probably went out on a binge, Flinn was imprisoned for being drunk and disorderly, and for the rest of his time in the army his service record is simply a calendar of the years he spent in military prisons. He was discharged finally in 1869 and returned to Athlone in Ireland where he lived in total obscurity, dying a pauper in the workhouse in 1892. He was just fifty. Sadly, his drunken decline following the highest award for courage is not unique in the history of the Victoria Cross.

3
Fighting for the Empire

The Victorian wars of the second half of the nineteenth century, like the Mutiny, do not from today's standpoint reflect very well on Britain. An expansionist imperial power, however reluctantly pushed into the responsibilities of government by the greed of merchants and the ardour of missionaries, does not look attractive to anyone, not even to itself after a sufficient lapse of time. To the natives of the various countries which Britain annexed into the Empire the troops who crushed their resistance, sometimes with considerable brutality, must have seemed like agents of the devil. But British servicemen, especially the ordinary soldiers and seamen, cannot too easily be blamed for the actions of their superiors. Many of them signed on to escape great poverty and deprivation. And, fighting many months away from home, against enemies whom they usually regarded as primitive savages and backed by a prevailing ethos which wholly endorsed the attitudes of their masters, British servicemen did their duty as they saw it and often far more.

Britain's various wars against China would all now be seen as somewhat disreputable. Although no imperial ambitions as such were involved, Britain had already attacked China twice in order to force the administration to permit British traders to use opium as a medium of exchange for tea. (For many years the Honorable East India Company had been the biggest drug-growing and drug-peddling enterprise in the world.) Following a treaty imposed upon the Chinese in 1858 an attempt to establish a British diplomatic mission in Peking was rejected, and when the British party persisted in trying to reach the city they were attacked and several of their number were killed. By 1860 Britain and France were both determined to force China to make abiding trade agreements on their own terms and a joint expedition was sent to march on Peking.

The first major obstacles which the Europeans faced were the Taku forts near the mouth of the Pei-Ho river, which effectively blocked the route to the Chinese capital. The forts dominated an area of low-lying marshland intersected with streams and drainage ditches. They were strongly built and equipped with artillery, and the allies had great difficulty bringing up their own guns to engage the enemy. On 21 August two battalions of British Infantry, the 44th and 67th, assaulted the fort on the north side of the river together with a regiment of French troops.

The action opened with an artillery bombardment and, although the guns at first made little impression on the walls of the fort, a lucky shot hit the Chinese magazine. The explosion did a great deal of damage and also deprived the Chinese artillery of their supply of ammunition, but the attacking forces did not have everything their own way. Enemy rifle and musket fire was heavy and persistent. The attacking forces had to advance across pontoon bridges which offered an easy target to the defenders and then run scaling ladders up the walls in order to storm the battlements, while other assault parties tried to breach the walls with charges of gunpowder. All these operations were extremely hazardous and it is not surprising that seven Victoria Crosses were won on that day – three to the first men on the battlements and three more to those storming a breach in the walls. But perhaps the most heroic action on that day was not in the cut and thrust of action at all.

As the assault parties drew close to the fort, the majority of the 67th Regiment were brought up to within five hundred yards of the walls where they waited under cover for orders to move forward. With them was a hospital apprentice of the East India Company named Thomas Fitzgibbon. While crossing an open stretch of ground an India stretcher-bearer was hit by a bullet and Fitzgibbon went out, under heavy fire, to tend to his wounds. When the regiment itself advanced across the same ground towards the fort Fitzgibbon saw another man fall and ran forward to help him. There was no cover of any kind. The wounded man and the medical

29

The Origins of the Victoria Cross

apprentice were exposed to a murderous hail of bullets, and before he reached the fallen soldier Fitzgibbon was himself hit and severely hurt. He was just fifteen years and three months old, and, together with Thomas Flinn of Cawnpore, was one of the two youngest boys ever to win the Victoria Cross.

The campaign in China was followed by others scattered across the world. In New Zealand a series of land disputes brought the British into conflict with the native Maoris, which continued on and off for nearly sixty years. Each time the Maoris rebelled in desperation as their lands and forests dwindled before the onslaught of cows, sheep and settlers, a contingent of British soldiers and sailors would have a bloody and difficult little war on its hands. The Maoris were brave and resourceful, masters of guerilla warfare and also skilled at fortification, building wooden stockades called *pahs*, so ingenious and well designed that they often resisted British artillery at point-blank range. Many Crosses were won in bloody hand-to-hand fighting as British soldiers stormed the Maori *pahs* and accounts of these actions make it plain that those awards were well earned.

But there are some nineteenth-century VCs which look a bit too easy when set against the high standards of more modern times. There was, for instance, a curious episode in the Andaman Islands in 1867. Seventeen soldiers had been landed on one of the islands to try and track down a party of British sailors who were missing, presumed killed at the hands of the natives. There was a heavy sea running and the Indian Ocean surf thundered on the beach. The rescue party themselves were soon in danger of attack by the Andaman islanders and their boat had been swamped when they tried to run it through the surf, so a fresh boat was sent to try and bring the shore party back to the ship. The rescue boat was manned by four soldiers of the 24th Regiment, and in command was Assistant Surgeon Campbell Douglas. A picture, now hanging in the RAMC headquarters on Millbank in London, shows Surgeon Douglas standing in an extremely precarious position in the bows of the boat, where he must have got extremely wet and probably found it tricky to exercise any influence on the steering.

With great difficulty the small boat made three trips through the surf and successfully brought off all of the stranded men. Today, this kind of surf boating is some people's idea of a fun way to spend the afternoon, so it does seem a little excessive to reward the exploit with no less than five Victoria Crosses, especially since none of the hostile natives were anywhere in sight and the action was certainly not 'in the presence of the Enemy'. It is true that there was provision, in an amendment of 1858, for deeds of heroism far from the front line to be eligible for the Cross, and one such award had already been given to a Private Timothy O'Hea, who had put out a fire in an ammunition wagon in Canada – an action which certainly required enormous courage. What seems curious, at this distance in time, is that rowing a boat through heavy surf should inspire quite so much admiration, though one should perhaps remember that few Victorian Englishmen, even those who made a living on the sea, could swim a stroke. Whether or not anyone at the War Office ever thought better of the awards for this action, this was the last time that anyone was decorated with the Victoria Cross far from the blood and smoke of battle.

There was no shortage of battles on the frontiers of the Empire. In the second half of the nineteenth century British forces saw action in many different parts of Africa; in India, especially on the northern frontiers both east and west; and even in Japan, where two officers of the Royal Navy both won the Victoria Cross in 1864. But it was the various campaigns in Afghanistan which most caught the public imagination, partly because the Afghans then, as now, were fighters who commanded respect and partly because Afghanistan was the gateway to India, the home ground for the Great Game between Britain and Russia for control of the sub-continent, a bloody and remorseless conflict which continues, with a slight change in the teams, to this day.

Fearful of Russian interference in Afghan affairs, the British delivered an ultimatum to the Amir, Shere Ali, in 1878. Either he would accept a permanent British mission in Kabul or the British would decide the matter by force. The Amir refused and on 20 November 1878 the British invaded. Three columns threaded their way up through the mountains and defeated the Afghans in a series of engagements throughout the winter

The Origins of the Victoria Cross

and spring. One British force, incidentally, was under the command of Sir Sam Browne VC, inventor of the sword belt of the same name, and another was commanded by General, later Field Marshal, Lord Roberts VC. On 2 April the cavalry of the Guides, a famous Indian Army Regiment, charged a much larger force of the enemy near Futtehabad. The cavalry commander, Major Battye, was shot dead and a Lieutenant Walter Hamilton took command of the attack. As he rode neck and neck with a Guide named Dowlat Ram, the sowar's horse was shot beneath him. The man fell and was instantly attacked by a group of Afghans. Instead of continuing his headlong charge, which he might honourably have done, Hamilton reined in his horse and turned to rescue the sowar. In a swift and violent little battle he cut down three Afghan soldiers with his sabre, caught a runaway horse and saw to it that Dowlat Ram was safely remounted before riding on to victory.

This would seem to have been the very stuff of action of the kind for which the Victoria Cross was ordained, but the Duke of Cambridge, Commander-in-Chief of the British Army, declined for some months to recommend the award. While the authorities dithered, Hamilton went on to greater glory, eternal glory one might say. The old Amir, Shere Ali, had died and his place had been taken by one of his sons, Yakoub Khan, who had to be released from the prison where his father had very wisely kept him for many years. Yakoub sued for peace and the British entered Kabul in triumph in May. A British mission was duly established in the city under a gentleman with the rather un-British name of Sir Lewis Cavagnari as Minister Plenipotentiary. A small escort of Guides under the command of Lieutenant Hamilton was left to guard the embassy, and the army, satisfied with a job well done, marched back to India.

Almost as soon as the army's backs were turned the little group in the British Embassy were in trouble. The new Amir was no friendlier than his father, and for obvious reasons the British were thoroughly unpopular with the people at large. After a number of unpleasant incidents a huge mob, helped by the Amir's soldiers, stormed the British Embassy on 3 September 1879. Instead of retreating from room to room as the enraged mob burst into the building, Lieutenant Hamilton mustered a little group of his Guides and charged the attackers. Brandishing a sword in one hand and a pistol in the other he fought his way out of the building, carved his way through literally hundreds of Afghans in the courtyard and was last seen by one of the Guides who managed to escape, hacking away at the enemy soldiers in the main gateway. There was no possibility of escape for a uniformed European in Kabul, so what exactly he was trying to achieve will never be known, but if young Walter simply wanted to die gloriously he got his wish.

Back home the War Office was still hesitating over whether or not to recommend the award of the VC to Hamilton for the action back in April of the same year. The news from Kabul decided the matter, but the dispatch did not reach London until nearly four weeks after Hamilton's death. Under the terms of the Royal Warrant the Cross would of course have to be put to the Queen for her confirmation before it could be awarded but, also under the terms of the Warrant, it could not be awarded to a dead man. In a masterly piece of official jiggery-pokery the Secretary of State for War, Lord Stanley, put forward a recommendation backdated to 1 September, two days before the unfortunate young officer was killed. The Victoria Cross was sent to Hamilton's father and nobody asked any awkward questions.

There was another anomaly in the original Warrant which also stemmed from the notion of Orders of Knighthood demanding high standards of conduct from their members. A man who had won the Cross could be deprived of the award and the pension that went with it for 'treason, cowardice, felony or any infamous crime'. This catch-all phrase led to the expulsion of eight offenders between 1861 and 1908 for crimes ranging from the theft of a cow to 'desertion to avoid investigation of a disgraceful offence', though what the disgraceful offence actually was, the Royal Navy were not prepared to reveal. In another case the unfortunate Gunner James Colliss, who, like Lieutenant Hamilton, won his Victoria Cross during the Afghan wars, lost it again for being caught out at bigamy.

Gunner Colliss was with the Royal Horse Artillery under General Burrow's command when the army returned to punish

33

the Afghans for the slaughter of the British at the mission in Kabul. The main force were successful and eventually reoccupied Kabul, but General Burrows was cut off at Maiwand and heavily defeated by a large Afghan army. The Artillery distinguished themselves at Maiwand by bringing out most of their guns while Afghan cavalry raged around them and British and Indian soldiers were fleeing the battlefield. Colliss himself was with a battery which was almost dismembered by a cavalry charge. Clinging to the limber, as it jolted furiously over the rocky ground, he was wounded and nearly killed by a sabre stroke from an Afghan sowar. Snatching up a carbine, he shot the Afghan dead and continued to ride shotgun on the back of the limber until his troop was clear of the battlefield.

When the pace slackened Colliss, although wounded himself, took on to the limber a number of men whom he considered to be in a worse state than he was. Continually harried by enemy cavalry, he was in constant danger as he tended to the wounded, stopping off to find water for them whenever possible. On the second day of the retreat, while fetching water from a village well, he spotted a troop of Afghan cavalry who threatened to overtake the gun. Urging his comrades to make a quick getaway, Colliss grabbed a rifle from a retreating infantryman and took up a position alone among a pile of rocks barring the way to the enemy cavalry while the rest of the British fled. There followed a Western-style shoot-out between Colliss and the Afghan sowars. His accurate fire forced them to dismount in order to shoot back, and he killed two of them as they gradually crept up on his position. Meanwhile the gun and limber, with its load of wounded men, was able to escape. At the last moment as the Afghans closed on him from several directions at once, a troop of Indian cavalry under General Nuttall rode up and put the enemy to flight.

Colliss was able to rejoin his troops, and he served with them during the siege of Kandahar that followed. In August he again attracted notice by volunteering to carry a message to a detachment outside the walls, shinning down a rope under enemy fire, running across two hundred yards of open ground with the Afghans sniping at him all the way, then back and up the rope again. As he began the climb to safety an enemy bullet clipped off the heel of his boot. When General Roberts arrived with the relieving column from Kabul he recommended James Colliss for the Victoria Cross, and himself presided at the investiture in Poona in 1881.

Only fragments of the rest of Colliss's story have survived. After his discharge from the Army he lived in Bombay for a while and then returned to England, where he served in the Corps of Commissionaires, which presumably gave him an opportunity to wear his medals from time to time, but in 1895 he was convicted of bigamy. He was imprisoned, his Victoria Cross was forfeited and his name was erased from the register of the award. The War Office even went so far as to relieve him of the actual Cross as well, but he had already hocked it at the local pawnshop and the police had to redeem it before they could return it to the War Office, where it disappeared into the recesses of the system. But that was not the end of the story.

Colliss lived until 1918 and when he died his sister sent a petition to the King requesting that his name should be restored to the register. George V was sympathetic. 'The King,' wrote his private secretary, 'says that most certainly Gunner Colliss's name should be inscribed with those of other VCs on the tablets of the Royal Artillery Victoria Cross memorial.' To his undying credit the King expressed his views most forcibly on the subject of forfeiture when it was raised again in 1920. 'The King feels so strongly,' runs another letter from his secretary, 'that no matter the crime committed by anyone on whom the VC has been conferred, the decoration should not be forfeited. Even were a VC to be sentenced to be hanged for murder, he should be allowed to wear the VC on the scaffold.' Although in theory it is still possible for the Cross to be forfeited, no man's name has been erased from the roll from that day to this and those names which were once removed have now been restored to all the published lists.

Ironically, Gunner Colliss could probably have got his medal back if he had asked for it, since the War Office abandoned the practice of demanding repossession of the actual Cross as early as 1908. However, if he had applied to the War Office there would have been some embarrassment. The records of the London auctioneers, Sotheby's, show that James Colliss's VC was sold at auction in 1910 for just £50 and the identity of

35

the vendor is, as always, discreetly cloaked in anonymity. Colliss himself was buried in Wandsworth cemetery 'with full military honours' but his body was stacked in a common grave together with those of fourteen other paupers. His grave is unmarked and he is somewhere in a plot of rough grass, close to the elaborate monuments of wealthier clients. His Cross was sold again in 1984 for £7000 – enough, one might feel, for a gravestone.

The story is not altogether unique. Many other dead heroes lie in unmarked graves and many other Crosses have been sold over the years – either by the men themselves, fallen on hard times, or by their relatives after their death. The wars of the nineteenth century are not fashionable with collectors and the older medals tend to bring lower prices, but there are some battles so famous that they still command interest. One of these is the battle of Isandlwhana and its sequel at Rorke's Drift in South Africa against the Zulu Warriors of King Cetawayo, an action in which the 24th Foot won seven VCs in twenty-four hours. This was of course the same regiment that provided the crew for the surf boat in the Andaman Islands, one of the most successful of all regiments of the line in terms of winning the Victoria Cross.

Isandlwhana was one of the worst disasters to be inflicted on ordinary soldiers by the incompetence of their officers until the First World War broke all records. At Balaklava there had at least been some heroic flair in the useless charge of the Light Brigade. At Isandlwhana there was nothing but a bloody waste of lives, though to the Zulu nation it ranked, and rightly so, as a great victory.

The Zulus were a people devoted to warfare. In their short history they had emerged from obscurity as a small tribe near the eastern sea-board of South Africa to become a powerful nation, with the young people of both sexes organised in *impis*, or regiments. The Zulus' fighting skills had been drilled into them through three generations of soldiers, beginning with the bloodthirsty King Chaka, who made his men shorten the hafts of their spears so that they would be forced to close with the enemy, and taught them one of the most effective of all aggressive manoeuvres – the advance of a solid phalanx in the centre, with two great enveloping horns spreading out on the flanks to encircle and annihilate the enemy. The discipline of the Zulus was legendary. When one *impi* of 3,000 men failed to fulfil the task allotted to them, Chaka ordered the regiment to march off the edge of a precipice. They obeyed, to the last man. Fortunately, when this frightful martinet ordered a regiment of women to perform a similar act of self-destruction, the girls hesitated long enough for Chaka to be assassinated by his own officers.

As Dutch and British settlers moved closer to this warlike people's homeland there were inevitable clashes. Sir Bartle Frere, governor of the British colony based on Cape Town, sent orders that the Zulus should hand over their weapons, which they of course ignored. Then, following a British demand for the surrender of the sons of a Zulu chief on a charge of murder, Sir Bartle sent an ultimatum to the Zulu King Cetawayo. The ultimatum too was ignored. In January 1879 a force of about 5,000 British soldiers, with 1,200 irregular cavalry and a half-trained levy of 10,000 Africans, invaded Zululand under the command of Lord Chelmsford. Considering that he was faced by an extremely aggressive and highly disciplined enemy with about 50,000 men under arms (not to mention the women), Lord Chelmsford then committed a classic blunder. He divided his forces into three columns, not one of which was powerful enough to take on the Zulu army by itself. Had the British been mobile and well co-ordinated this might have been a wise decision, but they were not. The British throughout their history have often tended to underestimate the fighting prowess of their enemies, a habit which has plunged whole armies into disaster more than once. Cetawayo was not at all overawed by the advance of the British. His spies could see their wagons and the steady march of the red-coated soldiers from miles away. The fleet-footed Zulus could move from one position to another at three times the speed and far less conspicuously than their enemies and their courage in battle was every bit as great as that of their opponents.

On 19 January Lord Chelmsford halted his column on the slopes of Isandlwhana ('the little hand'), a high and sinister-looking cliff which dominates the undulating country around it. The position he selected was not badly placed for defence,

37

but he made no attempt to fortify it and he had his men pitch camp, complacent in the belief that his column was too strong to be attacked. Three days later, however, he again divided his forces, moving off himself early in the morning with about half his troops in the hope of taking the Zulus by surprise. The camp was left with a garrison of about 800 soldiers, mostly of the 24th Regiment, and a contingent of 400 half-trained Africans. The Zulus watched until Chelmsford's column was several miles on its way and then began to close in. Even then, disaster might have been averted if the British had learned from the Dutch settlers and formed a defensive laager with their wagons, but they did the opposite.

Colonel Durnford, an officer of the Royal Engineers, arrived to take command with a squadron of irregular cavalry. He began the process of scattering the defending forces by ordering one company of the 24th to take up a position on high ground nearly a mile away from the camp. Then Durnford moved off, taking most of the African levy with him to scout for the Zulus and leaving Lieutenant-Colonel Pulleine of the 24th in command. Realising, as the day wore on, that the Zulus were moving in to attack, Pulleine sent a desperate series of messages after Lord Chelmsford, but most of these appear to have been ignored. Something like panic seems to have set in at the British camp, though it would have been almost treasonable to suggest such a thing in Victorian times. Instead of drawing in his perimeter as much as possible to confront the Zulus with a solid wall of rifles and bayonets behind a barricade of wagons, Pulleine sent two more companies of the 24th to join the outpost, a mile away from the main camp and even further from their ammunition supply. At the last moment Colonel Durnford realised the extent of the danger and rushed back into the camp to try and organise the defence, but he was too late. In any case it is doubtful whether he would have managed things any better than the unfortunate Pulleine. By one o'clock the British were spread out over a wide area and the Zulus were upon them.

They advanced, 20,000 of them in their great phalanx with the huge enveloping horns extended on either side. Scattered in small groups, open to attack from all sides, the British soldiers were overwhelmed by the rush of spears. Many of them died bravely. Some dead soldiers were found with Zulu corpses scattered around them, but of the 1,300 or so men in the camp only a handful escaped. The rest were killed. Zulu warriors did not take prisoners.

Three Victoria Crosses were won at Isandlwhana, two of them in rather curious circumstances. When it was obvious that all was lost, Lieutenant Melvill of the 24th took the regimental Colour and fought his way on horseback out of the mêlée. Hotly pursued by Zulu warriors who could run almost as fast as a man could ride, he galloped across country to the river Buffalo and plunged his horse into the current. Two other fugitives were with him, another subaltern named Coghill and Lieutenant Higginson of the Natal Native Contingent. Coghill reached the far bank in safety but Melvill and Higginson were both swept off their horses. For a while they hung on to the Colour, emblem of the regiment's pride, but it was torn from their hands and disappeared downstream. The two officers were left clinging to a rock in the river bed when the Zulus arrived and started firing at them with rifles, some of them newly taken from the dead at Isandlwhana. At this point Coghill could have got clean away and, considering what he had just been through, he might have been forgiven for doing so. Instead, he turned his horse and forged back into the river, intent on rescuing his brother officers. Before he could reach them his horse was shot from underneath him and he half swam, half scrambled to the rock where the other two were clinging and somehow got them across the river to the far bank, all the time under fire from the Zulus at the river's edge only a few yards away. Higginson managed to get away, but before he did so he saw the two officers of the 24th, both of them badly wounded, preparing for a final stand. When their bodies were found, three days later, there were twelve dead Zulus in a ring around them.

Both men were cited for gallantry in the by-now classic form of a memorandum in the *London Gazette* that they 'would have been recommended to Her Majesty for the Victoria Cross had they survived'. But more than twenty years later, during the Boer War, it was finally decided to make allowances for the posthumous award of the Cross, and the relatives of Coghill and Melvill applied to the War Office to have the question of

39

the dead heroes' awards reopened. The Secretary of State for War took the matter up with King Edward VII, who refused to grant the Crosses – fearing a flood of applications from widows and children. There the matter rested until 1906 when Mrs Melvill addressed a direct petition to the King. The personal approach seems to have moved him where official correspondence had no effect, and he finally consented to allow the posthumous award of the Victoria Cross to six men, one of whom had been dead for nearly sixty years. The *London Gazette* of 15 January 1907 announced the granting of the Victoria Cross to the surviving relatives of all six, including the two officers who died together at Isandlwhana.

The British Army's disaster in Zululand was followed very quickly by a story of heroism which did a great deal to restore the faith of the public in the virtues of British grit and determination, though it did not greatly impress the Dutch settlers who had fought many such battles themselves. This was the defence of Rorke's Drift, a small mission station at a river crossing a few miles from Isandlwhana. The British had taken over the station and turned the sturdy chapel into a store for food and ammunition. The dwelling-house was doing temporary duty as a field hospital and there were thirty-five wounded or sick men in the place at the time. The whole depot was garrisoned by a company of the 24th under the command of Lieutenant Gonville Bromhead, but the senior officer in the post was Lieutenant John Chard of the Royal Engineers. The Zulu Indunas, or war chiefs, who had taken careful note of the size and strength of all the British positions, quite rightly decided to hit the enemy supply lines. As soon as they had overwhelmed the defenders of Isandlwhana, the Indunas sent an entire *impi*, the Undi Regiment, to wipe out the post at Rorke's Drift.

At about three o'clock in the afternoon of 22 January a bunch of mounted fugitives, mostly from Durnford's irregular cavalry and the Natal Native Contingent, came pounding into the post bringing news of the disaster and warning that the Zulus were close behind them. Wisely, Chard and Bromhead declined to try and make a run for it. Instead they fortified the post, piling up a breastwork of upturned wagons and sacks of corn, cases of tinned meat, furniture, anything they could find, in two parallel barricades connecting the two buildings. Every man who could move was put to work, and twelve of the hospital patients rose from their beds to join in, including a little man named Schiess, a Swiss-born adventurer who had been serving in one of the native levies. As the Undi Regiment closed in on the little mission station, the missionary himself, the Reverend Otto Witt, decided he had urgent business elsewhere. Later he was to send a bill for repairs to the British authorities. A few of the fugitives from Isandlwhana elected to stay, but most of them took off for Natal; one of them was shot by an officer for desertion as he fled the camp. This left 104 men able to hold a rifle against 3,500 superbly fit fighting men of the Zulu nation, full of confidence from their recent victory and some of them armed with the rifles of the British soldiers they had slain, others with old-fashioned muskets, all with the short spear, the deadly thrusting assegai of the Zulus.

The vanguard of the Undi Regiment attacked silently at the run, rushing the barricade in front of them, the horns spreading out on the flanks to envelope the little post. But Bromhead and Chard had been wiser than Pulleine and Durnford at Isandlwhana. The makeshift barricades prevented the Zulus from closing with their assegais, and the Martini rifles of the defenders, firing at point-blank range, wrought fearful carnage in their ranks. Only at one point, close to the mission orchard which provided cover for the attackers, was the barricade incomplete. Here there was fearful hand-to-hand fighting, with the men of the 24th plying their bayonets until the pile of bodies was so thick that the warriors could make no further headway. Those who did break through were shot or bayoneted. Little Schiess, the Swiss hospital patient, stabbed three Zulus in quick succession as they tried to clamber over the barricade.

The Indunas drew off their men. Taking advantage of the mission orchard and the rocks and ant hills which littered the slopes of the hills around Rorke's Drift, the Zulus now took cover and began to use their rifles on the defenders. They had the advantage of high ground but they were not trained marksmen, and although some of their bullets found a mark, they continued to suffer heavy casualties. Private Hook, for instance, a Gloucestershire man who had been set to guard the hospital patients, stuck his rifle out of the window and picked off five Zulus at 300–600 yards' range as they emerged from cover to fire at the mission.

As darkness gathered the Zulus left the shelter of the rocks and resumed their rushes on the barricade. One storming party set fire to the thatched roof of the hospital. This building formed one side of the fortified enclosure and there was only a small window connecting the hospital with the barricaded yard. The Zulus burst their way into the building, killing several of the patients and two of their guards, but a private soldier named John Williams broke some holes with a pickaxe through the walls separating one room from another. Henry Hook, the marksman at the window, now took to the bayonet while Williams dragged the patients through one hole after another and the Zulus came stabbing after them. One patient had a broken leg, and Williams had to break the other to get him out of the window and into the yard while Hook kept the Zulus at bay. There were fearful struggles in and around the building, spear against bayonet in the fitful light of the blazing hospital. At the barricades the firing went on all night as the Zulus strove, with incredible courage, to overwhelm the defenders. Rifles grew too hot to touch. Those too badly hurt to shoot propped themselves up as best they could and reloaded the guns of those who were still on their feet. In the open courtyard, Surgeon-Major Henry Reynolds tended to the wounded, oblivious to the life-and-death struggle going on all around him.

Late in the night it proved impossible to hold the original perimeter, but Chard and Bromhead had wisely prepared a second line of defence, another barricade around a little cluster of buildings. Here they dragged the wounded and piled up spare ammunition as the Zulus occupied the burnt-out hospital and poured into the enclosure on all sides. But the last barricade held. With the defenders fighting shoulder-to-shoulder and back-to-back even the reckless Zulu charges wavered and broke. As dawn began to lighten the sky the Undi Regiment drew off, taking their wounded with them. Another large body of Zulus arrived at about six a.m., and for a while it looked as though the post was doomed, but Lord Chelmsford, who had returned too late to save Isandlwhana, now arrived on the scene just in time to save Rorke's Drift.

The heroics at Rorke's Drift helped to distract public attention from the disaster at Isandlwhana. Just over a hundred men had held off an attack of over three thousand Zulus – an example, if one were needed, of the capacity of trained and well armed troops in a well prepared position to defeat a much larger body of men, no matter how brave, as long as their officers knew what they were doing. Lieutenants Chard and Bromhead were both awarded the Victoria Cross, as were the redoubtable Privates Henry Hook and John Williams who had fought off the Zulus in the hospital. Surgeon-Major Reynolds got the Cross for tending the wounded under fire, as did the Swiss volunteer Scheiss and four other men of the 24th South Wales Borderers. Around the barricades 350 Zulus lay dead and perhaps as many more died of their wounds. A few weeks later, at the battle of the Ulundi, Cetawayo and his brave warriors were finally defeated.

The same imperial expansion which had brought the British into conflict with the Zulus also brought them up against an even more intractable enemy, the Afrikaners of the interior of South Africa. These frontier farmers, Boers as they were known, were the descendants of Dutch settlers in the Cape of Good Hope. Both Britain and Holland first established colonies there in order to have staging posts for their possessions in the Far East, but as British power increased many of the Dutch-speaking colonists moved out of the Cape and trekked into the interior. They wanted to be free of British political interference and also free to pursue their own strict Calvinist way of life beyond the corrupting influence of the city. Significantly, one of the evils which the Dutch settlers decried (even as far back as 1685) was inter-marriage – not to mention casual mating – between black and white. To the Afrikaners the blacks were serfs to be kept in servitude or exterminated. On the South African veld they farmed the lands and fought the natives, especially the war-like Zulu and Basuto peoples, who understandably resented this invasion of their territory. Every man, every woman, every child in a Boer farmer's family knew how to handle a rifle. A rigorous code of morality and a tough outdoor life combined to turn them into formidable

43

fighters – expert at guerilla warfare, but also disciplined in defence.

Eventually the Boers sought to set up independent republics in the Transvaal and the Orange Free State. Britain would not accept their demands for independence, but in 1880 the relatively small army in South Africa became embroiled in another war with a Bantu people – this time the Basuto, who were almost as formidable as the Zulus. The Boers seized their opportunity, overwhelmed the small British garrison in Pretoria and marched into Natal, defeating a force sent to oppose them at a mountain pass known as Laing's Nek. They followed up their initial successes with a series of well co-ordinated attacks and inflicted a serious defeat on the British at Majuba Hill.

In July 1881 the Boers were granted 'self-government subject to the suzerainty of Her Majesty' and an uneasy peace was agreed. It did not last long. In 1885 gold was discovered near Johannesburg in the Transvaal and there was a rush of foreign prospectors, 'uitlanders' as the Boers called them, into the independent republic. For very sound reasons the uitlanders were thoroughly distrusted by the Boers, who denied them political rights and treated them in some respects as second-class citizens. The scheming Cecil Rhodes, bent on creating a British hegemony from Cairo to the Cape, sought to exploit the discontent of the uitlanders and sent his crony Jameson, with a bunch of hired thugs, to provoke them into an armed uprising. This conspiracy was a total failure but it united the Boers behind their President, the stern Paul Kruger, and against the British. Always connoisseurs of good firearms, they began to buy large numbers of excellent Mauser rifles and Herr Krupp's Quick-Firing Field Guns from the Germans.

The British Governor in Cape Town, Sir Alfred Milner, backed by the Colonial Secretary, Joseph Chamberlain, adopted an intransigent attitude towards Afrikaner ambitions for independence and maintained the principal of British suzerainty over the Transvaal and the Orange Free State. In October 1899 troops arrived from India to reinforce the small imperial force already in South Africa, and Milner issued an ultimatum to President Kruger. But it was the Boers who struck first. In a series of rapid manoeuvres they invaded

Natal and the Cape Province and laid siege to Mafeking, Kimberley and Ladysmith. The war which followed was long, bitter and almost completely pointless, since the Boers achieved their self-government within five years of the ending of hostilities. The scorched-earth policy which the British eventually adopted, and the confinement of Boer women and children in concentration camps (where hundreds died), left a legacy of bitterness which accounts in part for the intransigence of Afrikaner attitudes to this day.

At first, the war went badly for the British. The Boer commandos with their Mauser rifles and the new smokeless ammunition were more than a match for the regular soldiers who opposed them. Many British regiments still wore red coats at the beginning of the war. So, concealed in rocks and gullies or dug into trenches, the skilled Boer marksmen, camouflaged in the grey or brown of their ordinary working-clothes, were able to pick off their enemies at long range as they advanced in parade-ground fashion over the bare veld. As usual, the British were apt to underestimate their opponents and it took several severe reverses to get them out of their red coats and into khaki.

The British were commanded by Sir Redvers Buller, a brave but incompetent officer, who had himself won the Victoria Cross during the Zulu war. One of his generals, Sir George White, was also a VC. In the winter of 1899 White and his forces were besieged by the Boers at Ladysmith. Buller marched to relieve him and launched an attack on the enemy fortifications near Colenso on the Tugela River. Two batteries of the Royal Field Artillery, the 14th and the 66th, went forward in support on the infantry attack. The commander of the artillery, Colonel Long, was one of those dashing soldiers whom Britain produces from time to time, possessed of a high degree of courage and little common sense. He raced ahead of the infantry and brought his guns to within less than a thousand yards of the main Boer position, known as Fort Wylie, and only about five hundred yards from the front line of enemy trenches. The batteries were set up in the open in plain view of the enemy and within minutes horses and men were falling like flies under well-aimed rifle fire. Instead of immediately abandoning the position, Long ordered his guns

45

to open fire and the men went through their drill as calmly and efficiently as though firing a salute in Hyde Park, the only difference being that men were dying while they did so. The Boers responded to the British Artillery with their quick-firing Krupp guns and kept up their accurate fusillade on the batteries. Soon there was hardly a man left standing to serve the guns. Long himself received a bullet through the liver and was dragged off, protesting, to the shelter of a gully, or donga, five hundred yards behind the guns. A junior officer with more sense than his commander then attempted to limber up the guns and get them out, but as soon as the horses were brought forward they were shot dead. Survivors of the carnage took shelter in the donga and waited for the infantry to come up.

Eventually, two companies of the Devons and a small party from the Scots Fusiliers reached the donga, but without artillery support they were unable to get any further forward. The two batteries still stood in the open surrounded by a welter of dead or dying men and horses and it seemed inevitable that the guns would be taken by the Boers. At this point Sir Redvers Buller arrived in the donga with his staff and called for volunteers to rescue the guns. Three young staff officers, anxious for glory, immediately offered their services. They were Captain Congreve of the Rifle Brigade, Captain Schofield of the Royal Artillery and Lieutenant Roberts, son of Field-Marshal Lord Roberts, who had himself won a Victoria Cross during the Indian Mutiny.

This gallant trio was soon joined by Corporal George Nurse, six gunners of the Royal Field Artillery and Private George Ravenhill of the Scots Fusiliers. Limbering up a gun in those days and for many years to come was a tricky exercise even for trained men and horses in parade-ground conditions. The limber, which carried ammunition for the gun, was a box on wheels drawn by a team of six horses. The gun, which was itself mounted on large wheels, had to be manhandled into position and the trail – the long 'tail' at the back of the gun – attached to the back of the limber, like a caravan on the back of a car. The whole cumbersome articulated vehicle could then be towed to wherever it was wanted, with gunners riding postillion, that is riding on the near-side horses to steer the gun on its way. On the parade ground this was difficult enough, but on the battlefield – if one of the six horses was shot, or if it simply stumbled and fell – the whole contraption could easily be brought down in an ugly scrimmage of heavy metal and flying hooves. Injured horses would have to be cut free of their traces and the gun righted by hand if necessary before the whole thing could be put on the road. Even the routine handling of artillery on the battlefield therefore called for great skill and daring. The gunners themselves made easy targets as they wheeled the gun into position behind the limber or as they rode postillion on their horses. Under heavy close-range gun and rifle fire the attempt to rescue the guns at Colenso was tantamount to suicide.

Since many of the horses were already dead the little party of volunteers only took out two limbers, but as soon as they emerged from the cover of the donga they came under murderous fire. There were five hundred yards of bullet-swept ground to cross before they even reached the batteries; then the frantic manhandling of the guns themselves, clearing dead men and horses and broken gun carriages out of the way as they limbered up (all the time with more men and horses falling to the Boers' fire); then the mad dash back to the shelter of the donga. Against all the odds they succeeded. Captain Schofield got his team back with one gun and Private Ravenhill, who was not even an artillery man, helped with the other, but young Frederick Roberts was shot and mortally wounded. Congreve and Nurse saw him fall and, when they had seen the guns safely back under cover, they went back for him. Congreve was hit by four rifle bullets and his horse was shot in three different places, but both horse and man survived. Roberts died two days later.

Recommendations for the Victoria Cross appear to have been made on the spot. Congreve (whose son was also to win the Cross in the First World War), Schofield, Corporal Nurse and Private Ravenhill were all gazetted on 2 February 1900 and, even though he was now dead, so was Lieutenant Roberts. Since his father, Lord Roberts, had just been appointed Commander-in-Chief of the British forces in South Africa, it seems likely that the War Office felt able to bend the rules without misgivings. From 1900 onwards it was tacitly acknowledged that the Victoria Cross could be awarded to men who

47

died winning it. A Royal Warrant of 1920 eventually gave official recognition to what had long been established practice.

Ladysmith was finally relieved a few weeks after the Colenso VCs were gazetted and the relief of Mafeking followed in May of the same year, but the war dragged on in a series of guerilla actions by Boer commandos until a slow process of attrition at last brought resistance to an end in 1902. Seventy-eight VCs were won by troops under British command, including detachments from Australia and New Zealand – the 'cubs', as contemporary posters rather coyly put it, 'coming to the mother lion's call'. The last VC of the war was also one of the most remarkable, because it was awarded to the first man in history to win the Cross twice.

As often happened, a small party of Boers had ambushed a British column. A number of soldiers were killed and several seriously wounded. Efforts to reach them were rendered almost impossible by constant and, as always, accurate rifle fire from the Boer positions, which were only a hundred yards from the wounded men. Despite the extreme danger Arthur Martin-Leake, a surgeon serving with the rank of captain in Baden-Powell's South African Constabulary, went forward to tend the wounded. Dodging the bullets, he managed to get one man under cover and patch him up as best he could. He then went out again and was in the act of helping a badly wounded man into a more comfortable position when he was hit three times by rifle fire and seriously wounded in the left arm and right leg. Instead of collapsing on the spot, he continued to do his best to help those he considered to be in a more serious condition than he was himself and only gave up when his wounds stiffened and he found himself unable to move. Even then he refused to drink any of the detachment's small supply of water until all the other wounded men had received their ration first. The citation for the VC which followed stated that he 'collapsed with exhaustion' – which is, as is often the way with citations, something of an understatement.

Twelve years later at Zonnebeke in Flanders during the first battle of Ypres, Martin-Leake was serving as a lieutenant with the Royal Army Medical Corps when a British attack went in against the German trenches. The attack failed in the teeth of heavy machine-gun and rifle fire and the survivors withdrew to the British lines, leaving hundreds of dead and wounded men in no-man's-land, many of them close to the enemy positions. The Germans were jumpy and fearful of another attack, and anything that moved in front of their trenches was immediately subjected to furious bursts of fire. Despite the enormous risks, Martin-Leake crawled out into the charnel house of the dead and dying and dragged back one wounded man after another. Any man who has himself been wounded in similar conditions knows how fearful it is to have to take the same risks again, but Martin-Leake did so, not once but many times. On 18 February 1915 the *London Gazette* announced that he was granted what they rather curiously called 'a clasp' to his Victoria Cross. Surprisingly enough he survived to wear it for many years. After a long career with the Indian Railway Service he returned to England and, when well into his sixties, served with an ARP unit during the Second World War. For him, as for many others, the courage that won the Victoria Cross was not a sudden burst of adrenalin, but a steady and enduring capacity to suppress his own fear and risk his life for the sake of others.

Part II
The First World War

The First World War

The First World War changed the whole scale of warfare. Where previous conflicts had counted combatants in thousands, this great eruption numbered them in millions. The industrialisation of war, with entire national economies and whole populations totally engaged in the effort to defeat the enemy, had been foreshadowed in previous upheavals, but it was now on a scale that had never before been imagined. The First World War was the last in which fleets of battleships confronted one another, the first in which the submarine emerged as a powerful weapon of blockade and destruction. For the first time, too, men fought for supremacy in the air as well as on land and sea; the aeroplane developed in four years from a harmless box kite with a tiny engine to a high-speed flying machine with synchronised machine-guns and built-in bomb racks. And on land, where armies had once wheeled and manoeuvred over wide areas, the Western Front quickly became a stalemate of trench systems from the North Sea to the Swiss frontier.

It was a war of dull endurance, of brave but futile advances costing hundreds of thousands of lives, to advance the line a few miles or a few yards in this direction or that. It was a matter of men against machine-guns, of earth-shattering artillery barrages, of tanks and poison gas. After the first few weeks there were no more brilliant cavalry charges or dashing deeds with the Colours. Even to talk of honour and glory in the mud of Flanders would have been obscene if it was not also ridiculous. For most men it was enough simply to try and stay alive. And yet there were countless deeds of great heroism in these horrific conditions, and during those four long years the Victoria Cross was awarded almost as many times as in

53

the whole of the rest of its history from the Crimea to the present day.

Historians still argue about the causes of the war, but most of them agree that the decaying Hapsburg empire of Austria and Hungary merely provided the spark for the powder-keg. For the past fifty years the great European powers – Russia, Germany, France and Britain – had all been engaged in expanding their empires, competing aggressively with one another whenever their interests seemed to conflict. The continental nations built up huge conscript armies and forged alliances and counter-alliances, always ready to back up diplomatic moves with a threat of war. Germany was in a high state of readiness in 1914, with a vast and well-trained army, a brand new navy and a national identity newly forged in Bismarck's 'blood and iron'. France too had a large standing army, each man conscripted for three years' service and the nation as a whole anxious to avenge the humiliation of the Franco-Prussian war. Russia had also steadily advanced her frontiers throughout the nineteenth century with the biggest army of all exercising dominion over the Eurasian land mass from Poland to the Kamchatka Peninsular. Britain compensated for a small professional army by keeping afloat the largest navy in the world to keep watch on its far-flung empire, and eyed the expansionist aims of the others with deep suspicion.

Even if they were not very sure which of the others to hate most, all the great powers were in a sense spoiling for a fight and Germany in particular had found that aggressive diplomacy, backed by the threat of force, was a useful means of getting their own way. When the Archduke Ferdinand of Austria was shot by what we would now call an urban terrorist in Sarajevo on 28 June 1914, the implications for the fragile Hapsburg empire brought about a flurry of threats and ultimata between Germany and Russia – bluff calling bluff, mobilisation in one country countered by mobilisation in another, so that diplomatic confrontation escalated into war almost without the conscious volition of any of the participants. Once a great army starts marching it is very difficult to call it back without a catastrophic loss of national pride and political power for those in command.

4

The War on Land

Germany struck first, but not principally at Russia. Fearful, as a later generation was also to be, of fighting on two fronts, the German High Command chose to eliminate France from the arena before taking on the vast spaces and endless hordes of Russia. They acted on the precepts of Schlieffen, a much admired strategist, who had advocated a swift advance through Belgium to the industrial heart of northern France. Britain, as usual the least well-prepared of all the combatants, reacted sharply to the German threat to Belgium and declared war as soon as the Kaiser's troops invaded. Fear of expanding German power certainly played a part, but so, just a little, did idealism. In 1914 the British still believed, as some Americans still do, in making the world 'safe for democracy' – even if this was not clearly apparent to most of the citizens of her empire.

The result, for six divisions of Britain's very small Regular Army, was that they just about had time to polish their boots and pack their kit-bags before taking the first boat to France as the British Expeditionary Force. One of the elderly British generals dropped dead before catching sight of the enemy and his replacement also collapsed within days of his arrival in France. The British commander, rather confusingly named Sir John French, alternated between aggressive optimism and gloomy timidity. In support of the French Army on his right he advanced northward to the Belgian town of Mons, where on 23 August 1914, in a feat of highly disciplined musketry, the small British force met and held a German Army three times its size. But the French Army began to fall back and, with their flanks unprotected, the British were also obliged to retreat. In the days that followed, before the German advance was checked and turned on the River Marne, a number of heroic rear-guard actions brought glory to several units of the

55

retreating British forces and earned the Victoria Cross for a number of outstanding men.

At Audregnies in Belgium on 24 August the 9th Lancers tried to stem the German advance by galloping full tilt at a solid mass of enemy infantry. The odds against them were if anything rather greater than those against the Light Brigade at Balaklava. The Germans immediately brought heavy rifle and machine-gun fire to bear on the cavalry and the 9th Lancers were cut to pieces. Captain Francis Grenfell rallied the survivors and prevented their retreat from turning into a rout. When a troop of Horse Artillery were also shot up and their guns in danger of being taken, Grenfell took a party of volunteers forward under fire and, in an action also reminiscent of earlier wars, they manhandled the guns free of the carnage so that the artillery men could limber up and make their getaway. Grenfell lived long enough to receive his Victoria Cross from the King, but was killed at Ypres the following spring.

The cavalry and the guns of the Royal Horse Artillery also featured in another remarkable action at Nery on 1 September. It was a foggy morning and the teams of horses had been unhitched from the limbers of 'L' Battery so that the horses could be taken to a nearby stream to drink, oblivious of the fact that an entire German cavalry brigade had ridden up to within a few hundred yards of their position. The guns were scattered in an orchard, totally unprepared for action. As the fog lifted the Germans saw their opportunity and opened up on the British battery with artillery and machine-gun fire. Heavy volleys of shrapnel exploded among men and horses and caused fearful damage, killing all the officers except the battery commander, Captain Bradbury. The survivors managed to get two of the guns into action, but one was quickly knocked out, leaving only one British gun against eight of the enemy. Sergeant David Nelson later wrote a report of the events of that day.

> During the awful carnage the groaning of dying men and horses were audible amidst the terrific thundering of cannon; the scenes were in most cases beyond description. One man in full view of me had his head cut clean off his body, another was literally blown to pieces, another was practically severed at the

breast, loins, knees and ankles. One horse had its head and neck completely severed from its shoulders.

There were now three serving the gun, Captain Bradbury, Sergeant-Major Dorrel (who up to now had been using a rifle under cover) and myself twice wounded; we still maintained a quick rate of deadly accurate fire until our ammunition supply began to wane and the two men carrying it to us disappeared.

Captain Bradbury went to get ammunition from an adjacent wagon, but he only got about four yards from the gun when a shell from the enemy completely cut both his legs off midway between knees and body, thus leaving Sergeant-Major Dorrel and myself in action.

We fired the two rounds remaining with the gun and with them silenced the only German gun which appeared to be shooting when 'I' Battery RHA opened fire on the enemy from a position behind us and completed their destruction.

I was ordered to leave the gun by Sergeant-Major Dorrel, but asked him to remain with me, when he said it was useless to do so and went away. I followed him reluctantly and seeing the 'Bays' in action I took up a rifle and fired at some straggling German infantry, I believe accounting for two of them. The kicking of the rifle greatly intensified the pain in my right side and also increased the bleeding so I had to drop the rifle.

Shortly afterwards the 4th Cavalry Brigade arrived on the scene and opened fire on the enemy from the flank. It was now the Germans who were in trouble. They abandoned their guns and fled. Only three men in 'L' Battery were still on their feet and the wounded, including Sergeant Nelson, were evacuated to field hospital. However, the hospital itself was overrun by the Germans a few days later and Sergeant Nelson, his wounds still unhealed, made a daring escape to the French lines. Against all the odds he survived to be evacuated to England and receive his Victoria Cross in November 1914. Captain Bradbury, who died of his wounds on the battlefield, and Sergeant-Major Dorrel both received the VC for the same action.

Towards the end of the same week in which 'L' Battery were surprised at Nery the German generals made a series of mistakes which brought about the first significant Allied victory of the war. Believing that they had outflanked their enemies, the Germans broke off their headlong advance to

The First World War

wheel across the Allied front north of Paris, hoping to roll up the right wing of the French Army. In doing so they left themselves open to counter-attack and General Gallieni, commander of the garrison in Paris, made brilliant use of the opportunity. Marshal Foch quickly exploited the advantage and Sir John French rather timidly joined in. In the so-called 'miracle of the Marne' the Germans were forced to withdraw and try, rather late in the day, to outflank the Allies by moving further to the west. The British and the small Belgian Army responded and soon the opposing lines extended all the way from the coast of Belgium to Alsace and Lorraine.

And there the Front remained, with gains and losses of only a few miles on either side, for the next four years. The history of those years is the history of extraordinary endurance in the mud and cold of the trenches, of massive offensives in which hundreds of thousands of men died – the names of the places where the battles were fought all now redolent of massive slaughter: Ypres, the Somme, Messines, Passchendaele. Many Victoria Crosses were won in those terrible offensives, many others in repelling similar disastrous attacks by the enemy. Men were guilty of all the actions of cowardice and brutality which war has always encouraged, with the added assistance of poison gas and trench mortars, heavy howitzers and tanks. But some of them also performed those fine acts of self-sacrifice which are occasionally recognised by the award of the Victoria Cross – rescuing comrades under fire, falling on a live grenade to save the lives of others, charging a machine-gun single-handed to avoid further casualties. One action will stand for all of them, because it summed up in so many ways the futile waste of lives and the absurd incongruities of war on the Western Front. And also because the man concerned is still alive to tell the tale – Major Edward Cooper vc, who still lives quietly in South Shields where, except for a few extraordinary years, he has lived all his life.

The battle known in the official history books as Third Ypres, because two other frightful battles were fought in the same place, was better known to the men who fought there as Passchendaele, though Passchendaele itself was not reached until the closing stages of what was in reality a campaign rather than a battle. It was fought for the wrong reasons in the

58

wrong place and at the wrong time, a four-month slog through mud and blood which achieved nothing except the death or wounding of 300,000 British troops and rather less than that number of Germans. In a war distinguished by bad generalship it was perhaps the most fatuous in terms of strategic objectives, and the most stubbornly pursued in the face of disaster of the entire British war effort. But, as in so many other campaigns, the incompetence of the high command was matched only by the courage of the junior officers and men who had to carry out their orders. Over sixty VCs were won during Third Ypres. When it was over, General Haig's chief of staff came forward for the first time and surveyed the terrible swamp through which he had sent over half a million men and turned astounded to his ADC. 'Do you mean to say that we sent men to fight in this?' he asked.

'It's worse further forward' said the young officer. The general broke down and wept, but it was of course too late for tears.

For many months before the summer of 1917 General Sir Douglas Haig, commander-in-chief of the British forces, had been planning a great offensive in Flanders. His strategic objective looked sound enough to him. The British 2nd and 5th Armies, with the support of one corps of French troops, would burst out of the Ypres salient and drive through the plains of southern Belgium in a great right-hook which would roll up the right wing of the German Army, seize the Channel ports and destroy the bases of the U-boats, in order to ease the losses of shipping which were threatening to starve Britain into surrender. In fact by August 1917 the losses in shipping had already fallen as the Royal Navy at last adopted the convoy system. There were few U-boats on the Belgian coast anyway and the Belgians had flooded their nice level plains, so the German flank was secure, but an awareness of these facts had not percolated through to General Haig. Nor had he learned the lessons of his previous offensives, like the great slaughter at the Somme the previous year which had cost over 400,000 casualties – 60,000 on the very first day. In fact none of the attacking battles, Allied or German, had made any serious impact on the enemy's overall position since 1914 and all had been at a terrible cost in lives. Nevertheless Haig went

59

boldly forward with his plan. The place he chose for the battle that he hoped would bring him success and acclaim could hardly have been worse.

The old Flemish town of Ypres was surrounded to the north-east by a flat plain of drained marshland, intersected by streams and canals. Junior officers clearly perceived that an artillery barrage would turn the entire area into a swamp, impassable to men, guns, horses or tanks. They tried to warn the general, but he did not hear them. General Foch, the French commander, called the projected battle 'the ducks' march'. Haig did not hear him either. The Germans had sensibly withdrawn almost all their troops from this slough of despond and had dug themselves in on the high ground which overlooked it on three sides. The curving British front line, the so-called Ypres Salient, wallowed beneath these hills. Every movement of troops and supplies could easily be discerned from the ridges above and pounded by German artillery. Haig took two months to prepare his offensive, so the Germans had plenty of warning. They established an elaborate system of in-depth defence, protected by almost impenetrable cordons of barbed wire. Beyond the wire the first line consisted of concrete block-houses – pill-boxes the British soldiers called them – which commanded all possible approaches with interlocking fields of machine-gun fire. Behind the pill-boxes were trenches with deep dug-outs, more trenches, more wire, more dug-outs, increasing in size and strength the further they were from the British, so that even if the first line was overrun the Germans could counter-attack from positions of strength. When the British were finally ready to attack the Germans were ready for them. In fact General Ludendorf was so confident that he released some of his divisions and packed them off to help the Austrians against Italy.

The British advanced through the swamp on 31 July. The preliminary artillery barrage, as predicted, left the pill-boxes intact and made the ground impassable to the attacking troops. As they waded forward, each footstep sucked deep into the slime, they faced appalling concentrations of enemy artillery and mortar fire, poison gas, barbed wire and the deadly hail of the machine-guns. Men died in groups, in platoons, in entire companies as they advanced, some blown literally to pieces by the artillery, many more machine-gunned, some even drowned. The shell holes quickly filled with a viscous brown soup, an evil-smelling fluid concocted of mud, blood and water, deep enough to swallow men, mules, even the hopelessly bogged-down tanks. By the end of the first day everyone but the general and his staff knew that it was insane. The quartermaster sergeant of the 1st Battalion of the Hertfordshire Regiment went forward with the rations for 660 men at the end of the first frightful day. When he eventually got through he found that his battalion had ceased to exist. Five hundred and thirty-six men had been killed or wounded; the rest were prisoners, shell-shocked, or simply lost somewhere in the mud. But instead of stopping, reconsidering, even pausing, Haig pressed on with the offensive, not for a week or a month but for 104 days from 31 July to 12 November 1917.

So it was as a small part of Haig's great offensive that Sergeant Edward Cooper's platoon of men of the 12th Battalion of the King's Royal Rifle Corps advanced in the pre-dawn light of 16 August towards what had once been the Belgian village of Langemark. Like most of his fellow soldiers, Edward Cooper was a conscript, called up in 1914 when he was twenty years old to train in Field-Marshal Kitchener's new army. Cooper was a devout Christian, a man who never used foul language, rarely if ever had a drink, with a strongly developed sense of responsibility for his fellow men. Three years of war had hardened him to the sight and smell of death, but had done nothing to diminish his determination to do what he thought was right. He was a small and inconspicuous man who had won promotion partly through solid merit, partly because of his extraordinary capacity simply to stay alive while others died all around him. He had been through the lot and he was still on his feet, so he was now platoon sergeant, the effective leader of about thirty men (the number at any one time depending of course on the number of casualties). In nominal command was a young officer, a newly commissioned second lieutenant, fresh out from England. It was the officer's first battle. In his hand he carried a brand new revolver, a going-away present from his parents.

The troops were already dog tired. Laden with an extra 60 pounds of equipment, 150 rounds of ammunition, picks and shovels, emergency rations, they had already walked, or rather waded, nearly eight miles through the marsh that morning. In Cooper's platoon the soldiers were strung out in a long line on either side of their officer. Even though machine-gun and artillery fire had already torn wide gaps in their ranks they kept walking slowly forward. Not one of them tried to take cover. Cooper recalls:

> You couldn't lie down. Your instructions were that if you were resting you couldn't lie down and take cover. There was none. But even so, you couldn't lie flat in the mud – you'd never have got up again with the equipment, you were absolutely laden. Anyone going down in the mud or falling into a shell hole, he had to be left to his own devices and of course we lost dozens of men due to this happening. There was this line of block-houses, a line of them protecting these rear positions of the Germans, and they could fire on to us with impunity because the shell fire had no effect on the block-houses themselves. It would take a direct hit from a six-inch gun, which was very unusual, to disturb one of those.

As the barrage lifted and the line of pill-boxes came into plain view, the machine-guns began their pitiless hammering through the frail lines of men. The attack wavered and halted.

> They had held up the advance of the first line of the attack, and of course we piled up behind them so that it was like doubling the number of troops getting it. The machine-guns were just playing havoc. At this point I lost three or four officers, my company commander was killed; my own officer was killed; the colonel was wounded; the intelligence officer was killed; the Lewis-gun officer was killed and we lost about seven officers and up to fifty men at this immediate area where I was at that time.

Cooper knew he must take charge of the shaken remnants of his platoon. On an impulse he went over to the body of the young second lieutenant and took the shiny new pistol from his lifeless fingers. He thought he would take it back to England and return it to the young subaltern's parents, a good intention which long afterwards he actually fulfilled. He slung his rifle over his shoulder and took the unfamiliar pistol in his hand. Almost useless as a weapon at anything but point-blank range, it was perhaps a kind of talisman, a symbol of command in action. Angry at the waste of lives, Cooper decided he had to do something to save the rest of his men. Looking carefully at the block-house, his experienced eye could tell that one of the machine-guns firing through a narrow slit was limited in its arc of fire – a factor which had so far saved their lives and now gave him an opportunity to attack.

I knew that if we stayed there long enough we would all be killed and I decided that if I got into a certain position, the Germans' arc of fire couldn't reach me, and I set off diagonally to get into this position. I called on my men to follow me. Four did rise and follow me and we got to within about a hundred yards of the block-house when I ordered them to fire and give me cover, while I stole up and put the machine-gun out of action. There were only two machine-guns actually firing and the crews were inside the block-house itself. One was still firing to the front, but of course it couldn't reach me because I'd got into such a position that they couldn't fire at me. And all the other men were under cover, so the Germans didn't know how many men were there.

I then stole up to the front of the block-house and fired my officer's revolver down the barrel and the machine-gun stopped firing. I didn't bother with the other one; when one stopped firing the other automatically ceased firing for some reason so that they were both out of action. I then rushed round the back, put my head into the block-house and called on them to surrender. There were two entrances to this block-house and when the first German eventually appeared I was watching the other opening. So when I turned and looked at this other opening [and saw] a German in front of me – twice my size and with his hands up – I got such a shock that I pulled the trigger of the revolver and down he went. And of course everything then started all over again.

The Germans rushed back into the dug out and they opened up again with another machine-gun. I had to go through the whole procedure again, but by then I had tucked the revolver under my belt and got my rifle and bayonet in front of me, and I stood out in between the openings and shouted some more and they all came out again. The next man out, as he passed me I just clipped him across the ears and kicked him up the pants and the others just came out quietly without their equipment . . . I called them out to surrender and I formed them up facing their own lines instead of taking them to the front of the block-

house, where they were out of view of their German comrades.
I had them all lined up there and then of course my men came
up and took charge of them.

Without in any way diminishing the immensely courageous
spirit which had led him into a one-man attack on an
apparently impregnable German position, it is fair to say that
he had succeeded almost by accident. One small and rather
frightened man had captured a strongpoint which could easily
have defeated a hundred. By the book Cooper had done almost
everything wrong. At his first approach, forty-five men, with
seven machine-guns, all uninjured except for the unfortunate
man whom he had accidentally killed, surrendered to him in
full view of their comrades in the trenches nearby. He should
have thrown a grenade into the pill-box to kill or stun as many
of the enemy as possible before attempting to force a surrender.
He should also have waited for reinforcements, but he didn't
call up the rest of his men until all the enemy soldiers had
given themselves up. And he should not have formed the
Germans up in front of their own trenches, because the rest of
the enemy could and did see what was going on.

> The Germans, soon as they saw all these prisoners getting ready
> to march away, they opened fire again and killed one or two of
> their own men and wounded some of ours. I had a lance-
> corporal on my right and a corporal on my left, brothers, they
> were both wounded and I was left unharmed again. And
> eventually the prisoners moved away and I formed the men up
> ready to go forward with the advance. I'd lost touch with the
> troops on my right and left now and the advance continued, and
> the adjutant appeared on the scene.
>
> On the battlefield he started telling me off because I was off
> my line of advance. I knew that of course, but the troops that
> were left were having a good laugh at me, being told off on the
> battlefield for being off my line of advance, so I had to mention
> to him what had happened, that I'd captured these prisoners
> and this block-house . . . Eventually we caught up with our
> barrage, we continued the advance and reached our objective.

At the time, Cooper was thoroughly embarrassed at being
shown up in front of his men and he was also very much aware
that he had tackled the pill-box in less than text-book style.
He also knew that he had been afraid.

64

Of course I was frightened, but that's what bravery's all about.
You hide your fears and share your courage with the men. They
look to you as an NCO, as a sergeant, for example and
discipline. And I suppose it was just discipline and *esprit de corps*
that made me go on . . . The men expected leadership and if I
hadn't gone forward and led them of course they'd have had to
stay there. There was nobody else capable of taking charge.

The following day Cooper was in action again. Following a
German counter-attack, one of the positions which had been
taken on the first day had been overrun by the enemy and it
was up to Cooper and the thirty or so men remaining in his
company to take it. Cooper was assigned all that remained of
the battalion's 'D' Company to help him. 'D' Company
consisted of four men. But through all the fighting that
followed over the next weeks, Cooper seemed to bear a
charmed life; even when those all around him were killed he
survived unscathed. So he was one of the very few men in his
battalion to be present at a ceremonial parade behind the lines
later that autumn.

The brigade was drawn up and formed into a square and there'd
be roughly a thousand men there. The decorations were
announced, the people who were being awarded DCMs first and
then MMs and so on, but my name was never mentioned. At the
end of the parade the general sent for me. He said, 'I want to
compliment you, Sergeant Cooper, on your part in this action
and in the work you did.' He said, 'I've already told your
parents of this and sent them off a – diploma.' (I don't know
what they called it, announcing that you've been mentioned in
dispatches and so on for outstanding work.) 'But,' he said, 'I
have a complaint to make against you.' I said, 'I'm sorry to
hear that, sir. What was it?' He said, 'You remember when you
captured the block-house? Well, one of the Germans complained
– and he was an officer, this German who complained – that
he'd been treated very roughly by a sergeant in the British
Army, that he'd been clipped across the ears and kicked up the
pants, and what do you have to say about that?' Well, I'd
forgotten all about the incident. I said, 'Well, I remember it
now, sir, now that you've mentioned it, but it wasn't viciously,
it was just in the excitement of the moment that I did this.' He
said, 'I understand, Cooper. The only mistake was that he
should have been out first and got the bullet.'

The First World War

Cooper went back up the line again after the parade with a vague idea that he'd been mentioned in dispatches, but that was all there was to it. A few weeks later he was marching his platoon down the road behind the lines when a heavy shell landed. Nine of his men were killed instantly and eighteen wounded. He was the only man left standing, an event which confirmed him in his almost superstitious belief that he bore a charmed life.

He was not sent on leave until 15 January 1918, nearly five months after the action in front of Langemark, and when he left the front he still did not know anything about an award. It was not until he was sitting in a YMCA café at King's Cross that he happened to see a newspaper carrying a list of the new VCs. The name of Chavasse caught his eye – Captain Noel Chavasse who had just won a Bar to his VC, one of only three men ever to do so and the poor man had died shortly afterwards. Next in alphabetical order was Cooper, E. It was not until he had read and re-read the name and the regimental number that he realised that it was his own citation that he was reading.

> It never struck me at the time that everybody else knew but myself about this VC . . . and when I got on to the station and into the train there was nothing to distinguish me from anybody else. It was filling up rapidly with troops from overseas and camps in the south and everybody was talking about Sergeant Cooper. Some were professing to know him and I was listening to all this conversation. I was sat in the corner and I found out later that on the station, on the hoardings there were notices [saying] 'If Sergeant Cooper's on this train will you report to the *News of The World* or any one of the other national papers', you know, they were all advertising for me. They'd learned that I was in between front and home. I didn't see these things but I don't think even if I had seen them I would have stopped, that I would have delayed going on this train to go home.

The small, shy sergeant in the corner of the carriage said nothing, but when the train finally reached Darlington, where he had to change, Cooper was astonished to find his father and his elder brother waiting for him. Then, to his enormous embarrassment, a civic reception awaited him at South Shields. He was paraded through the streets, speeches were

66

made in his honour, he lost all the buttons of his uniform, his cap was stolen, his rifle disappeared, everything that anybody could get hold of as a souvenir was taken off him and he arrived home almost in tatters. Then there was further embarrassment. His uniform was not just torn, it was lousy. All the men in the trenches were infected with lice, but somehow he could not explain this to his mother, just as he could never bring himself to explain to anyone at home just how frightful war in the front line really was. Somehow he felt that he must protect their innocence, even over the lice. Quietly, he burned his underwear in the back yard and set off the next day to try and get a uniform from the local Territorial Army. The quartermaster greeted him with scorn, and it wasn't until an officer intervened that he was able to extract new kit from the reluctant guardian of the Territorial Army's stores.

After his investiture, Cooper returned to the front line and was granted brevet promotion to lieutenant. His luck held and he came through the rest of the war unhurt. But after he was demobilised he never mentioned the fact that he had won the Victoria Cross. He did not like the way that other men would try and press drinks on him and get him to talk about the war. In any case he felt that they expected 'a strapping six-footer, not a little fellow like me'. The few people who knew his record gradually forgot. For thirty-five years he lived in modest obscurity until the Victoria Cross Association was formed in 1953 and someone hunted him down. Suddenly he was a hero all over again. In 1957, forty years after the events in which he had won the Cross, the Corporation of South Shields finally put up a plaque to Edward Cooper, the shy VC.

5
The Royal Navy

The Royal Navy's vital function during the Great War was demanding but unexciting – the blockade of ships carrying food and supplies to Germany. Since the Germans and their allies had few merchant ships of their own, this effectively meant stopping and searching neutral vessels, a policy which, because it interfered with international big business, made the Royal Navy highly unpopular with non-combatants, especially with the United States. At the onset of war Britain held back from blockade on the high seas, precisely for this reason, but the Germans brought these measures upon themselves by a campaign of submarine warfare which by 1917 had become completely unrestricted; any and every vessel which might be carrying goods to Britain could be torpedoed without warning. Each of the major combatants tried to deprive the other of essential supplies. Ultimately the adoption of the convoy system much reduced the effectiveness of the German U-boats, but before the end of the war the Royal Navy had a total of 3,000 vessels operating the blockade all over the world, making this one of the most important factors in the eventual Allied victory.

In 1914 naval actions were more dramatic. Within days of hostilities opening, a daring raid on the German fleet in harbour at Heligoland lured half a dozen enemy light cruisers into the North Sea, where a squadron of British battle-cruisers under Admiral Beatty promptly sank three of them. This sharp lesson so alarmed the Germans that for the next four years they rarely risked their larger vessels out of harbour. However, a few German cruisers were already far from home when war broke out, and the cruiser *Emden* did much damage to British shipping in the Indian Ocean before she was tracked down and sunk by the Australian cruiser *Sydney*. Off Cape

Horn in October 1914, a small British squadron under Admiral Cradock attacked a superior force of enemy vessels under the capable German Admiral von Spee and, entirely predictably, he got himself and two ships blown out of the water. This catastrophe was avenged at the battle of the Falklands early in December, when Admiral Sturdee sank four of the German cruisers, including the flagship, the *Gneisenau*. Von Spee himself went down with his ship.

In both encounters the braver actions were in the defeated vessels. In naval battles of this period a ship that went into action against a vessel with superior armament could expect only to be sunk, usually with all hands. Cradock was brave, if ill-advised, to attack von Spee with only two cruisers against five. The Germans, at bay off the Falklands, also turned on a more powerful squadron and tried to close with them so that their lighter guns could be brought to bear, but the British stood off and pounded the smaller vessels to pieces at long range. Royal Naval commanders, unlike their opposite numbers in the army, had a high regard for the safety of their own men and possibly an even higher regard for their ships. Throughout the war Admiral Jellicoe's Grand Fleet, which spent most of its time at anchor in Scapa Flow, lost a total of two men killed and four wounded in direct action against the enemy. Total casualties to all ranks in the Royal Navy were under 40,000 in four years, against 60,000 lost to the army in a single day on the Somme. This is not to say that the Grand Fleet did not serve its purpose, which was to act as a deterrent. Its task was to keep the German High Seas Fleet in harbour, and it succeeded very well.

With the possible exception of the battle cruisers under Beatty, which saw action again at the Dogger Bank in 1915, the most daring and audacious engagements were not in the big ships at all, but in some of the much smaller vessels under naval command all over the world. It was in these less conventional craft, in submarines, in torpedo boat raids on shore installations, in landing parties on even smaller boats, as airmen, even as infantry in the trenches, that most of the Royal Navy's Victoria Crosses were won. The first naval VC of the war was awarded to Lieutenant Norman Holbrook, who was in command of a near-obsolete submarine in the Straits of the Dardanelles. The channel, no wider than a sizeable river, was heavily mined, and the ageing B.11 only had enough power in her batteries for two hours' travelling under water at six knots. Under the nose of Turkish shore batteries, Lieutenant Holbrook guided his craft up the narrow channel at less than walking speed to conserve the batteries as long as possible; and at enormous risk to himself and his crew succeeded in torpedoing the Turkish battleship *Messudiyeh*. As the big ship began to settle she opened fire on the submarine, which very nearly came to grief when her compass was flooded and Holbrook was unable to tell which way he was heading. For the rest of his journey home, as he inched down the narrows, he had to keep coming up to periscope depth to check his position. When he finally brought his crew to safety the submarine had been submerged for nine hours and the air was so foul that his main engines were unable to start. For sustained courage under intense stress Holbrook won the Victoria Cross, and the entire crew was awarded the DSM.

British submarines were on the whole neither as numerous nor as essential to the Allied war effort as the U-boats were to the Germans. In April 1917 losses to Allied shipping from submarine attack were so catastrophic that there was a strong likelihood that Britain would be starved out of the war. Until Lloyd George at last pushed the Admiralty into accepting the idea of convoys, all kinds of methods were tried to combat the U-boat menace. The most ingenious of these were the 'Q'-ships, heavily armed cargo vessels disguised to look like harmless freighters, sailing alone and unprotected and simply asking to be attacked. If, as sometimes happened, the U-boat attack was unheralded until the torpedo hit the ship the elaborate deception was a waste of time and lives, but torpedoes were expensive and the submarines could only carry a limited number. The captains often preferred to surface and sink their target with gun fire, especially if the first torpedo missed its mark.

On 22 March 1916 the 'Q'-ship *Farnborough*, commanded by Lieutenant Gordon Campbell, was attacked by the submarine *U.68*, in mid-Atlantic. The torpedo passed astern and the crew of the *Farnborough* lay low and pretended they had seen nothing. The submarine surfaced to close on its prey, and Campbell ordered a 'panic party' of naval men disguised as merchant seamen to take to the boats. Totally deceived, the U-boat came to within 800 yards of the apparently doomed freighter. Suddenly, a 'steering house' in the stern of the *Farnborough* swung open to reveal a 12-pounder gun, and two 6-pounders appeared on either side of the bridge. As the submarine tried to submerge, a number of shells found their target. Campbell made sure of her by dropping a couple of depth charges, and the submarine foundered with all hands.

The U-boat commanders soon grew too wary to be caught so easily, and 'Q'-ship commanders had to take even greater risks if they were to succeed. The next time the *Farnborough* (now renamed *Q.5*) was attacked, in February 1917, Campbell deliberately manoeuvred to allow the torpedo to strike home, taking care only that it should hit aft of the main bulkhead, which would prevent the ship from filling too quickly with water. But as the 'panic party' got away, the ship began to settle and it looked as though it was only a matter of time before she sank. Not daring to man the pumps for fear of being seen, Campbell and his men lay hidden. Cautiously, the submarine *U.83* approached and circled the ship with only the periscope showing, carefully examining her for signs of malicious intent. The nervous strain on captain and crew must have been intense. At last the submarine came to the surface and edged cautiously around to the stern of the 'Q'-ship, until she was only 100 yards from the sinking vessel.

Then Campbell sprang into action. The covers were thrown from the guns and the submarine was hit a dozen times in the first half minute. She sank almost immediately, and only two of the German crew (an officer and a rating) managed to struggle to the stern of their erstwhile victim. Hopelessly crippled and still settling slowly in the water, the *Q.5* was eventually towed to safety with all her triumphant crew alive and none seriously injured. It was one of the last triumphs of the 'Q'-ships and brought Commander Campbell a much deserved VC.

Only once during the entire war did Admiral Jellicoe succeed in bringing the German High Seas Fleet to battle, and the result of the meeting was inconclusive. On 31 May 1916,

The First World War

Admiral Scheer, the new and aggressive German commander, sent his battle-cruisers under Admiral Hipper to lure the British out into the North Sea. Scheer's intention was to instigate a confrontation between Hipper's squadron and Admiral Beatty's battle-cruisers, then move in himself to crush the lighter British ships with his own heavy Dreadnoughts. What he did not know was that the Royal Navy had cracked his codes early in the war and had some idea of his probable intentions. So, as Hipper and Scheer left the shelter of the German coast, it was not just Beatty that sailed to meet him, but the Third Battle-Cruiser Squadron under Admiral Hood and the whole of Admiral Jellicoe's Grand Fleet steaming at full speed out of Scapa Flow. Three formations of British ships, many of them bigger, faster and more powerful than their adversaries, converged on the High Seas Fleet.

It should have been the greatest naval battle that the world had ever seen, an Armageddon of the oceans. In the event, however, confused and inadequate signalling, defective British shells which failed to penetrate the German armour and his own reluctance to risk unnecessary losses combined to rob Admiral Jellicoe of victory. But if Jellicoe was cautious, his subordinate Beatty was not. As soon as one of his light cruisers sighted Hipper's squadron at about half past two in the afternoon, Beatty took his battle-cruisers into the attack, leaving his four heavy battleships far astern. Instead of standing off and engaging the enemy at extreme range, where his own heavier guns would have had the advantage, Beatty closed within nine miles of the enemy and it was the Germans who fired first. Within minutes two British battle-cruisers had blown up under the impact of accurate enemy salvos, while Beatty's own fire had hardly dented the German vessels.

'There's something wrong with our damned ships today,' Beatty is said to have remarked. Indeed there was. A defect in design allowed sparks to follow the trail of cordite straight from the gun turrets to the magazines below. At about four o'clock Beatty's own flagship, *Lion*, received a direct hit on one of the midship's turrets. At that instant an officer of the Royal Marines, Major Francis Harvey, was mortally wounded. But, hideously burned and suffering from shock, he was still alert for the safety of the ship. With the last of his strength he

72

supervised the closing of the doors to the ammunition chambers and the flooding of the magazine. Admiral Beatty continued to attack, oblivious of the danger, while the dying marine officer saved his flagship for him. Harvey was rewarded posthumously with the Victoria Cross.

As Scheer's battleships came up to close the trap on Beatty, they were appalled to see the entire Grand Fleet bearing down on them. Admiral Jellicoe had come to the rescue. With great skill, the German battleships promptly reversed their direction, each ship turning virtually in its own length as the Grand Fleet steamed across their path. Some of Scheer's battleships took a battering as they fled, but not before they had managed to sink yet another British battle-cruiser – Admiral Hood's *Invincible*. None of the big German ships were sunk and Jellicoe did not go in hot pursuit. Fearful of mines and submarines, he steered a course to the east of the enemy, confident that he could cut off their retreat. As if to prove him right, Admiral Scheer's battleships suddenly reappeared from the west, heading straight for the centre of the British line, though whether by accident or design has never been satisfactorily explained. Again the Germans turned about and fled, this time sending a shoal of destroyers in with a torpedo attack. The British turned aside to avoid the torpedoes and Scheer made good his escape by ordering Hipper to charge the Grand Fleet with his battle-cruisers. They did little damage to the British and took a terrible hammering in return, but somehow most of the German ships managed to stay afloat and the whole of Scheer's fleet escaped during the night. This was the beginning and the end of the great Battle of Jutland.

The Royal Navy retained its mastery of the sea, but at heavy cost. In total, 14 British ships were sunk (3 of them battle-cruisers) as against 11 of the enemy, most of them much smaller vessels. And 6,000 British seamen died against 2,500 Germans. The enemy had inflicted more damage with fewer and lighter guns. They could and did claim a victory. There was no glorious triumph for the Royal Navy to bring hope to the soldiers in the trenches and strike terror in the hearts of their enemies. Worse still, the British did not dare to invade the Baltic in force as long as the High Seas Fleet was still there, and so could not bring relief to Russia – a failure which contributed to the 1917 revolution, the rise of the Bolsheviks and the withdrawal of Russia from the war. Jutland was not a good battle for the British.

And yet, as always, there had been great heroism, especially on board the little ships, the destroyers and light cruisers that had harried the retreating enemy. Commander Loftus Jones of the destroyer *Shark*, for instance, valiantly defended his ship to the last, manning one of his guns himself. When his leg was shot away he kept fighting and ordered a new White Ensign to be hauled aloft when the old one was destroyed by enemy fire. And finally when he could see that his ship was doomed, Loftus made sure that as many of his men as possible reached the relative safety of the boats. Like Major Harvey, his VC was posthumous. In fact, as the war progressed, it became increasingly difficult to win the Cross without dying for it.

But the most famous VC won at Jutland, perhaps the most famous ever, was that awarded to Boy Cornwell of the light cruiser *Chester*. The *Chester* was in the van of Admiral Hood's squadron when it first came up on the German fleet, and took heavy punishment during its first encounter with the enemy. One in five of her men were killed or wounded and half her gun crews badly knocked about, including the crew of the forward 5.5-inch gun, where sixteen-year-old Jack Cornwell worked as sight-setter. While two men crawled to safety and the others lay dead or dying around the gun, the former grocer's delivery boy stood by his post and stayed there throughout the long horror of the action. It was not until the battle was over, many hours later, that anyone realised that he was dying. When they did it was too late. His body was taken ashore and buried with little ceremony in a common grave at Grimsby.

When Admiral Beatty came to write his report, however, he described Boy Cornwell's action in particularly glowing terms. There is, after all, nothing like a heart-rending tale of heroism to take people's minds off uncomfortable failures. The adulation that followed was one of the most extraordinary demonstrations of public sentiment in a war which was often sentimental on the home front. The unfortunate boy's body was disinterred from its communal resting place and given a hero's funeral, with gun carriage, White Ensign, an escort of

Naval Cadets, and troops of Boy Scouts lining the route of the former Boy Scout's funeral. When his VC was gazetted in September, the public adoration was like the mass hysteria surrounding a pop star. Boy Cornwell was as famous as the Beatles. Society painters competed to depict the most moving portrayal of the action, though they had some trouble getting a likeness until someone suggested his little brother. Copies of one picture or another adorned every school-room and Scout-hut in the land. A special day was set aside in his honour and tales of his heroism appeared in hundreds of different papers and magazines to be read aloud to impressionable children. A Cornwell Memorial Fund was launched by the Scouts for Cornwell Badge winners.

It would have been nice if his parents could have had some of the money, but his father did not survive to see his son's VC and his mother died in 1918. His sister got a little of the cash when she emigrated to Canada after the war, but otherwise that was that. Public interest died down after a while and only lingered on in the Scout Movement. When the war is over, heroes tend to become redundant, dead heroes most of all. Only a few years later, a letter in a national newspaper complained that the wretched boy's grave was neglected and overgrown.

In retrospect it does appear that there is something slightly nauseating about the adulation of Boy Cornwell, and even something questionable about his VC. The gun by which he stood was wrecked, and there was no possible contribution he could make to the battle by standing by a useless gun. If he was able to move he would have been a hundred times more useful carrying ammunition or tending to the wounded. If he did not move from his post, it was perhaps because the poor dying boy was unable to do anything but stand where he was and hope, by standing, that he would not die.

So what was the Cross awarded for? The terms of the Warrant allowed for 'outstanding devotion to duty in the presence of the enemy'. Here then was an example of outstanding devotion, the kind of devotion that was needed if boys of his age or a little older were going to continue to advance into the machine-guns of the Somme or Passchendaele. At a time when questioning voices were being raised about the useless

75

slaughter of youth, it may have seemed appropriate to make a hero out of just such a victim – to encourage the others perhaps. There is also room for a rather different interpretation, however. The public, in willingly joining in the adulation of Jack Cornwell, were perhaps giving expression to a collective sense of mourning quite independent of any possible cynicism on the part of national leaders. In praising him they could mourn him, not in the kind of defeatist way which would only have drawn censure in those stirring times, but with the pride appropriate to a dead hero. A little of his glory could then rub off on all the other boys who died in the bloody squalor of war, unrecognised and inadequately mourned. Boy Cornwell stood for them all.

6
The VC in the Air

Despite the appallingly heavy casualty rate for pilots in the struggle for air supremacy over the Western Front, the air battle retained some of the glamour which was quickly lost on land. In all the combatant nations, most of all in France and Germany, 'aces' who could claim many victories over enemy planes were hailed as national heroes. Men like Immelman, von Richthofen and Georges Guynemer, with scores of enemy aircraft to their credit, became household names throughout Europe. And, on the whole, aerial combat also retained some elements of chivalry. Despite the German 'terror' attacks on British cities, the Allied air forces did not attempt to bomb non-military targets and only took to bombing enemy transport and lines of communication at a comparatively late stage in the war. The most important role for aircraft was reconnaissance, and the second most important was that of shooting down enemy aircraft. In the air, if in few other theatres of war, there was still room for good, clean heroics.

None of the British aces clocked up quite the same astronomical numbers of enemy planes shot down as their rivals in Germany and France. The most famous pilot of the Royal Flying Corps, Albert Ball, only scored a relatively modest forty-four, but he did it in a very short space of time and had, in any case, other qualities to make him a popular British hero. He was in the first place extremely young – barely nineteen when he began his career as a fighter pilot and only twenty when he died. He also had the good fortune to reach the peak of his extraordinarily aggressive career when British disasters, especially the great offensive on the Somme, were creating widespread disillusionment on the home front. Heroic deeds are a great help to morale on the home front when all the news is bad; and some PR-minded general made sure that

77

The First World War

Ball's successes were in the news, but he also had another asset which may have helped him appeal to the British public.

Albert Ball was not a gentleman. His father was a plumber, a highly successful plumber who built up a big business and eventually became Lord Mayor of Nottingham, but a plumber for all that. So although young Albert was sent to good schools, he did not acquire a classical education; instead he developed a keen interest in engineering and a passionate love for machines. Popular legend later claimed he worked as a blacksmith, but in fact, while still a boy, he went into business with his father's help as a mechanical engineer. When war broke out he was eighteen and immediately volunteered for the army, enlisting as a private on 21 September 1914. Helped perhaps by his mechanical aptitude and his experience in an Officer Cadet Training Corps, he was commissioned as a subaltern within a month.

Much to his irritation he remained in England throughout 1915, so he seized the opportunity to train as a pilot at his own expense at Hendon Aerodrome. He was not a brilliant student but his enthusiasm made up for his lack of expertise. He wrote to his sister, 'I am getting on ripping with my flying. I went up yesterday at four a.m., one hundred feet and landed ripping. You would love the sport.' Then, a little later, 'Yesterday a ripping boy had a smash and when we got up to him he was nearly dead. He had got a two-inch piece of wood right through his head and died this morning. If you would like a flight I should be pleased to take you any time you wish.'

Albert Ball was evidently not an unduly nervous boy. He eventually succeeded in gaining his Royal Aero Club Certificate, but he had to wait another three months before he was accepted by the Royal Flying Corps. At last, in February 1916, he was transferred to France, but was disappointed to find himself flying slow two-seater BE2c's which were not at all suitable for the kind of aerial combat he longed for. He clamoured for a faster machine and in May he was transferred to No. 11 Squadron, which was equipped with Nieuport 17s. These manoeuvrable little aircraft had a Lewis-gun mounted on the upper wing which could fire directly forward over the propeller – a device which made them more or less a match for the German fighters, particularly the much feared Fokker,

with its forward-mounted machine-gun synchronised to fire
between the propeller blades.

In June, following a succession of inconclusive but highly
aggressive sorties, Ball brought down an enemy observation
balloon and was awarded an MC. He followed this up with a
victory over a German Roland, but the aggressive tension of
his flying had begun to take a toll on his nerves. In July he
wrote home:

> I am now getting a taste of real army thanks. I will tell you the
> circumstances. The day before yesterday we had a big day. At
> night I was feeling pretty rotten and my nerves were feeling
> quite pooh-pooh. Naturally I cannot keep on forever. So at
> night I went to see the CO and asked him if I could have a short
> rest, and not fly for a few days. He said he would do his best. He
> asked General Higgins and now what has taken place? Well,
> GH has sent me to No. 8 Squadron, back on the BE2c's. This
> is thanks after all my work, and not even the major can stop it.
> Three majors have done their best, for they all think it is a cad's
> trick. However, here I am. Now I think I shall ask to go back to
> my regiment. Will you advise me, write soon. Address to No. 8
> Squadron BEF. P.S. Oh, I am feeling in the dumps.

The childishness of this letter suggests a kind of *Boys' Own
Paper* mentality, a schoolboy resentment of authority, but this
was combined with an equally boyish enthusiasm for derring-
do. Certainly, this is how Ball seemed to see life in the early
months of the war. He volunteered for an extremely hazardous
mission, flying across the German lines and landing behind
their rear positions to drop off a secret agent. The mission was
a failure, but Ball had restored himself to the General's favour.
He was soon back with No. 11 Squadron and his favourite
Nieuport. In this plane he swiftly won a series of spectacular
successes, taking on enemy aircraft in batches of half a dozen
at a time, and by September he had been credited with twenty
victories and had won for himself the freedom to fly as he
pleased and fight as often as he liked. His plane rarely seemed
to be on the ground, except for essential servicing and the
patching of innumerable bullet holes. He quickly won a DSO
and Bar and was promoted to Lieutenant.

Unlike some of the other great aces (Captain James
McCudden, for instance) Ball was not known for bestowing

protective care on the less experienced pilots in his flight. He was not very sociable, he took his job very seriously – and that job was, as he saw it, to destroy as many enemy planes as possible. He was highly professional, lavishing great care and attention on his machine, but his greatest gift was for sustained, single-minded aggression. The curious thing is that he also began to feel considerable remorse. 'I do not feel anything bad about the Hun,' he wrote to his father. 'Nothing makes me feel more rotten than to see them go down, but you see it is either them or me, so I must do my duty best to make it a case of them.' His English had not improved, but he was certainly forced to grow up very quickly.

He continued a spectacular run of successes with another eleven victories in the autumn of 1916, which brought him another Bar to his DSO in November and made him the first man ever to win two Bars to the award.

At this stage he again asked for a transfer and was sent back to England as a pilot instructor. His home town, Nottingham, honoured the most highly decorated pilot in the country by granting Albert Ball the freedom of the city. He could easily have stayed safely at home for the remainder of the war, but like many other men who win the Victoria Cross he quickly began to yearn for a return to active service. In April 1917 he got his wish and returned to France with No. 56 Squadron, the same unit with which McCudden was later to win so much fame. The squadron was equipped with the latest SE5s, which were bigger and faster than the Nieuport but not so manoeuvrable, and Ball clamoured for a Nieuport. The higher powers were willing to indulge their star pilot and he was issued with one of these beloved machines for his own personal use.

Ball was highly successful both with this machine and with the SE5, which he carefully modified to his own specifications. He remained a loner, with his own strange eccentricities like never wearing goggles or a flying helmet because 'I like to feel the wind in my hair'. Although some of the great aces were still to clock up enormous numbers of victories in the last two years of the war, the era of the lone hero was drawing to a close. To overcome their numerical inferiority, the Germans in 1917 began to group their planes into 'wolf pack' formations, with whole squadrons in the air at the same time. In his first sortie with No. 56 Squadron Ball brought down an Albatros two-seater, but in the afternoon he came up against a group of five Albatros scouts. He shot down one and then got into difficulties with the other four, returning to base with his plane riddled with bullet holes. Towards the end of April he dropped a message over an enemy airfield challenging two German fighters to meet him the following day, but the Germans unsportingly laid a trap for him and he found himself once again up against five Albatroses instead of two. Again, he was lucky to escape.

At the beginning of May he scored his forty-fourth victory, which put him two ahead of his main Allied rival, the French ace Guynemer; there were great celebrations, but this was to be his last successful combat.

On 7 May 1917, after flying bomber escort duty in the morning, he took up a group of SE5s in the afternoon looking for the enemy. They found Jagdstaffel 11, the famous German 'wolf pack' commanded by Manfred von Richthofen, though on this occasion the Albatros fighters were led by his younger brother Lothar. The two groups of fighters were well matched and the battle raged for the rest of the afternoon and on into the evening. Four German planes were forced down. One of the SE5s was blown up in mid-air; two other British planes were forced to land, but the pilots eventually made it back to base. Only Albert Ball's plane was not accounted for. He had last been seen fiercely engaging an Albatros, but both planes had disappeared into a bank of cloud and none of the other pilots had seen him come out.

Two weeks later a German fighter dropped a message over the British lines: 'RFC Captain Ball,' it read, 'was brought down in an air fight on 7 May by a pilot of the same order as himself. He was buried at Anoeullin.' Albert Ball was dead, but there were no signs of combat damage to his plane when the Germans found it, and the pilot who had claimed the victory – Lothar von Richthofen – had himself been forced down with a damaged engine. The exact circumstances of Ball's death are still unknown. The Germans gave him a funeral with full military honours and his VC was gazetted on 8 June 1917. His last letter to his father, written two days before his death, is a kind of epitaph.

The First World War

'I do get tired of living to kill,' he wrote, 'and I'm really beginning to feel like a murderer. Shall be so pleased when I have finished.'

Ten other British pilots ended up with higher scores than Albert Ball, but none achieved so many victories in so short a space of time. His Victoria Cross was awarded, like many other VCs in the air, for sustained action over a period of time, but in Albert Ball's case the period of successful combat activity was little more than four months – three in the summer and autumn of 1916 and one in the spring of 1917. This is of course not to diminish the achievement of others. Edward Mannock, the highest-scoring British ace with seventy-three victories to his credit, was scarcely given any official notice during the war and was only awarded with a posthumous VC after much agitation by his former colleagues. James McCudden, whose fame almost equalled Albert Ball's, had an admirable reputation as a caring flight commander as well as a fighting record of fifty-seven enemy aircraft brought down. But the VC is not responsive to mathematics. Captain Freddy West had shot down fewer German planes than any of these, but his VC was none the less deserved.

Ferdinand West, known always as Freddie, was born in 1896. Unlike Albert Ball, he was born an aristocrat and a cosmopolitan and remains so to this day – urbane, charming and very much amused by the absurdities of life. He was born in London, the only son of Lieutenant Francis West and grandson of Admiral of the Fleet Sir John West; but his mother, Comtesse Clemence de la Garde de Saignes, was French. When his father was killed in the Boer War, Comtesse Clemence moved to Milan and it was in Italy that Freddie spent most of his youth. (It is remarkable, incidentally, how many future Victoria Cross winners lost one or both of their parents in early childhood.) By the time Freddie was eighteen he was tri-lingual, a student of international law at Genoa University and looking set for a legal career, but as he himself observes, 'I was secretly hoping for adventure and excitement.' The war looked like an ideal opportunity and he travelled back to England as quickly as possible to volunteer for the armed services. To his irritation he found himself a private in the Royal Army Medical Corps, but after several months he succeeded in obtaining a commission in the Royal Munster Fusiliers. More months of training followed, and it was not until November 1915 that he finally reached France. But instead of the 'adventure and excitement' he craved, he found himself in the filth and boredom of the trenches.

> I lived like a rat for about twelve months. I was shot at but I could never see who was firing at me, and during the many months of doing nothing I used to watch the sky and see these aeroplanes flying, having a wonderful time in the immensity of the sky. And when they fought it was a real fight between two individuals and I said to myself, if I get a chance to be a pilot that's what I want. And one day a message came through the trenches that the army wanted particularly army fellows with army experience to join the Royal Flying Corps as observers. I was first on the list and that's how I joined the Royal Flying Corps.

After only four weeks' training as an observer, Freddie returned to France and was posted to No. 3 Squadron equipped with Morane two-seater Parasols. These were fragile but manoeuvrable monoplanes, which were used for reconnaissance and the bombing and strafing of enemy positions. By volunteering for every possible mission Freddie quickly built up an impressive number of flying hours as an observer in combat, in order to gain acceptance as a trainee pilot. His experience in the Moranes taught him two valuable lessons. The first was that when flying a slower and more vulnerable plane, the observer should scan the skies constantly for enemy aircraft and leave the pilot to do the ground-spotting. The second was that if attacked it always pays to be the first to open fire.

Freddie was accepted for pilot instruction in October 1917, by which time he had flown 225 combat hours as an observer. He wanted to be a fighter pilot, but because of his spell in the trenches and his experience in reconnaissance he was trained for an army co-op squadron. Air tactics were still in their infancy, but the idea of close liaison between aircraft and troops on the ground was beginning to gain general acceptance. Early in January 1918 he was posted as a pilot to No. 8 Squadron near Amiens, under the command of Major Leigh-Mallory. The squadron was equipped with the big, solid

The First World War

Armstrong-Whitworth FK8, known to its crews as the 'Big Ack'. It is not nearly so fast or manoeuvrable as the fighters but it was dependable and, for its period, well armed, with one machine-gun mounted forward and one (sometimes two) Lewis-guns on a ring mount for the observer.

The duties of the squadron were varied, ranging from spotting targets for the artillery to bombing and strafing enemy troops and transport, but the job which all the pilots disliked most was photographic reconnaissance, because in order to bring back a coherent series of pictures, they had to fly at low altitude in a dead straight line. This meant of course that the enemy anti-aircraft gunners could predict exactly where the plane would travel and aim off in front of it. 'To fly straight, being fired at, particularly by Archie [anti-aircraft guns],'as Freddie puts it, 'is no great fun.' Almost every time he and his observer completed such a mission, they brought their plane back peppered with holes from rifles, machine-guns and shrapnel.

Against the German fighters Freddie resorted to the tricks he had learned as an observer.

> They invariably followed the same tactics. Once they spotted you they went up to about five or six hundred feet above you and then they tried to dive on you, all guns blazing, and shoot you down. Our way to answer was that the observer should open fire immediately he saw the German pilot put his nose down. Often the pilots didn't like being fired at; they broke combat. Occasionally, you had a tougher fellow who wanted to go on fighting. In that case I would try to do a very unpleasant flat turn and try to face the direction the enemy was coming from, because that compelled him to do large turns to the left or to the right and give my observer a chance to fire on him. That's the way we tried to save ourselves.

Freddie's self-deprecating modesty is legendary. Not only did they try to save themselves, they were often highly successful at shooting down the enemy. On one occasion, when the Big Ack was attacked by a group of Pfalz fighters Freddie made his turn and shot one of the enemy planes out of the sky. A few moments later his observer brought down another and, although they were hotly pursued by the rest of the pack, Freddie managed to shake them off and get safely back to his

1a Mate Charles Lucas, an Irishman from County Armagh, winning the first Victoria Cross on board HMS *Hecla*, on 21 June 1854, during the opening stages of the Crimean War

1b Like many VCs, Lucas did well in the services and rose to the rank of rear admiral. He died in bed at the age of eighty in 1914

2a Queen Victoria demonstrating great equestrian skill at the first investiture of the Victoria Cross in June 1857

2b The Charge of the Light Brigade at Balaklava. The incompetence of the High Command, coupled with the heroism of junior officers and men, resulted in a magnificent disaster during which nine VCs were won

3a *above* Thomas Kavanagh receiving the finishing touches to his make-up before leaving the Residency in Lucknow

3b *below left* Ross Mangles rescuing a wounded soldier during the Indian Mutiny, 1857. Like Kavanagh, Mangles was a civilian

3c *below right* Former drummer-boy Thomas Flinn, who won the Victoria Cross at the age of fifteen

4a Assistant-Surgeon Campbell Douglas getting extremely wet on the coast of Little Andaman Island in 1867

4b Lieutenants Melvill and Coghill trying to save the Regimental Colour at the battle of Isandlwhana, 1879

5a The mission station at Rorke's Drift under attack from the Zulus. Several VCs are visible in the picture, including Lieutenant Chard, Surgeon-Major Reynolds and Privates Hook and Williams

5b *left* Private Henry Hook

5c *right* Private John Williams

6a Gunner James Colliss, who forfeited the Victoria Cross after being imprisoned for bigamy and died in poverty

6b Saving the guns at Colenso, December 1899. Corporal Nurse in centre foreground, Lieutenant Roberts falling, mortally wounded, from his horse on the right

7a Sergeant, later
Major, Edward Cooper
vc destroying a German
machine-gun during the
attack on Langemarck,
August 1917

7b Edward Cooper
receiving the Victoria
Cross from King George V

8a John Cornwell became a national hero after his death at the battle of Jutland in May 1916

8b Cornwell standing mortally wounded by his gun on the deck of HMS *Chester*

8c Captain Gordon Campbell, the commander of *Q5*

own lines. They were also successful at their vital role of
reconnaissance. He and his colleagues, operating in the
Amiens sector, were able to give early warning of the German
offensive of March 1918. It was not their fault if General Haig
consistently ignored or misunderstood the significance of the
warnings they sent him. For the two weeks of the great German
thrust in their sector, No. 8 Squadron were airborne every day
in a series of bombing raids on enemy lines of communication.
Since virtually all rapid movement of men and supplies
depended on rail transport, these raids could and did have an
important effect on the rate of the German advance. During
this extremely dangerous time for the British, Freddie West
and his observer, Flight-Lieutenant John Haslam, made many
raids on German transport and both were awarded the MC
for their part in the battle.

The Germans put the last of their strength into two more
attempts to break the Allied line in Flanders in April, and on
the River Aisne (near Reims) in May, but although these
offensives also achieved initial successes, they did not result in
the expected breakthrough. By mid-summer the initiative was
back with the Allies, and Haig planned another offensive to
recover some of the ground lost to the Germans on the front
near Amiens. Mercifully, he had learned something from the
needless slaughter of Passchendaele and the Somme, perhaps
because he now had fewer troops to sacrifice. This time he
would make proper use of tanks and would not force vast
numbers of men to their deaths against impregnable positions.
Haig had also begun to learn the value of aerial reconnaissance.
On 7 August, the day before the expected battle, the commander-in-chief of the newly formed Royal Air Force, Sir John
Salmon, paid a visit to No. 8 Squadron. Freddie West recalls
the occasion:

> He told us that the army would launch a very big offensive
> which he hoped would be the end of the war. The commander-
> in-chief – Earl Haig – had asked him to get the earliest possible
> information as to the location and direction and movement of
> German reserves. If we could do this it would help enormously.
> So Sir John Salmon turned round to us: 'Now boys, I rely on
> you, it's up to you to bring this information.' So all of us – all of

us were most anxious on the 8th, 9th and 10th of August . . . to obtain this information.

On 8 August Freddie, now promoted to captain, and his observer, John Haslam, took the Big Ack through the mist over the German positions as the British offensive began. Because of the mist they had to fly at very low altitude and they were constantly exposed to enemy small-arms fire. On their way back they were unable to see their landing strip and eventually located it only with the aid of rockets fired from the ground. The damaged aircraft crashed on landing and Freddie was bruised and shaken. Despite this setback he and Haslam were out again the following day, scouring the countryside for enemy troop concentrations. Since these were usually camouflaged from the air and laid up in thick woodland, the most effective way to find them was to fly low over wooded areas and deliberately draw their fire. They practised this hazardous form of reconnaissance so effectively that the engine was shot out of action and again Freddie had to crash-land his aircraft.

In the circumstances, after two extremely narrow escapes, one might have thought that West was pushing his luck to try again, but on 10 August he and Haslam were airborne once more. They flew at 1,500 feet, trying to locate the German reserves.

I was lucky, or unlucky, whichever way you want to look at it, and I was delighted to find at last an area where I saw many German troops, a large amount of transport, a large amount of guns – and I thought, this is the information that the army needs. And so, having got this information, I made straight for my aerodrome. Unfortunately, German fighters were also of the opinion that I should not bring back this information and so I was attacked. During one fight I received some explosive bullets in my left leg, which was almost severed, but you know when you are young you are an optimist, and I think the combination of youth, health and optimism got me back. I am also grateful to my observer who did first-class work with his Lewis-guns and I'm glad to have this opportunity to pay a tribute to him, because he is still alive. We may be, for all I know, the only alive team from the 1914–18 war in the air. He became a group-captain and a parson. He's a reverend, probably due to my bad language in the aeroplane.

The VC in the Air

Freddie's laconic humour obscures all but the bare essentials of the episode. The fact was that he was under continual attack from German fighters almost from the moment he first discovered the enemy concentration. A burst of machine-gun fire hit him in the foot. His plane was damaged and he had a useful report to take back to base, but still he insisted on making another wide slow turn under the noses of the German fighters to make sure of the exact location of the enemy. When he finally headed back to base he had to take on five German planes and, within minutes, a burst of enemy fire had almost completely severed his left leg. Twisting his underwear into an improvised tourniquet with his left hand, Freddie flew on with one hand and one foot through a mist of pain, back towards his own lines, still under attack from a persistent German scout. Knowing he could not reach his home field, he somehow managed to put his plane down on a patch of grass close to some Canadian positions. But even when first aid had been administered and his rescuers were trying to get him to hospital, Freddie insisted on waiting until he could make his report to an officer from No. 8 Squadron. Only when he was sure that his information was properly conveyed to the right quarters did he allow himself to be taken to hospital.

Freddie's left leg was amputated shortly afterwards. In hospital in London a few days before the Armistice was signed, he was taken off to the theatre to have a minor operation on the stump.

> When I returned to my bed under anaesthetic I was semi-conscious. I heard a considerable amount of noise which was due to all the other boys rattling, using spoons in their metal mugs and making a colossal noise in that way, and there was an orderly saying something about the Victoria Cross, followed by most uncomplimentary words, but I didn't know what it was all about, until later – about an hour later when I was conscious – the senior surgeon of the hospital, the matron and one nurse turned up and they said congratulations. I said, but what are you talking about? They laughed, said nothing, but they dropped a newspaper on my bed. Later, out of curiosity, I glanced at the newspaper and there on the front page I saw my name in the awards for the Victoria Cross. That's all I know. I was most surprised.

The First World War

If a man's courage lies not just in the sudden surge of adrenalin-induced energy on the battlefield, but in his sustained capacity to overcome his own fears and weaknesses, it was in the aftermath of the war that Freddie showed what he was worth. The artificial limbs generally available at the end of the First World War were not sophisticated, and he was fortunate in meeting a Swiss engineer named De Soutter, who fitted him up with an aluminium leg – a modified version of which he wears to this day. Thus equipped, Freddie quickly learned to walk again and rather gloomily resigned himself to returning to the legal profession.

> I was a member of the Inner Temple and was going to be a lawyer; never for one moment did I think I could be accepted for the Royal Air Force. And suddenly I got a typical message from Sir Hugh Trenchard, later Lord Trenchard, which read as follows: 'Can you fly with a tin leg?' And I replied, 'Yes, sir, and I would very much like to do so.' Shortly afterwards I was posted to Air Commodore 'Stuffy' Dowding, later Lord Dowding, who was extremely kind to me and arranged for an instructor to fly with me and give a report on my flying ability. After about three weeks, or a month, the report was satisfactory and I must say I was very happy and very proud to have the opportunity to serve most of my life in the Royal Air Force.

Not only did he learn to fly again, but he found a new role in the Royal Air Force, first as a base commander and later as air attaché in Finland, Estonia and Latvia – all sensitive postings in the aftermath of the Russian Revolution. When war came again in 1939 Group-Captain West led a formation of Blenheim bombers to the aid of the British Expeditionary Force in France and landed once again near Amiens. It is said, though not by Freddie, that it was his skill and courage in managing an aircraft with his 'tin leg' that inspired Douglas Bader to return to active service after the loss of his legs at the beginning of the war. But West's career took a different turn. His air attaché experience and his language skills led to his appointment as a somewhat mysterious official at the British Legation in Berne.

Details of this appointment have still not been made public, but it is known that he ran a secret 'underground railway' for RAF pilots who had managed to make their way across the

Swiss frontier. The Gestapo wanted him dead and put a price on his head, but Freddie did not offer anyone the opportunity of collecting the money. The element of risk must have appealed to him and he would probably have offered high odds on his own survival, because he has always regarded life as a bit of a gamble. 'Of course,' he says, smiling benignly, 'life is a roulette game. What else?'

Part III
The Second World War

The Second World War

The Second World War is still too close to us to need elaborate explanation. The story of Adolf Hitler, the rise of the Nazi Party, the persecution and attempted genocide of the Jews, the unprovoked invasion of Czechoslovakia and Poland – none of this needs retelling here. But the story of the Victoria Cross does illuminate some moments of that terrible war which might otherwise be forgotten, just as the courage of the men whose stories follow might easily be forgotten.

Many, too many, of the men who won the Cross during the Second World War died winning it. The award has grown progressively more difficult to achieve as other medals have proliferated and as the nature of modern warfare has reduced the opportunity for outstanding courage 'in the presence of the enemy'. Only those actions so evidently heroic that they carried more than a high chance of death in battle could hope to qualify in the struggle with Germany and Japan. The stories told here are those of a few men who survived and were able to recall the circumstances of the action themselves, but to place those memories in a clear context I also talked to other men who were there at the time. With their help it has been possible to reconstruct quite accurately sometimes more accurately than the citations recorded at the time – the events which led to the award of a Victoria Cross.

The other advantage of approaching those who have survived is that it is possible to seek answers to other, less easily defined questions. Is the VC just one bright moment in an otherwise dull career for the man who has won it? Is that bright spark of courage simply generated in a flash of anger, of high adrenalin, even of fear? Or if there is some more enduring aspect to it, can it be perceived even in childhood and does it survive the shock of war and continue to enhance

The Second World War

the whole of a man's life? These brief accounts do not begin to do justice to the complex fabric of six men's lives, but there are clues, sometimes strong indications that the qualities necessary to win a Victoria Cross can be discerned in many other aspects of a man's life, both before and after the event.

The men whose lives are briefly explored here were chosen almost at random. The chief criterion was that they should represent the major countries of the British Commonwealth who came to our rescue in 1939. Even given that prerequisite, there were still many others who could, perhaps should, have been chosen to demonstrate the whole gamut of heroism in the many different theatres of war. Unfortunately, the precise details of some of those events are now difficult to establish, either because the men concerned have since died or because the details were never properly recorded. There is no other reason why some were chosen and some not, other than that these are a few of the surviving VCs I happened to meet and these are their stories.

7
Ganju Lama

His Majesty the King has been graciously pleased to approve the award of the Victoria Cross to:

No. 78763 Rifleman Ganju Lama 7th Gurkha Rifles, First Battalion.

In Burma on the morning of 12 June 1944, the enemy put down an intense artillery barrage for an hour on our position north of the village of Ningthoukhong. This very heavy artillery fire knocked out several bunkers, caused heavy casualties and was immediately followed by very strong enemy attack supported by five medium tanks. After fierce hand-to-hand fighting the perimeter was driven in in one place and enemy infantry, supported by three medium tanks, broke through, pinning our troops to the ground with intense fire. 'B' company of the 7th Gurkha Rifles was ordered to counter-attack and restore the situation. Shortly after passing the starting line, they came under heavy enemy medium machine-gun and tank machine-gun fire at point-blank range which covered all lines of approach. Rifleman Ganju Lama, the number one of the PIAT gun, on his own initiative and with great coolness and complete disregard for his own safety, crawled forward and engaged the tanks single-handed. In spite of a broken left wrist and two other wounds, one in his right hand and one in his leg, caused by withering cross-fire concentrated on him, Ganju Lama succeeded in bringing his gun into action within thirty yards of the enemy tanks and knocked out first one, then another; the third tank being destroyed by anti-tank guns. In spite of serious wounds he then moved forward and engaged with grenades the tank crews, who now attempted to escape. Not until he had killed or wounded them all, thus enabling his company to push forward, did he allow himself to be taken back to the regimental aid post to have his wounds dressed. Throughout this action Ganju Lama, although very seriously wounded, showed complete disregard for personal safety, outstanding devotion to duty and determination to destroy the enemy, which was an example and inspiration to all ranks. It was solely due to his prompt action and brave conduct that a most critical situation was averted, all positions regained and very heavy casualties inflicted on the enemy.

Ganju Lama has an air of permanent good humour. His face is so deeply creased with smile lines, especially around the eyes, that it is difficult to see how he could possibly rearrange his features into a frown. Although he is now in his sixties and spent two years in hospital towards the end of the war, he also has immense physical vitality. Like most men from the eastern Himalayas he is quite short, but his shoulders are broad, he is strongly built and positive in his movements. When he talks he moves his hands in great sweeping gestures so vigorous as to discourage close proximity. It is over forty years since he won the Victoria Cross, but one still gets the feeling that it would be a mistake to cross him. Smile or no smile, he might still be a dangerous man with a kukri.

Ganju Lama was born Gyamtso Shangderpa, the second eldest boy in a family of four brothers and two sisters, in 1924. The family home was in a remote village of Sangmo, high in the foothills of the Himalayas, within sight of the great mountain, Kanchenjunga. It is a beautiful spot, with high rain forest clothing the hillsides round about and, on the rare occasions when the sky clears, spectacular views across the valley below. Sangmo is not far from the border with West Bengal near Darjeeling, but in those days the village was part of the independent kingdom of Sikkim, a tiny state sandwiched between Tibet, Nepal and Bhutan. In common with many other men who have shown exceptional courage in their lives, Gyamtso faced tragedy in his early years. When he was two his mother died. His father was mandel, or head man, of the village and there was no lack of female relatives to help with the child's upbringing, but young Gyamtso's childhood was austere, at least by western standards. His father, an old friend recalls, never corrected his children when they did wrong. He simply beat them with his stick.

Despite this parental severity, Gyamtso seems to have had

a vigorous and enjoyable boyhood. The hills are rocky, steep and thickly wooded, an exciting and challenging environment for an adventurous child. Although he had to work hard for his father, there was still time to explore the forest, to climb the tallest trees in search of the beautiful orchids which abound in this part of the world and to take part in wild and sometimes warlike games with other village boys. There was no possibility of going to school in Sangmo in those days as the only available school in the whole of Sikkim was in the capital, Gangtok, and that was at least three days' journey from the village. So Gyamtso, in common with the other boys in the village, spent his days helping with the farmwork, tending the livestock and working in the narrow terraced fields.

The Shangderpa family were Lamas – a clan of people sharing the same name, rather than a family in the western sense. They belonged to the Bhutia people, a tribe speaking a Tibetan dialect who came to Sikkim hundreds of years ago and learned their agriculture from Nepali immigrants who settled in the same area in the eighteenth century. The two peoples lived harmoniously side by side, together with the earliest inhabitants of Sikkim, the Lepchas. But while the majority of Sikkimese were Hindus of one kind or another, the Bhutias were Buddhists and have remained Buddhist to this day.

As mandel of the village, Gyamtso's father was deeply involved in religious ceremonial. There was a small shrine on the hillside close to the family home and a special room reserved for religious ceremonies within the house itself. The boy's education, insofar as he had one, was imbued with Buddhist precept and example. But there were other more tempting influences which were gradually making themselves felt in Sikkim during the 1930s. The boy longed to travel and see the wide world. His elder brother had joined the army and one day he came home on leave; his smart uniform and assured, worldly manner made a deep impression on his younger brother. At first the war was only a distant menace in the peaceful valleys of Sikkim, but by 1942, when Gyamtso was nearly eighteen, the Japanese were on the march and the British sent recruiting officers into the hills to look for volunteers for the Gurkha regiments. A recruiting office was

97

set up in Darjeeling, only two days' march through the hills, and one day a party of Gurkhas came to Ravangla, a small town a few miles away from Sangmo. At his first attempt to join up, Gyamtso was turned down. It was known that his father was a village mandel and that he was strongly opposed to his son leaving home because he wanted him to stay and work on the farm. But Gyamtso was only biding his time. One evening when he was playing a surreptitious game of cards with his friend Karma Chettri, the old man came in and caught them at it. Immediately he began to beat his son. Without stopping to protest, Gyamtso grabbed a few possessions, left home and went straight to Darjeeling.

> 'Name?' snapped the clerk at the recruiting office.
> 'Gyamtso,' replied the boy, mumbling with embarrassment.
> 'Ganju,' wrote the clerk. Then, 'What clan are you from?'
> 'Lama,' said the boy.

From the military point of view this was an important question. Traditionally, the Gurkha regiments were recruited from the so-called martial peoples of Nepal (the Rais, Limbus, Thapas and so on) – all clan names with a long history of warfare behind them, whose past military adventures had taken them far beyond the boundaries of Nepal. The Lamas, however, had no such military tradition. They were Bhutias, not Nepalese, and their Buddhist faith, with its emphasis on peace, usually disqualified them from military service. In 1942, with Singapore and Malaya in Japanese hands and their armies storming northward through Burma, there was not much time for nice distinctions of this kind.

The name of Gyamtso's regiment was scrawled across his bare chest, he was put through a medical, his head was shaved and within hours he was recruit Ganju Lama of the 7th Gurkha rifles. Gurkha basic training was rigorous. The young men were not allowed to smoke or drink alcohol. Their scalps were shaved, except for a small pigtail on the crown of their heads and they were put through a tough course of drill, weapon-training and physical exercise. In Ganju Lama's words: 'I wanted very much to become a really smart soldier. To me it was like the games we used to play at home, or the work I did in my home village. I just worked hard and obeyed my officers.

98

It did not seem to me so very different from home. I felt at home in the army.'

At the time when Ganju Lama joined them, the first battalion of the 7th Gurkha Rifles were resting and re-fitting after a long and bitter fighting withdrawal through Burma, but unlike many of the British and Indian units which had been cut to pieces and thoroughly demoralised by the Japanese, the 7th Gurkhas did not feel they had been beaten. In just one action at the Burmese town of Kyaukse, 'B' company under Captain O. R. Gribble had attacked a large force of Japanese and routed them completely, killing more than a hundred of the enemy for a loss of only one Gurkha life. Two battalions, the 1st and 3rd combined into one, had reached the Indian frontier with over eleven hundred men and the bulk of their weapons and equipment intact, feeling that they had beaten the Japanese all ends up in straight confrontation. It was only the overall strategic situation which had forced their withdrawal.

After training at the regimental centre in Palampur, Ganju went with the reinforcements to the 1st battalion near the town of Imphal in Manipur in January 1943. Following their triumphant advance through Burma, the Japanese had consolidated their position roughly along the line of the Chindwin river at the foot of the great mountain range separating India from Burma. For most of 1943 they were kept busy on other fronts and did not attempt to storm the formidable obstacle in front of them. British and Indian forces then began to take the initiative. In December the whole of 48 Brigade, which included 1/7 Gurkhas, went into battle against the Japanese near Kennedy Peak, a prominent feature in the Chin Hills, close to the Burmese Town of Fort White. It was here that Ganju Lama saw action for the first time. The Japanese were adept at concealment, the jungle was thick on the hills and during his first battle Ganju did not catch sight of a single enemy soldier although he fired several rounds from his own rifle. But one morning he went out foraging on his own, hoping to find a chicken or a goat which had escaped from one of the devastated villages in the area.

All of a sudden in the bamboos I saw a Japanese soldier. Later, they told me he was an intelligence officer trying to spy on us, but at the time I did not know if he was an officer or just an ordinary soldier. So I fired at him and he fell to the ground. I thought if I don't kill him properly he will wake up and shoot me. So after he had fallen down I kept on firing at him; many shots I fired.

Shortly after this incident Ganju was made batman to Roy Gribble, a tall young officer who had distinguished himself in action against the Japanese and enjoyed high prestige in the battalion. It was the batman's job to clean his officer's kit, keep him fed and watered and look after his welfare in every way. Roy Gribble recalls:

I wanted somebody tough and able to keep up with me on the march and my second-in-command produced this eighteen-year-old recruit, Ganju. . . . He had two days with the old batman to learn the ropes, so as not to inconvenience the Sahib, and then he took over. Ganju came into my dug-out at four o'clock the next morning with a mess-tin full of tea and just said 'get up'. No 'good morning,' no 'sir' or anything and I thought well, this chap is rather extraordinary. No Gurkha had ever treated me like that before. My heart warmed to him and I thought, well I've really got something here. . . . Our relationship was very good in fact. He was a very good young soldier, very smart.

At this time the Japanese were very firmly dug in on top of Kennedy Peak and 1/7 Gurkhas, together with their comrades in the brigade, 2/5 Royal Gurkha Rifles, made repeated efforts to dislodge them. One attack came close to success when two companies of Gurkhas established themselves on top of the Japanese position.

We dug in on top of the Japs. The Japs were underneath in their bunkers and we dug in on top, which was a very embarrassing position to be in and a very dangerous position. One of the forward platoons sent back a message wanting some ammunition, so that night I sent Ganju off with a box of ammunition. In due course he came back and told me he'd killed a British soldier. I couldn't believe it. But what he'd actually done was killed a Jap dressed as a British soldier. . . . This man had attacked him on the track going up with the ammunition and Ganju turned round and killed him with the bayonet and that was one of the first times he'd been in action. It was quite obvious then that he was a brave man. . . .

Early in March 1944 British intelligence warned of a big build-up of Japanese forces on the central front in North Burma. It was obvious that a big offensive was on the way and General William Slim, the officer commanding the 14th Army, decided to withdraw his forces to the strategic town of Imphal, where he had already accumulated large reserves of men and supplies and where he could fight the Japanese on ground of his own choosing. Accordingly, 48 Brigade were withdrawn back along the road through Tiddim towards Imphal. On 17 March the Japanese 15th Army launched a major assault across the Chindwin River and within five days they had crossed the frontier into India. A hundred thousand men in three divisions converged on the British garrison towns of Imphal and Kohima, and 48 Brigade had to fight every inch of the way as the Japanese sought to cut off their line of withdrawal by encircling movements through the hills. Many times the Gurkhas had to blast their way through Japanese road blocks established in their rear and many times they were ambushed by small parties of Japanese, concealed in the undergrowth by the side of the road. In one of these Captain Roy Gribble was badly wounded and Ganju Lama was shot through the calf. Both men were evacuated to Imphal, and Ganju further impressed his officer by ignoring his own wound and devoting himself to looking after those more seriously wounded than he was. Within a few weeks Ganju's own wound was healed and he returned to duty with his battalion.

The Japanese plan called for the conquest of Imphal and Kohima by 30 March. So confident were they of victory that when the chosen date arrived there were great celebrations in Tokyo and triumphant announcements on the radio, but Imphal and Kohima did not fall. Besieged on all sides, the British and Indian forces held out and inflicted terrible losses on the advancing Japanese. Using their superior air power, the allies were able to supply their garrisons with food and ammunition, while harrassing the enemy supply lines by bombing and strafing the roads and railways through Burma. Meanwhile, General Slim brought reinforcements up from

India which would eventually turn the tide against the Japanese.

By the beginning of May, after a heroic fifty-day stand, Kohima was relieved and the 14th Army was ready to take the offensive. Imphal lay in the centre of a great fertile plain surrounded on all sides by hills, and the Japanese had taken up strong positions dominating the town from vantage points on high ground. They had by no means given up the struggle. The Japanese 33rd Division, a crack force who had fought their way up through Burma, were determined to take Imphal or die.

'The coming battle will decide the success or failure of the war in Asia,' ran a famous order of the day. 'Regarding death as something lighter than a feather, you soldiers must seize Imphal. You must expect that the division will be annihilated.' Faced with such a determined enemy, the commander of the 17th Indian Division, General Cowan, devised a plan to break the enemy front on his sector to the south of Imphal. 48 Brigade, which comprised 1/7 Gurkhas, their old comrades in battle, 2/5 Royal Gurkha Rifles and a detachment of artillery, was sent in a wide looping march across country to cut the Japanese line of communications on the Tiddim Road. From there they would march northward, back towards Imphal, where another brigade was advancing southward to catch the Japanese between two fires.

On 16 May 1/7 Gurkhas swooped down on the Tiddim Road. They surprised a party of Japanese soldiers near a bridge at Milestone 33 and killed them. Then they in turn were surprised when five Japanese tanks started to rumble over the bridge from the north. Up to this point no one had seen Japanese armour anywhere in the Imphal area and the Gurkhas were totally unprepared. The attack halted and they raced for cover. Fortunately, the battalion had recently taken delivery of four PIAT guns. This cumbersome weapon was basically a giant pop-gun with a strong spring, capable of lobbing an anti-tank grenade about fifty yards or so, although in practice it was only accurate (approximately) at much closer range. Rifleman Ganju Lama had been issued with the weapon and given a swift course of instruction, but few people, not even the officers of the battalion, had any real idea of its capabilities.

In the confusion of the moment, Ganju kept his head. He heard the tanks approaching, loaded his PIAT and got it into a firing position close to the bridge. As the first vehicle rumbled forward, he fired and scored a direct hit. The tank lurched to a halt with smoke pouring from a gaping hole in its armour. Ganju reloaded as fast as he could, just in time to blast a second tank as it came up behind the knocked-out vehicle. Together, the two tanks now blocked the advance of the others and the Gurkhas were able to withdraw in good order and set up a defensive position, digging in on either side of the road and effectively blocking it completely. For this quick and successful action, Ganju Lama was later awarded the Military Medal.

The same night the Japanese attacked the road block from the north and again the battalion's PIAT guns were in action. Two more enemy tanks were knocked out, and one so badly crippled that it was later abandoned, but the night's events had only just begun. Although the Gurkhas had been holding the road block for over twelve hours, the Japanese north of the block failed to alert their comrades to the south and at midnight a convoy of enemy troops and supplies in eight lorries came blundering up the hill, straight into the position held by the 1/7th. The Gurkhas let them drive past their front line, then closed the trap. Ganju Lama blasted the leading truck with his PIAT and the rest of the battalion opened up with everything they had. Fifty-two Japanese were killed and a large quantity of enemy supplies fell into the Gurkhas' hands.

1/7 Gurkhas held on to their position for another five days, while the Japanese made frantic efforts to dislodge them. The commander of the battalion, until he was wounded later in the same battle, was Lieutenant-Colonel (later Major-General) J. A. R. Robertson.

> The Japs were quite hysterical in their attacks. Every night they came in approximately at the same time and in exactly the same way and really went quite mad. They threw themselves on the wire and we really butchered them. . . . They didn't seem to come round us or try to get at us in any other way. They were

incredibly brave and dedicated. . . . Loss of life seemed to mean
nothing to them.

The 67th Regiment of the Imperial Japanese Army lost
nearly three hundred men at Milestone 33, 1/7 Gurkhas less
than thirty. But the Japanese held the high ground on all sides
and the Gurkhas were under continual artillery and mortar
fire both by day and by night. It also became apparent that the
rest of 17th Division were too fully occupied fighting the
Japanese further to the north to be able to put the original
plan into effect. So, on the night of 23 May the brigade
withdrew northward, each man following the other in single
file along a narrow track through the hills. Each village along
the road was held by the Japanese and the brigade had to fight
all the way back to the town of Ningthoukhong, where a
battalion of the West Yorkshire Regiment was locked in
confrontation with a strong force of Japanese. Unable to take
Ningthoukhong, which was heavily defended with machine-
gun bunkers and a squadron of Japanese tanks, the 1/7th and
their comrades bypassed the village and linked up with the
rest of their division to the north of the town.

By June 1944, although the British and Indian forces had
made great progress in clearing the enemy from the hills
around Imphal and Kohima, the Japanese 33rd Division –
freshly reinforced and equipped with more tanks, which they
had somehow managed to drag up the hills behind them –
remained on the offensive on the Tiddim Road. The town of
Ningthoukhong and the adjacent village of Kha Kunou was
now its principal stronghold. The West Yorks, the 2/5th and
the 7th Gurkhas had all made valiant attempts to seize the
town, but it remained firmly in Japanese hands. Early on the
morning of 12 June the Japanese suddenly launched an attack
on the positions occupied by 2/5 RGR. The defenders were
well dug in and in normal circumstances they would have had
little difficulty in repelling the attack, but this time the
Japanese infantry were supported by tanks. Lieutenant-
Colonel Basil McDowell was in command of 1/7 Gurkhas.

I was standing outside my bunker washing my face in a canvas
bucket, when, without any warning, two high-velocity shells –
tank shells – roared overhead and down came an artillery

barrage on 2/5 Gurkhas. So I realised there was a major attack and got on the blower to connect up with the Brigadier and with Colonel Eustace, who commanded the 2/5th. . . . It soon became apparent that the 2/5th had been surprised by the tanks. Somehow the Japs must have bridged the stream during the night and got the tanks across and I think they caught the 2/5th off-balance a bit. And I heard Eustace saying, very deliberately and slowly, 'There are two tanks, not very far from here and they're making too much progress towards me. . . .' And then he said, in the tone of voice one might use discussing stock exchange prices, 'You can't really fart against thunder'.

In fact an anti-tank gun manned by the 2/5th did succeed in knocking out two of the tanks and the other three were having difficulty making progress in the boggy ground near the stream, but they had succeeded in giving close support to the infantry attack on the Gurkhas; the two leading platoons had been overrun and the remainder of 'A' and 'D' companies were forced to withdraw. Meanwhile, the Brigadier had got on to Basil McDowell.

He was pretty laconic. He said, 'Do you mind putting in a counter-attack with two companies and restoring the situation?' So I gave the necessary orders and off went the two companies. Well, then of course the battle noises rose to a crescendo, shells were flying all over the place and small arms fire all over the place and then suddenly, without any warning, it all died out and there was a sort of deadly hush, except for perhaps the odd desultory bit of firing here and there and I realised that the battle was over by that time. Of course I didn't know why.

What had happened was that the tanks had been knocked out, and without their opposition the Gurkhas of the 1/7th had made short work of the Japanese infantry. But the story of the destruction of the tanks was the story of Ganju Lama's VC.

The two companies of the 1/7th, 'B' Company to the left of the main track and 'D' Company on the right, advanced through the lines of the 2/5th. On the right, 'B' Company made good progress, killing most of the Japanese in their path and sending the remainder scurrying back across the stream. On the left, 'B' Company regained the forward positions which had been overrun, but then found themselves pinned down by shell and machine-gun fire from two tanks to the left of the track. The Commander of No. 7 Platoon, a Gurkha officer named Narjit Rai, called up Ganju Lama with his PIAT. Alone, Ganju crawled forward. To begin with he could not see the enemy tanks, but he could hear them rumbling towards him. He cocked the cumbersome weapon, loaded it with its projectile and waited until the first vehicle lumbered up the slope towards him. At thirty yards' range he fired, and scored a direct hit. The crew bailed out and ran for cover as their vehicle caught fire. Warily, Ganju crawled forward again. He could hear the second tank coming closer. As it came up behind the knocked-out vehicle, Ganju fired again. This time he missed the body of the tank but hit the track. The vehicle lurched into a spin on its own axis until the crew, realising that they were likely to be hit again, scrambled out and took cover in the bushes.

Growing in confidence, Ganju stood up and advanced on foot. He could hear another tank approaching, but it was still some distance away. As it came into view he stood in the open, loaded the PIAT and fired his third bomb at extreme range. This time he missed and his target disappeared into a gully. Once again he re-loaded the gun and began to stalk his quarry. As he did so, he heard a machine-gun open up and at the same moment the PIAT seemed to fly out of his hand. Half jumping, half falling, he rolled over into a hollow in the ground. He tried to crawl out again and found he could not move. Slowly, he became aware of the extent of his injuries. Machine-gun bullets had pierced his right hand, his left wrist, and both legs had been hit, the right leg severely. He was almost completely disabled. As he became aware how helpless he was, he heard men approaching on his left flank. For a moment he thought it was his own platoon moving forward to the rescue, but as he peered out from the shelter of his hollow he could see the sun glinting on bayonets as three Japanese soldiers, the crew of one of the tanks, moved towards him. He explains what happened in broken English.

> I thought, what can I do? I am hurt. I need some protection. I have got to push up my fist to open my pouches. Here is three hand grenades. I push out one grenade, but the pin is sticking. My hand is broken. I take the pin in my teeth and pull, like this. I throw grenade.

The Japanese soldiers threw themselves to the ground and opened fire, but their bullets passed over Ganju's head. As they began to crawl towards him he hurled another grenade. They flattened themselves to the ground and inched closer still, one firing to cover the approach of the other two. Ganju could hear them slithering through the grass, only a few feet away. He hurled his last grenade. The Japanese soldiers froze. The last explosion had been too close for comfort and if they made a dash for him another grenade might kill them all. But had he got another grenade? If not, a quick charge and it would all be over. In the hollow Ganju waited. Stealthily, the Japanese soldiers prepared to spring.

At that moment, like the US Cavalry in the closing reel, Narjit Rai and the Gurkhas of the leading section burst into the open and charged the enemy. The Japanese died before they could fire another shot. Narjit Rai crossed to the hollow and saw Ganju lying there.

> I hear him calling my number, 763, then he see me. 'Hello,' he said, 'you won, Ganju, you won.' Then he tried to push me up standing, but I could not. My leg is broken. Then someone give me water. Another section comes. . . . They bring stretcher-bearers, laid me on there, carry me away.

Ganju was taken back to battalion headquarters and from there he was transferred to a field dressing-station and ultimately to a hospital in India, while the officers of 1/7 Gurkhas deliberated as to what should be done. Basil McDowell takes up the story:

> That evening, under cover of darkness, the two company commanders came to me. One of them, Morris Wyatt, who was the company commander of Ganju Lama said, 'Do you remember Ganju Lama who earned a Military Medal with his PIAT gun at the 33rd Milestone road block? Well,' he said, 'you wouldn't believe it, but he's done the same thing all over again. He engaged those two tanks at a range of about thirty yards, knocked out one, deliberately stood up and re-loaded his PIAT gun and then shot the second tank.' And then Morris went on to say, 'And I think we should recommend him for a bar to the MM.' I said, 'Nonsense, this is a VC matter. Nothing less than a VC.' So we sat down and we produced a citation and I tried in the citation to highlight the balance of the battle being on the

work of one man and one man only, for he was really the man of the moment, and it was Ganju Lama. But when the citation went up to higher command, they became very wary of purple prose and sort of ironed it out and made it into the usual rather dull, drab prose which you associate with VC recommendations and citations.

When the award was approved it was some time before Ganju Lama could be found. He had disappeared into the recesses of the hospital system and it was not until General Slim himself intervened that the machinery was set in motion which eventually tracked him down in Lucknow.

> After a few months in this Lucknow General Hospital, I hear this person say you've got this medal, or that, but I don't know what is this medal, the Victoria Cross, because I am simple soldier. And that day comes to my bed so many officers, so many gentlemen running there and here. Then they are taking me from my bed and putting me in another barrack, officers' barrack.

Upgraded to the officers' ward, fussed over by nurses and senior army officers, Ganju was brought in an ambulance to Delhi Hospital, while preparations were made for the investiture at the Red Fort. Ganju's family was sought and eventually found, and his father and elder brother created a minor sensation when they put in an appearance in Delhi in the embroidered purple caps and robes of Bhutia gentlemen. The mandel caused another sensation when the anxious authorities discovered that he needed a bottle of whisky a day by way of sustenance.

The investiture was a grand affair on the Maidan between the Red Fort and the River Jumna. Several other awards were to be made on the same day. The viceroy himself, Lord Wavell, presided over the ceremony, and the regiments of all the Victoria Cross winners (including the 7th Gurkhas) had an honour guard on parade. Seated on the dais, close to the viceroy were Earl Mountbatten, then Supreme Commander of Allied Forces in the Far East, and the victorious General of the 6th Army, now Sir William Slim. According to some reports, Bill Slim himself insisted on taking a turn at pushing Ganju's wheelchair. In later accounts of the Burma campaign

Ganju Lama

Earl Mountbatten was to say of Ganju Lama's Victoria Cross that it was the most richly deserved VC won in the whole of the Far Eastern theatre of war.

When all the excitement had died down and the war against Japan came to an end, Ganju Lama was still convalescing in hospital. Although he made a splendid recovery, one bullet lodged in his thigh and did not emerge until twenty years after the action. The army was anxious to keep him and, because he was still illiterate, sent him during his convalescence to an educational unit where he learned to read and write. When India won its independence in 1947, the 7th Gurkhas became a British regiment and Ganju elected to transfer to the 11th Gurkha Rifles, an Indian Army unit, with which he was to stay for the rest of his army career. He was promoted to havildar, or sergeant, in 1948 and fulfilled his wish by serving as education sergeant for the regiment. His interest in education led to his first marriage with a school teacher in 1949 and the couple had three daughters. But the marriage did not work out, and he and his wife were divorced in 1958.

By this time Ganju was a subedar – a junior commissioned officer in the 11th Gurkhas; this is a rank somewhere between a sergeant major and a second lieutenant, but with no precise equivalent in the British Army. Promotion for Ganju Lama did not come fast. Despite his fame and the prestige the Victoria Cross gave him he was not sufficiently well educated to gain rapid promotion, but in 1968 he was honoured by being appointed Honorary ADC to the President of India, a post he held through the period of tenure of six different presidents, and still holds today.

Determined not to over-reach himself on the domestic front, Ganju chose for his second wife a partner arranged through the time-honoured process of negotiating through members of his family for a suitable girl. On the pretext of visiting another member of the family, Ganju travelled to North Sikkim to have a good look at his prospective bride. He liked what he saw and in 1965 the couple were married. She spoke to me through an interpreter in her native Bhutia language.

When I was married I did not know much about him and after about three days I came to hear that he had won the Victoria

109

Cross, but I still did not know much about it. After a year or so I was invited to a friend's place for a party and there they discussed my husband. So I came to know more about it, and when I got home I asked my husband and he told me about it, more about the war. . . . In the beginning I was very frightened, thinking about the war and about how he had fought. I could not believe he had killed so many people. I used to get frightened, but now I am used to the idea.

Ganju has three children by his second marriage, a son and two daughters. He has one much older son, who is now an officer in a Gurkha regiment and there are also the three daughters, all grown up, from his first marriage. He is in contact with all his children and to those still at home he is a loving and affectionate father. He is something of a disciplinarian and expects to be obeyed in his own household, but he has never raised his hand to his children, though he has occasionally threatened to do so. To his daughter, Rinchin, a pretty sixteen-year-old, he is obviously quite a hero. 'I feel proud to be his daughter,' she says, 'he is a brave man.'

Ganju retired from full-time service with the army in 1972 with the honorary rank of captain and a small pension. The government of Sikkim had already given him a grant of land close to his native village in the Ravangla district of Sikkim. Ganju was able to add to it by purchase and he went into business as a farmer by planting the profitable, but labour-intensive crop of cardamom. This shrub needs heavy rainfall and shade from the tropical sun and conditions in the forest on Ganju's farm are ideal for it. The spice fetches a high price in the market. Prospering as a farmer, he was determined to do something for his community. While on leave from the army in 1956 he had already urged the local people to found an education committee and to start a school in Sangmo village. To begin with he paid the school teachers' wages himself, but as the school expanded it was integrated into the government system. Now he involved himself with a similar project and started a school in another area close to Ravangla, which was officially opened in 1972. He also did voluntary work for a government ex-servicemen's organisation, caring for the needs of old soldiers who had fallen on hard times. He interested himself in the building and maintenance of a school for destitute children in West Sikkim, a foundation that places special emphasis on maintaining traditional Buddhist culture, combined with a modern educational curriculum.

This concern with culture and religion is not superficial. In 1979 Ganju made a large donation towards the building of a new monastery close to an ancient shrine in the neighbourhood of Sangmo. Not content with subsidising the venture he personally supervised the construction of the monastery making the tortuous five-kilometre journey downhill from his home early every morning, despite the pain of his old wounds, and climbing back every evening. Now that the monastery is complete, he has organised the construction of a road down the mountain which will one day connect the whole of his native village with the outside world. These philanthropic works give Ganju a great deal of satisfaction, but his wife believes that his underlying motives are deeply religious and connected with Buddhist notions of death and re-birth.

> If he goes through some great labour, like building the schools so far from his own house and visiting and looking after them, he feels he is doing good for the villages. By building monasteries he feels he is doing good for religion. . . . We believe in re-birth, you know. So he feels he will get a better life later on. As you know, we are not allowed to kill animals even. Killing is prohibited. So he feels that since he did so much killing in war then he should now practise religion and good deeds. He feels he should cover up the bad deeds he did during the war, not knowing that it would win him so much fame. Now he should do good to people all round the village.

His wife's views are heavily influenced by her own religious convictions. It would be a mistake to think that Ganju Lama himself is ashamed of his Victoria Cross. On the contrary, he has served for many years on the committee of the Victoria Cross Association in London and has been their honoured guest on many occasions. He maintains close contact with the Indian Army and still urges young men to join the armed forces to learn discipline and see more of the world. It is more a matter of seeing different kinds of enterprise as being appropriate to different stages of life. A young man may fight for glory; a mature man should work hard and raise a family; an old man should turn his mind to good works and quiet contemplation, and as far as possible, make amends for what he has done wrong. This is not by any means exclusively a Buddhist notion. It owes much to Hindu philosophy. But it shows how it is possible for a courageous young warrior to bring his courage to quite different tasks once the battle is won and the war over.

8
Keith Elliott

The King has been graciously pleased to approve the award of the Victoria Cross to:

No. 6751 Sergeant Keith Elliott, New Zealand Military Forces.

At Ruweisat at dawn on 15 July 1942, the battalion to which Sergeant Elliott belonged was attacked on three flanks by tanks. Under heavy tank, machine-gun and shell fire, Sergeant Elliott led the platoon he was commanding to the cover of a ridge 300 yards away, during which he sustained a chest wound.

Here he re-formed his men and led them to a dominating ridge a further 500 yards away where they came under heavy enemy machine-gun and mortar fire. He located enemy machine-gun posts on his front and right flank and, while one section attacked on the right flank, Sergeant Elliott led seven men in a bayonet charge across 500 yards of open ground in the face of heavy fire and captured four enemy machine-gun posts and an anti-tank gun, killing a number of the enemy and taking fifty prisoners.

His section then came under fire from a machine-gun post on his left flank. He immediately charged this post single-handed and succeeded in capturing it, killing several of the enemy and taking fifteen prisoners. During these two assaults he sustained three more wounds in the back and legs.

Although badly wounded in four places Sergeant Elliott refused to leave his men until he had re-formed them, handed over his prisoners, which were now increased to 130, and arranged for his men to rejoin their battalion.

Owing to Sergeant Elliott's quick grasp of the situation, great personal courage and leadership, nineteen men who were the only survivors of 'B' Company of his battalion captured and destroyed five machine-guns, one anti-tank gun, killed a great number of the enemy and captured 130

113

prisoners. Sergeant Elliott sustained only one casualty among his men and brought him back to the nearest advanced dressing-station.

If ever an action in which a Victoria Cross was won can be said to be typical of the man, it was Keith Elliott's private war at El Ruweisat Ridge. To start with, he disobeyed orders and saved his men from certain capture by exercising his own initiative. If events had turned out differently he could easily have been charged with deserting his post. Then he began a battle of his own against infinitely superior numbers of the enemy and carried it through with such aggression and determination that he succeeded, against all odds, in achieving what he had set out to do. Most characteristically of all, the whole action was begun on the spur of the moment because another man was wounded and in need of help. In the space of a few hours the action exemplified the whole of Elliott's life.

Even today the Reverend Keith Elliott is not everyone's idea of an Anglican clergyman. The pugnacious zeal which won him the Cross is evident in his bearing, in his voice, in the power of his faith in God. To hear him in the pulpit as he roars out a sermon in support of New Zealand's commitment to a nuclear-free zone is to realise that this is a man sincerely dedicated to world peace. To see him in the bar afterwards, with his strong face thrust forward in loud conversation, his wide shoulders and huge belly making space for himself in the crowd, is to know that he would still be a dangerous man in a scrap. But when he laughs, as he does often, exuberant enjoyment of life bursts out of him. Then again, peacefully fishing on the shores of Lake Waikeromoana in the last great reserve of a native forest in the North Island, he talks quietly, reverently, of the beauty of the landscape and the peace which it brings to his spirit. Keith has fought many battles in his life and knows the value of peace. He has rescued many from the extremes of poverty and hunger and, quite possibly, from the devil as well. He is still a soldier, a soldier of the Lord.

Keith Elliott was born the eighth of nine children in the

backwoods settlement of Apiti in the North Island in 1916. His
father, Frank, was an English immigrant, a farmer and a lay
preacher in the Anglican Church. Frank Elliott had a great
deal of difficulty sticking to anything, especially money. He
inherited two large bequests from relatives in England, drank
some of it, gave a lot of it away and squandered the rest on ill-
considered business ventures. Yet those who knew him seem
to have liked him. He certainly handed on some of his qualities,
his generous and convivial nature and his love of fishing, to his
youngest son. Keith's mother Ethel put up with the vagaries
of her husband's fortune, his frequent absences from home,
and succeeded in bringing up her large brood imbued with her
resilience and determination to make the best of things.

For several years, after Frank Elliott had to sell the farm at
Apiti, the family lived in some poverty in an old house in the
town of Feilding. The depression kept farm prices down, work
was difficult to find and food was scarce. Fortunately Keith's
mother was not a woman to give up easily. The family had a
couple of acres of land, and they kept a cow, a few pigs and
chickens and grew their own vegetables. Keith remembers his
childhood as very poor, but extremely happy. He devoted a
great deal of time to fishing for crayfish in neighbouring
streams, raiding local farms for fruit or sweetcorn and generally
making a nuisance of himself, but he also attended the local
church every Sunday and went to school at Lytton Street in
Feilding. He does not seem to have been an outstanding pupil,
but he found there was more to school than writing and
arithmetic.

Many of the children from outlying areas were brought in
by their parents on horse-drawn traps and buggies and these
vehicles would be parked in a paddock on one side of the
school grounds. In this yard, ankle deep in horse manure, the
Lytton Street boys fought their first battles. Around the
perimeter of the yard were a number of tall pine trees which
the more daring boys used to climb. One day when Keith was
about ten the travelling dentist came to the school to inspect
the children's teeth. This lady had a fearsome reputation and
a habit of extracting wobbly milk teeth which filled the
children with understandable horror. Keith made an instant
decision. Up he fled to the top of the nearest pine tree. The

115

Principal came out to the yard and shouted up to him to come down but Keith merely shifted a little farther up the tree. His elder brother, named Frank like his father, was dispatched to bring him down, but Keith was lighter and more agile and scrambled into the next tree along. Threats and entreaties were useless; Keith would not budge until the dentist was well quit of the school and the last of the watchers below had given up and gone home. Tactical withdrawal in the face of overwhelming enemy forces, coupled with his own daring and capacity for decisive action, was to serve him well in later encounters.

When Keith was thirteen he was sent to Feilding Agricultural High School where the headmaster, L. J. Wild, had instituted a remarkable experiment in pupil self-government, with a system of elected committees which took over a large part of the administration of the school. This seems to have been well adapted to the egalitarian nature of New Zealand society and the system was eventually taken up all over the country. For Keith it meant early experience in self-reliance, which was also reflected in other aspects of his life. The Feilding school was too far away from his parents' home for a boy of his age to travel to and fro every day, so Keith was boarded out with friends in Feilding.

One of the people with whom he boarded was a resolute old lady called Mrs Dermer, who kept a small herd of Jersey cows which Keith had to milk every day before going to school. But Mrs Dermer was also a keen church-goer and recognised in Keith a genuine religious enthusiasm which might eventually develop into a vocation. Keith himself approached his head-master with the idea of reading for the ministry; but Mr Wild rejected the proposal on the grounds that his parents did not have enough money and perhaps because he did not feel that the aspiring cleric was sufficiently clerical.

For Keith was not a sanctimonious boy. When he was sixteen he was selected to play in the school's rugby fifteen. He played rugby with such determination and gusto that despite his small size he quickly gained a reputation as a hard man to beat. A little later on in his rugby career a team mate, Joe Mahar, remembers him like this:

116

He wasn't a brilliant player; he was a hard player and he'd
bullock his way through where the ordinary player would give
up and pass the ball on, but Keith was in the thick of everything.
And he was really aggressive, perhaps a bit too aggressive at
times. But he was always very popular. He might have gone a
long way – he might even have reached All Black status, but
the war settled that of course.

When he was seventeen Keith was obliged to leave school.
His father had managed to lose most of his money all over
again and Keith had to go to work to help support the family.
A year later the Mount Biggs farm had to be sold and the
Elliotts moved to a much smaller and rougher farm at a remote
place called Marima, near the small town of Pahiatua. The
farm house was little more than a shack; the steeply sloping
land unfenced, still littered with the stumps remaining from
the original native forest and overgrown with weeds. By this
time, Keith's elder brothers had left home, his father was of
little practical help and he had somehow to break in the land
on his own. He was not yet nineteen.

For five years Keith worked to get the farm into shape,
levering out the great stumps one by one with a primitive jack,
ploughing the rocky ground with a team of borrowed horses,
re-seeding the land and fencing it off into neat five-acre
paddocks. To keep the money coming in while the farm was
still being brought into productivity Keith also had to go out
to work for other farmers. At times the huge work-load made
him ill and brought him close to despair. But somehow he
managed to keep going and even found time to play rugby on
Saturday afternoons. At the end of the five years the land was
stumped, fenced and re-seeded. There was a growing herd of
good milk cattle, a flock of sheep and a few pigs. The farm was
a paying concern. This achievement and the huge labour that
had gone into it developed in Keith the sturdy independent
spirit which he was to retain for the rest of his life.

It was now 1939. Sooner than most New Zealanders, Keith
realised that war was on the way and had no doubt about the
role he would play.

> We've got something here that is worth defending. It is a pearl
> of great price, New Zealand, and we have tremendous ties with
> the home country, with Great Britain. All our best stock, human

and animal, the best seed, it all comes from there and we respect that. We respect the Crown. And that's the reason I went to fight.

Together with his friend, Joe Mahar, he made the journey over to Palmerston North and tried to enlist in the summer of 1939. At first he was turned down, partly because the authorities did not want to take away the breadwinner of the family, but in January 1940 he reported to Trentham Camp, near Palmerston, and joined No. 11 Platoon of the 22nd Battalion, the unit with which he was destined to stay throughout his army career.

> We arrived in Trentham, all very inebriated, you know, and we were rounded up by these barking lance-corporals, and I thought it was quite interesting, to see these fellows straggle into the place. Coming from the country we were pretty rough material. But we had a wonderful colonel. He had won the VC in the 1914–18 war, Colonel Andrew VC, and he was a great soldier, a great disciplinarian. . . . He would stand out there on the parade ground like a statue, tremendously well controlled and disciplined, and he was a fellow who never expected you to do something he wasn't prepared to do himself. But he expected the best, the tops . . . second rate was no good to him.

After five months' basic training the 22nd Battalion embarked for England. The first echelon of the New Zealand forces was transferred straight to the Middle East, but the 22nd Battalion was sent to Mytchett near Aldershot, where they went into further training. By this time Keith had been promoted to lance-corporal and had been given command of a section of ten men, many of whom were to stay with him from then on. One of them, Jack Unverricht, remembers Keith's style as an NCO.

> He struck me as very aggressive, pig-headed. He was one of those chaps that if he said anything he meant it and you did it or you were in big trouble . . . but if you were short of anything he was an out-and-out scrounger. When we were on parade, he was on the job. When parade was over for the day he was just one of the boys . . . it didn't matter what we were doing. Keith was there.

More than once Keith's attitude to the job got him into

trouble. At Hollingbourne in Kent, where the battalion was stationed for a few weeks in 1940, Keith was appointed orderly sergeant one night, even though he was still only a lance-corporal. (The sergeant-major and the senior NCOs wanted to go out on the town.) When Lance-Corporal Elliott went round to take the roll-call that evening he found that only 13 out of a company strength of 120 were in their billets. He made a note of the names of those who were present and left it at that. The following morning he awoke to find that his entire section was in the guard-room. They had consumed a few pints of beer and had been arrested while wandering round the countryside, trying to ride a borrowed horse and trundling their kit in a borrowed wheelbarrow. The company sergeant-major demanded that Elliott should put his men on a charge for being absent without leave. Keith responded by saying that 107 men in the company had been absent without leave including the company sergeant-major, and either they all went on a charge or none of them did. When the CSM objected, Keith marched off to see the company commander. This officer sensibly declined to take any action and Keith won his point, but it was not the kind of attitude that made him popular with his superiors.

In the spring of 1941, the New Zealand 5th Brigade embarked again, first to Helwan in Egypt and then to Greece, to try and stem the southward march of the German forces, who had already taken control of the Balkans. The 22nd Battalion were moved into defensive positions overlooking the Mount Olympus pass. It was here that they were to see action for the first time. The battalion was dug in on the slope of a hill overlooking a stream and a bridge that had just been demolished. On the night of 14 April, a vanguard of German motorcyclists came quietly down the road on the far side of the broken bridge. As the Germans came to a halt, Alan Murray, who was the Bren-gunner in Keith's section, was the first to open fire. Jack Unverricht remembers:

> There was a whole platoon of Germans coming up with motorbikes and side-cars. . . . And we let them get underneath and then we let go with hand grenades . . . all we could hear was what was left of them running back to the road. They didn't even bother turning their motorbikes around.

The Second World War

The Germans left it at that until first light, but the following morning they advanced with tanks and bridging equipment under cover of fire from mortars and artillery. The New Zealanders' own 25-pounders responded, and soon the valley was filled with the dust and smoke of battle. Alan Murray was badly wounded, but he was still aware of Keith in the thick of the action. 'I saw him pumping away with a Tommy gun as though he was playing marbles in the middle of a school room. I was getting out of it. I was scared stiff myself, but he didn't look to be.'

Ron Jones, who was later to accompany Keith in the epic battle at El Ruweisat, was also trying to keep his head down. 'And there was Keith saying, "Let's go down and get them." Fortunately wiser counsels prevailed and said, "Let's wait and see what happens." But that was Keith's reaction. That was Keith.'

As so often during the first years of the war, the Germans were far better organised and better armed than the Allies. Rifles were of no use against tanks, and the British-equipped forces had no effective anti-tank guns at their disposal. The Germans also had a spotter plane which roved up and down the hillside giving accurate instructions to their mortars and artillery. No. 11 Platoon took heavy casualties.

> We were dead ducks for the German mortars and machine-guns. . . . We watched the Germans come across the stream. They just put flat-topped tanks into the stream bed, four of them, and drove straight over. So we got out of it that night and walked right back, right through the pass.

Beaten and dejected, hounded by German dive bombers, the 22nd Battalion marched back through Greece to be evacuated by Royal Navy 'Glen' ships from the little seaside town of Porto Rafti. But Colin Armstrong, who won an MC Commanding No. 11 Platoon on Mount Olympus, had been greatly impressed by what he had seen of Keith's actions during the battle and the subsequent retreat. 'He stood out as being one of the reliable men who commanded the respect and obedience of the members of the platoon. . . . He took kindly to discipline when he believed in it . . . when he accepted that

120

the orders were sound. If he thought they weren't, then he questioned them.'

The battalion disembarked at Canea Bay in north-western Crete and were marched along the coast to man defensive positions around the ill-fated Maleme airfield. On 20 May 1941 the Germans attacked from the air, beginning with a bombing raid as the New Zealand troops queued up in the open air before their breakfast. No. 11 Platoon were ordered back to their trenches, while the troops on the perimeter of the airfield were bombed and strafed by the Germans. Then wave after wave of transport aircraft came over, and the enemy parachutes billowed out of the planes and drifted slowly towards the ground. Each group dropped a canister full of weapons and equipment and then the paratroopers followed, each man trying to land as close to the canister as possible.

Lance-Corporal Elliott watched them come. 'The fact was we were told to stay in our slit trenches and I didn't think this was the way to deal with these paratroopers. So I just ordered my men out and we did bayonet-charge after bayonet-charge to get rid of these people.' Jack Unverricht was there too. 'Keith wasn't squeamish about using the pick . . . but we soon found out it was a case of them or us and when you find out a thing like that, you don't worry about what you're sticking it into. . . . Keith went in with a pick and they were good Jerries. They didn't move at all.'

Sickened by the defeat in Greece and by the death of many of his mates in the platoon, Keith went in for the kill.

> I didn't feel any qualms about it whatsoever. Here was the enemy and it was like playing a game of rugby . . . it was either them or me, kill or be killed . . . the thing was to get to the canister before they did and then they couldn't operate. A lot of people say they came down firing Tommy guns and throwing hand grenades, but they came down squealing when they saw what they were jumping into.

The New Zealanders met and held the first German onslaught on Maleme airfield. But poor communication and a lack of decisive action by some of the senior officers led to an Allied withdrawal from Crete. Keith Elliott felt indignant:

> You know the Germans got the biggest hiding they'd ever had,

up to that point in time . . . we defeated the finest fighting-machine of the German Army. . . . I suppose by ten o'clock in the morning it was all over in our area. And in the evening when Major Leggitt came and said we were going to pull out, Lance-Corporal Elliott said 'Why? Have you got the wind up, sir?' He wasn't very impressed.

Once on the retreat the Allied troops were again at the mercy of German fighters and dive-bombers. In a series of vicious rearguard actions, in which some of the New Zealand Maoris particularly distinguished themselves, the British forces managed to avoid total disaster and most of the New Zealanders were safely evacuated – this time to Egypt.

The 22nd Battalion was given a chance to rest, re-equip and train up their reinforcements. Keith was promoted to platoon sergeant and trained his men hard, but for several months they saw little action and were even able to get the odd few days' leave in Alexandria and Cairo. Then, on 11 November, they advanced across the Libyan border to the Menastir Ridge, close to the enemy-held port of Bardia. After a few days 'B' Company, which included No. 11 Platoon, was moved to the desert airstrip at Sidi Azeiz, to help guard Brigade Headquarters against surprise attack. Unfortunately Rommel chose this moment to launch his Panzers through a gap in the British defences. Colin Armstrong, Keith's platoon commander, describes what happened.

> There we were, a hundred strong, with rifles and bayonets and the next morning they came. They stood off, a thousand yards away . . . vehicles going up in all directions . . . ammunition going up all over the place and we couldn't do anything in return. Eventually a tank ran up against Brigadier Hargest, who had his red hat on by then, and took the surrender. There was nothing else we could do.

Abject humiliation followed. But what really gnawed at the guts of Colin Armstrong and the other New Zealanders was that the brigadier had not withdrawn to gain the protection of one of his battalions before the Germans struck.

> We had gone out on patrol in the darkness and told him that they were revving up their engines and coming towards us . . .

and at any stage the day before we could have gone over to join the shelter of the 26th Battalion. So we were always saying, 'When are we going?' and no one gave us any orders because the brigadier was told he had to stay there and defend that strip of desert at all costs and he couldn't get hold of Division to get another order. So that convinced Keith, I think, that it's a bad idea to wait for orders when that sort of thing happens.

No. 11 Platoon spent the next seven weeks in a makeshift prisoner-of-war camp in Bardia. At that time the port was almost entirely surrounded by British forces and the garrison had great difficulty in getting supplies for their own troops, let alone the POWs. Conditions in the camp were grim. It was mid-winter, wet and cold. The only protection the prisoners could lay their hands on were strips of corrugated iron which they used to cover holes and trenches in the ground. They were constantly exposed to bombing and shelling from their own forces besieging the port and there was a chronic shortage of food. As a responsible NCO Keith did his best to care for the men in his platoon, but it was a difficult time for all of them.

> I suppose I was eleven or twelve stone when I went in there and I came out at seven . . . I was the sergeant in charge of thirty-one men . . . and it was quite distressing, because you could see the blokes going downhill. We were lucky in one respect; had it been summer time we would all have died from dysentery, but it was winter and that saved us. And sleeping all together in a long line . . . we kept one another warm.

Keith said his prayers and quietly urged some of the others to join him.

> We used to hold church services. There was a fellow, Palmer, he became the Dean of St Peters in Hamilton, and he was our Padre. We'd have a communion without any bread or wine – a spiritual one – and that was a tremendous help to the fellows.

On 1 January 1942 relief came. In an elaborate combined operation with naval and air support, the British, South Africans and New Zealanders stormed the port and released the Bardia prisoners. Miraculously, or so it seemed to Keith, the thousand men in the tiny camp came through the bombardment unscathed (all except for one unfortunate man who had been allowed outside the compound to scavenge for wood). Keith felt that his prayers to God had been answered.

Many of the men, Sergeant Elliott among them, were sent off to hospital to recover from their experiences. There followed several months of short postings and transfers from one position to another with a brief spell with his own platoon in Northern Syria. Then at last, in the early summer of 1942, Keith and his men were back together in Egypt as the 22nd Battalion moved up the line, just prior to the battle of El Ruweisat Ridge.

The position, as so often in the western desert, where columns of trucks and tanks could manoeuvre freely over a wide area, was confused. Rommel was seventy-five miles from Alexandria and the British were loosely grouped in the neck of land between the El Quattara depression and the sea, close to a village which was later to become better known as El Alamein. The desert in the area was relatively featureless, and command of the high ground carried great tactical advantage. Accordingly, a division comprising the New Zealand 4th Brigade, Keith Elliott's own formation, 5th Brigade and three battalions of Indian troops were detailed for a night attack on a slight rise in the ground known as the El Ruweisat Ridge, which commanded the southern lines of approach to Alexandria. It was known to be held by the Italian Pavia division, but the exact strength and disposition of the Axis forces were unknown. What was certain was that the assault involved up to six miles of rough going, on foot and at night through enemy-held territory before the objective could be reached.

The attack on El Ruweisat was one of the minor epics of the war. On that night and the following day, the 15 and 16 June 1942, another New Zealander, Captain Charles Upham, was to make history by winning a bar to his VC. But in many ways the battle was a shambles. The New Zealand 4th Brigade and the Indians failed to make their objective until the following day and in the meantime, 5th Brigade, which did succeed in its allotted task, was out on its own with its flanks wide open. The 22nd Battalion, which was following up in support of the 21st and 23rd, was cut off behind the rest of the brigade, with disastrous consequences for nearly a third of its strength.

After a night of stumbling through the desert, fighting blind actions against an invisible enemy, mortared, machine-gunned and thoroughly exhausted, the battalion came to a halt approximately where it was supposed to be – about a mile behind the two leading units in the brigade which were strung out along the line of the ridge. The weary troops took up defensive positions and dug in as best they could on the rocky ground. Some of them even managed to snatch a few moments of blessed sleep, but as dawn came up Sergeant Elliott was wide awake and taking a keen interest in his surroundings.

> I wasn't a very good soldier really, but I was a very vigilant one, and I was taking a look around and saw these tanks coming in behind us . . . and of course as the daylight came I found that they had the wrong jerseys on; they had black crosses on.

Keith reported the fact to the two adjacent platoon commanders, but they were new to the desert and had never seen enemy tanks before. They refused to take his warnings seriously. Meanwhile the tanks were closing rapidly and it was obvious to Keith that the whole battalion would be taken prisoner, just as the troops at Sidi Azeiz had been. He went back to his platoon and 'called all my corporals together just like a good platoon commander should. . . . I said, "What's it to be, boys, Stalag or the Bush?" They said, "The Bush", so we took to our heels.'

On the face of it, Keith was utterly wrong to abandon his position, even in the face of overwhelming enemy forces. But two important points were in his favour. Incredibly, as it now seems, British and Dominion forces still had no effective weapons against German tanks – defeat and imprisonment were therefore inevitable. But the essential point in Keith's favour was that he led his troops forward, not back, towards the position held by the 23rd Battalion along the ridge a mile or so to their front.

As soon as Keith and his men started to move, the enemy tanks opened fire with machine-guns and shells. Only about two full sections followed their sergeant. The rest were too petrified to move.

> I blame myself a little bit for that . . . but there was a fair bit of hardware flying at the time. And the only reason I'm alive today

is because of this fellow George Fletcher. . . . George is lying in his trench and I'm walking down telling him to get going and run . . . and he questioned my birth, you know, he reckoned I was illegitimate, and I stopped to correct him in a nice way . . . and a bullet went across my chest, passed through one tit and out the other side. Now if I hadn't stopped for a moment it would have gone straight through me. I always thank old George for that.

Keith's two sections ran, dodging the bullets from the tanks until they gained the next stretch of high ground. There they seem to have come under fire from New Zealand artillery, but finally they joined up with elements of the 23rd Battalion on the El Ruweisat Ridge. Keith had his wound dressed and reported that enemy tanks were active behind the New Zealand lines and that most of the 22nd Battalion had been taken prisoner. It seems that the officer to whom Keith reported thought he had simply panicked and abandoned his position.

But no one was given much of a chance for enquiries or recriminations. There was still brisk action going on along the line of the ridge. Shortly after Elliott's platoon arrived, a lance-corporal stumbled weeping up the slope in front of them from the direction of the enemy positions.

They'd been out on patrol. His officer had been shot through the eye and was bleeding to death. The other runner had been killed and this fellow wanted us to go out and pick them up. The officer from the 21st said, 'We'll get a truck and go down,' and I said, 'Oh no you won't, you'll get blown to bits. We won't do that.' And with that I took Corporal Ron Garmonsway and about half the blokes and left the rest to give us covering fire and we put in an attack on the enemy machine-gun post to our front.

The ground in front of them was the same broken, rocky desert they had stumbled across the night before, and there were folds and gullies in the landscape to give cover. They knew the troops in front of them were Italians, with a slight 'stiffening' of Germans. But it was broad daylight. They had 700 yards to cross with only nine men against a well-prepared enemy position and their own small-arms support was too far away to be effective. They managed to storm the enemy trench and take half a dozen prisoners, but no sooner had they taken one position than they came under fire from another. Again Keith and his men put in an attack and again they took the enemy position without suffering any casualties.

By this time the handful of New Zealanders were deep within the enemy lines and they were being sniped at from all sides. A lesser man might have considered that his men had done enough for one morning and taken them back to the shelter of their own lines, but they still had not found the wounded officer and Keith was not a man to leave a job half done. He divided his forces in two. Ron Garmonsway with four men went off to the right to deal with a third machine-gun nest while Elliott himself with three men resumed his advance into enemy territory, taking their Italian prisoners with them. Encumbered as they were, it was almost impossible to operate, so Keith sent one man back for reinforcements.

Now there were just three of them: Keith, a tall Aucklander named Ron Jones who had been with No. 11 Platoon almost from the beginning, and 'Shorty Lancaster', a tiny little man who had made a part-time living as a deer hunter before the war. All they had in the way of weapons were their rifles and bayonets and a few grenades. This ill-assorted trio with twenty or more Italian prisoners marched forward to attack an entire battalion of the Pavia division, and at this point another machine-gun opened fire on them from the rear.

Leaving Ron and Shorty to deal with the enemy position to their front, while still guarding their prisoners, Keith sprinted 300 yards to the shelter of an abandoned water-truck, a short distance from the enemy behind them. There the Italian machine-gunner pinned him down – every time he tried to move round the front of the truck he was met by a burst of fire. He moved round to the back of the vehicle and was promptly wounded in the thigh by a bullet which ricocheted off the water tank, but another burst punctured the tank and Keith wallowed gratefully in cool water. Then, noticing that the enemy soldiers had their heads down for a moment, he made a dash for a mound of sand about five yards in front of the truck. The next time the machine-gunner raised his head, Keith shot him. Then, incredibly, considering the deep wound in his thigh, he charged the enemy trench with his bayonet fixed across nearly a hundred yards of open desert. By the

127

time he reached it most of the occupants had taken to their heels and run off to join the rest of the prisoners with Lancaster and Jones.

They too had been busy. Jones had been wounded by an enemy grenade and had thrown one of his own which failed to go off, but procured the instant surrender of another bunch of prisoners. Lancaster had been putting his deer-hunting skills to work, potting enemy soldiers at long range with his rifle. Then the enemy mounted an attack.

> It seemed like a platoon to me . . . it might not have been quite so many, but quite a few came at us and Jonesie and I drove them back. Keith must have been helping from the side too because they never came at us again . . . and they did more damage to the prisoners than they did to us. They killed quite a few of their own men.

Keith had indeed been helping from the side. Before he left the shelter of the enemy trench he shot another machine-gunner who was preparing to fire on Jones and Lancaster from the rear. Then he rejoined his two comrades. In his last attack, Keith had been wounded yet again, this time in the knee by a splinter from an explosive bullet. All three of them were exhausted after more than four hours of continuous fighting, quite apart from the long march the night before. So they rounded up their prisoners – by this time there were over sixty of them – and began the long march back to their forward positions. As they did so a truck full of reinforcements came down to meet them, but seeing a large number of Italians advancing towards them the reinforcements promptly opened fire and Keith had to wave a white towel in surrender to his own comrades. As if to underline the fact that the battle was still going on, one of the first reinforcements to get out of the truck had his leg blown off by an enemy anti-tank gun and died shortly afterwards. This unfortunate man was the only New Zealand fatality throughout this remarkable action.

Corporal Garmonsway, who had separated from Keith earlier on, had been equally successful. He and his four men had taken two enemy positions and captured a large number of Italians. The total tally for the morning's work was 130 prisoners and about 30 enemy killed or wounded. Privately, those who took part in the battle believe there were far more. An under-strength platoon, with only nine men actively involved throughout the engagement, had taken on an entire battalion of the enemy and had emerged victorious. To cap it all, the officer who had lost an eye was rescued by the reinforcements and recovered to live for many years.

Keith returned to his platoon, made sure they were in good shape, and reported to his superior officer before stumbling off to the field dressing-station. He spent the next three months in hospital. On 22 September he returned to duty. He had just settled down to supper in the sergeant's mess when there was an interruption. An officer had entered the mess and sought permission from the president to make an announcement. In Keith Elliott's words:

> He wasn't within a donkey's roar of me. He was down the other end of the table and I'm just sitting there, even had my back to him, I think, and he announced it then, that I'd been awarded the Victoria Cross. . . . The first thing I thought was I had to go to the loo . . . you know, you've still got to be normal and do all the things that normal people do. And then it sort of changed my whole life . . . until that time I suppose I was recognised as quite a formidable soldier, quite a good, tenacious bloke . . . and this sort of changed it. It became an awe, you know.

An investiture was held in the field, with General Montgomery presiding over the ceremony. Keith was reunited with his platoon for a while, but he never saw action at the front again. After a few weeks' leave he was sent on a special detail with a Maori charged with a disciplinary offence and happened to bump into General Freyberg, commander of the New Zealand division. Being Keith, he had no hesitation about marching up to the general and asking what plans were in store for him. The answer he eventually received was not at all what he had anticipated. He was to be commissioned in the field and returned to New Zealand to keep up morale on the home front.

Nothing would ever be the same again. Keith had always prided himself on his ability to mingle freely with his men, so when he had his new commission he went down to the canteen in his old battalion to buy a farewell drink for the men in his own company. He bought all the beer in the canteen, but the men were overcome with embarrassment. They could not drink with an officer, least of all with Second Lieutenant Elliott vc, and Keith had to leave them to celebrate without him.

In July 1943, he came home to the inevitable hero's welcome. He was overjoyed to be reunited with his family, but he found the ceremonial and adulation difficult. He was glad to get back to the farm at Marima, which he was delighted to find in good heart, there to pick up the pieces of his life as best he could. A few weeks later, by chance he came across Margaret Markham, a girl he had met briefly before the war, and within a few months Keith was a married man. At the same time, in February 1944, Keith was granted the lease of a 500-acre farm, Gairloch, only a few miles away from his home at Marima. The lease was made available to him under a New Zealand Government rehabilitation scheme for returned servicemen. Like most Commonwealth countries, New Zealand's provisions for its old soldiers make those of Britain look mean and shabby.

Before long Keith was hard at work on the new farm while Margaret settled happily into the role of farmer's wife. By late autumn their first son was born and it seemed that they could both look forward to a happy and prosperous family life. However, things are not that simple for a national hero. Time and again Keith was summoned to attend this celebration or that and it was, in any case, difficult to settle down after the tumultuous events of the past four years. There were also pressures upon him to take a greater part in public life, and for a time he considered becoming an MP.

> I was toying with the idea. You know, you want to help your fellow men, but which way are you going to go? However Margaret said, 'You'll never make a politician – you're too straight. You'll give the country back to the Maoris and apologise for the mess we've made of the show.' So she wasn't very keen.

Providentially perhaps, the Reverend Michael Underhill, a former army padre, happened to be in the area and had met Keith's sister, Lucy. They both came to see Keith, but at first

Margaret thought nothing of it, because all kinds of people came to see him.

> I was busy preparing afternoon tea and left them in the lounge talking, and when I went in the Reverend Underhill said to me, 'Well, Margaret, what do you think of Keith offering himself for the ministry?' I said, 'I'd think he was mad,' just like that – because I'd married a farmer. But as the days went by I got used to the idea and we talked it over, thrashed it out, and we decided that this was what he wanted to do and as I was his wife I would go with him.

So they left the fine 500-acre farm with its beautiful old house, the kind of property which Keith could only have dreamed about before the war, and went to live in a rented house on a miserable stipend of £300 a year, while Keith trained for the ministry. After some difficulty the lease was passed on to his elder brother Charlie, but Keith would never farm his own land again.

Keith's career in the Church was just as turbulent in its way as his life in the army. Shortly after he was ordained he was invited to work for the City Mission in Wellington – a refuge for down-and-outs, alcoholics and other social cast-offs. He went to work energetically, but was so determined to help that he once literally gave away the coat off his own back. Alan Murray, who was wounded during Keith's first action at Mount Olympus, tells a typical story of his generosity.

> Margaret was waiting to put the roast on and she said, 'I'll have to wait until Keith gets home with it'. Keith came home and she said, 'Keith, where's the roast?' 'Well,' he says, 'it's like this, dear. I met a poor fellow on the station. His mother was dying and he had to catch the express. I had to give him the money, so I didn't have any money to buy the roast.'

Sometimes the help that Keith gives is immediate and practical, carting in a load of logs for someone in need, or helping with a building job. Margaret recalls with some indignation how he once spent half a Sunday afternoon mowing a neighbour's lawn when their own grass was a foot long. On other occasions the help is spiritual. Alan Murray tells another story of how Keith, who was late for an important engagement in a distant town, turned his car around and headed in the opposite direction when told that an old man was dying and had asked to see him. Occasionally, though, the good deeds misfire. According to Alan Murray:

> He once brought me a load of manure for the garden, but he picked it up straight out of the cow yard. It was heavy and wet and you could have trailed him from Raumati to here from the muck on the road. . . . He had quite a job to get himself washed up and made respectable before he left – he was on his way to a funeral. . . .

Margaret's patience with this kind of thing is legendary. Not only did she have to put up with having no money, she also had to make house room for sundry alcoholics and vagrants whom Keith would bring home off the streets. Somehow she managed to survive it all and bring up four children as well.

After several years with the City Mission Keith was ill with exhaustion. His bishop moved him to a country parish where he promptly took on a total of four farms, which he managed for people who were unable to cope on their own – mostly divorced women or widows. But he yearned for greater challenges. When he heard at a diocesan synod meeting that there was a shortage of ministers to work with the Maoris he stood up and volunteered on the spot. Margaret was stunned, because Keith had never mentioned the matter before. She had to uproot herself and her family and move to a Maori mission, but much to her surprise she enjoyed the work enormously and so did Keith.

In due course Keith became something of a champion of Maori rights, fighting their land claims for them, contesting their legal battles and generally becoming a thorn in the side of the New Zealand establishment. Keith's style in church was also apt to give offence to delicate sensibilities from time to time. Jack Unverricht, who had been with him through so many of his wartime adventures, overcame his astonishment at Keith's becoming a parson and went to a reunion at which his old platoon sergeant was presiding.

> Keith was taking these civilian people all round the show. We were on one side, all standing to attention and Keith's addressing everybody. He stood up and he said, 'A fine pack of bastards,

aren't they?' . . . He never meant it the way those people think it. It was almost a term of endearment to us. It was always, 'You old bastard, where have you been all this time?' That was what Keith would say, but these civilians, I don't think they saw things that way. They were a bit disgusted, I think.

After some years working with the Maoris, Keith returned to the City Mission in Wellington, again to work with the down-and-outs. This time his immediate superior was a highly conventional Anglican pastor who was somewhat appalled by Keith's rough-and-ready approach. He was also a stickler for good book-keeping. When he examined the accounts and found that Keith had given away a few dollars without keeping scrupulous notes on every cent, he made a public issue out of it. Keith rode out the subsequent storm and stayed at the mission for another four years, but although no one who knew him could possibly have doubted his probity, the stuffier bishops in the Anglican communion refused him promotion. Some of his friends feel that the Church treated him shabbily and that he would have been a happier man if he had never become a priest, perhaps if he had never won the Victoria Cross. Shorty Lancaster agrees.

It was very hard for the children and also terrifically hard for Margaret too. You see, they had an image to live up to. There was a father, not only a VC but also a parson, and every time he moved his name was in the papers, it was on TV, it was on the radio. Simply because he was a VC and a parson, they focused on him. Well, the kids had to live with this and it's like the prime minister's family, you know, the family are the ones that suffer.

The children, all now grown up, deny it. They admit to occasional embarrassment when they were small and the two boys certainly found their father's reputation difficult to live up to, but on the whole they feel they had a very happy childhood. The elder daughter, Elizabeth, remembers one unhappy time during her teenage years, when her father showed great tenderness to her.

I went through quite a hard time during examinations and I found I wasn't able to sleep at night and I can remember going in to Dad and sort of tapping him on the shoulder and saying,

'Dad, I can't sleep, I can't sleep.' And night after night, week in and week out, Dad would come into the bedroom and he'd sit by the bed and he'd just stroke my head and talk to me and finally I'd go to sleep . . . to have him come in like that and lose his own precious sleep was tremendous.

Peter, the younger of the two sons, still lives with his parents at the age of thirty-four, even though he holds down an excellent job and earns far more money than Keith ever did. As a boy he suffered some ribbing from his schoolfellows because of his father's reputation. Even today, though he will joke freely with Keith and tease him about his weaknesses, he still admires his father tremendously.

I remember a time when we were fishing and I hooked him in the eye with a fishing fly. This was up at Lake Waikeromoana. We were miles from any hospital and he had this hook in his eye and I drove him all the way to Rotorua, forty miles on dirt roads, and he had to be brave not to whimper or show any sign of panic, you know. He was just sitting there with that hook in his eye and he wasn't going to get it out until he got to hospital.

Like her children, Margaret has no doubt of her husband's courage but she has needed a placid temperament of her own to put up with some of the vagaries of Keith's behaviour. He has given away some of their most cherished possessions to people he thought were more in need than they were and throughout their life together he has often sprung important decisions on her without any prior warning. Shortly before he retired, for instance, he suddenly announced that he was going to raise money for a new church in the poor parish where he was working by walking from the Cape to the Bluff, the entire length of New Zealand from the extreme north to the southernmost tip, a distance of 2,000 miles. For a man of sixty-one, who was already overweight and took little exercise, it was a brave, not to say a foolhardy, venture.

The first day he walked forty kilometres. By the third day his feet were raw. Margaret followed behind in a car.

The first week I wouldn't like to say what his feet must have felt like, but I saw them and they were blistered, great big blisters. . . . I don't know how he walked on them, I really don't, and I think that took a lot of courage. And I think the actual length of the trip also took courage, because it was a long way.

Characteristically, Keith finished the walk but he failed to raise all the money he wanted from his sponsors, perhaps because he acted too impulsively and expected all his supporters to have the same generosity of spirit as he has himself. Keith also acknowledges that he can be extremely obstinate in sticking to a course of action he has chosen. He himself has no regrets about following his vocation and no recriminations about his failure to ascend the hierarchy of the Anglican Church.

> There's other old soldiers who did much better than I, but I never read anything, you know. I was brought up in the university of hard knocks and they went to . . . some big university in England where they train Sky Pilots. And they had the background. I didn't have any background. I just relied more or less on my own personality. I was a doer of the word . . . I would go out and do.

Keith is still a doer of the word. Although officially retired, he travels all over the country taking baptisms, weddings and funerals, often for the children or parents of others whose lives he has ministered to at some time in the past. He officiates at his local parish church at least once a month and still preaches fiery and controversial sermons when the opportunity arises; he also holds a demanding post with the Wellington Fire Service, working as welfare officer for the men. He is not the kind of man who will ever retire completely, even though he also seizes every opportunity he can get to go quietly up into the hills to his beloved Lake Waikeromoana, where he can fish for trout and contemplate the glorious handiwork of his Creator all around him.

Margaret has no doubt of his greatest qualities. 'A loving disposition . . . a personal touch with people . . . he is able to help them . . . as he has said many a time, he is with people in their joys and in their sorrows and that, I think, is the greatest joy for him.'

Keith agrees. 'I suppose the greatest thing has been helping, and caring for people. You don't put up a flag every time you help someone, you know, but every now and then someone

135

The Second World War

reminds you of something that you've done. . . . That's what I'd like to be remembered for, as someone who helped people when the need arose.'

9
Sir Roden Cutler

The King has been graciously pleased to approve the award of the Victoria Cross to the undermentioned:

Lieutenant Arthur Roden Cutler Australian Military Forces.

For most conspicuous and sustained gallantry during the Syrian Campaign and for outstanding bravery during the bitter fighting at Merdjayoun when this artillery officer became a byword amongst the forward troops with whom he worked.

At Merdjayoun on 19 June 1941 our infantry attack was checked after suffering heavy casualties from an enemy counter-attack with tanks. Enemy machine-gun fire swept the ground but Lieutenant Cutler with another artillery officer and a small party pushed on ahead of the infantry and established an outpost in a house. The telephone line was cut and he went out and mended this line under machine-gun fire and returned to the house, from which enemy posts and a battery were successfully engaged.

The enemy then attacked this outpost with infantry and tanks, killing the Bren-gunner and mortally wounding the other officer. Lieutenant Cutler and another manned the anti-tank rifle and Bren-gun and fought back, driving the enemy infantry away. The tanks continued the attack, but under constant fire from the anti-tank rifle and Bren-gun eventually withdrew. Lieutenant Cutler then personally supervised the evacuation of the wounded members of his party. Undaunted, he pressed for a further advance. He had been ordered to establish an outpost from which he could register the only road by which the enemy transport could enter the town. With a small party of volunteers he pressed on until finally with one other he succeeded in establishing an outpost right in the town, which was occupied by the Foreign Legion, despite enemy machine-gun fire which prevented our infantry from advancing.

At this time Lieutenant Cutler knew the enemy were massing on his

137

left for a counter-attack and that he was in danger of being cut off. Nevertheless he carried out his task of registering the battery on the road and engaging enemy posts. The enemy counter-attacked with infantry and tanks and he was cut off. He was forced to go to ground, but after dark succeeded in making his way through the enemy lines. His work in registering the only road by which enemy transport could enter the town was of vital importance and a big factor in the enemy's subsequent retreat.

On the night of 23–24 June he was in charge of a 25-pounder sent forward into our forward-defending localities to silence an enemy anti-tank gun and post which had held up our attack. This he did and next morning the recapture of Merdjayoun was completed.

Later at Damour on 6 July when our forward infantry were pinned to the ground by heavy hostile machine-gun fire Lieutenant Cutler, regardless of all danger, went to bring a line to his outpost when he was seriously wounded. Twenty-six hours lapsed before it was possible to rescue this officer, whose wound by this time had become septic necessitating the amputation of his leg.

Throughout the campaign this officer's courage was unparalleled and his work was a big factor in the recapture of Merdjayoun.

A few years ago when Sir Roden Cutler was governor of New South Wales, even his close friends addressed him as Your Excellency. Today, when he is only the president of the New South Wales Bank, with a mere handful of other directorships, it would still take a certain amount of temerity to address him as anything other than Sir Roden. This is not just because of his distinguished record or because of the string of honours after his name; it is partly his sheer size. He is a big man, who looks even bigger because of his great physical presence. He walks with a limping stride, dragging the artificial leg which is a memento of the action in which he won the Victoria Cross but the limp only adds to his dignity. At first glance he looks distinctly forbidding, but when he smiles his heavy moustache lifts at the edges and his eyes almost disappear in folds of merriment. His manner is easy and relaxed; he jokes freely with anyone he happens to meet and he has the gift, possessed by many successful men, of giving his total attention (if only for a few moments) to the person he is addressing at the time. Even without trying he looks the kind of man who would command respect and admiration, but the story of his life suggests that he has tried – very hard – to be worthy of it.

Sir Roden was born on 6 May 1916 in Manly, one of the small suburbs which line the bay to the north of Sydney, the eldest of a family of four children – three boys and a girl. His father, Arthur, was for many years a travelling salesman with the Remington Rifle Company and was often away from home. So from quite an early age young Ro Cutler had to help his mother organise the smaller members of the family. The four children increased to five when Ruby Cutler took on the job of bringing up one of her nephews. Ruby was a strong and highly principled woman, absolutely devoted to her family and determined to bring them up with a good education and high standards of what Sir Roden calls 'common decency'.

Manly, in the early decades of this century, must have been an ideal place to live. Although it was only a twenty-minute ferry ride from the city centre, the little town had its own separate identity. Many of the houses were built overlooking the bay, and the Cutlers' home was on top of the low cliffs immediately above Little Manly Cove. To the east the woodlands around the old Naval Quarantine Station at North Head ran down to the water's edge. The coves and inlets were not as cluttered as they are today with water skiers and windsurfers, and the Cutler children enjoyed an idyllic childhood.

They played on the beaches, fished off the rocks, taught themselves to swim in the shark-proof enclosure in Little Manly Cove and paddled about in their father's old rowing boat. In search of more robust pleasures young Roden tried to make himself a sailing canoe.

> I'd taken a sheet of old galvanised iron and bent it over and nailed it together and pitched it to make a canoe out of it. I put an outrigger on it and a sail and I went out towards the Heads and turned around to come back to Manly with the sail fully set and a howling southerly with about three-foot waves.

> Unfortunately, my mother happened to be in the garden and
> she looked out. I suppose she was saying to herself 'Who is
> that stupid child?' and then she realised it was me. So I got
> into a lot of trouble when I got home.

Roden's father, Arthur, as befitted his calling, was a
champion rifle shot with a chest full of medals and a shelf-
load of cups. He taught the boys to shoot with a ·22 rifle,
potting crabs as they sunned themselves on the rocks. When
Arthur Cutler was off on one of his sales trips, Roden would
take advantage of his absence to mount his own shooting
expeditions.

> If I could sneak the ·22 away we'd go over through the bush
> and up past the old Cardinal's Palace as we called it . . . and
> into the woods of the old Quarantine Station, which were
> closed in those days of course, and we'd go up on the hill and
> try and shoot rabbits. . . . My father was very strict about the
> safety rules with a rifle. That's why I'd have got a wonderful
> hiding if he'd caught me taking the ·22 and going to shoot
> rabbits at North Head.

Despite these dangerous pranks, Roden was employed by
his mother as a kind of platoon sergeant to keep the other
children in order. Geoffrey was the next brother in line, but
there were still four years between them and young Geoff
held his elder brother in some awe.

> Sunday lunch was always a major meal. We'd often be swim-
> ming down at the beach and my mother used to come out and
> put a towel on the front fence to signal us to come home. My
> brother would then make sure we were all dressed in our
> Sunday best, ties on, hair done, shoes polished, faces washed.
> Then we'd all be paraded for inspection before we went into
> lunch to make sure we passed muster. . . . I think he being the
> eldest and my father being away a lot, my mother placed more
> responsibility on him than she would otherwise have done. But
> he always seemed to be a responsible fellow and possibly older
> than his years when he was young.

When he was thirteen Roden passed the examination for
Sydney High School, one of the most highly regarded boys'
schools in the city, and had to make the daily journey, by
ferry and bus, to the other side of the town. At Sydney High

he did well academically, swam for the school and was made captain of the rifle team. He also became a prefect in his final year and gained entrance to Sydney University as an economics student.

In Australia in those days it was not uncommon for students to work their way through university, taking a job during the day and attending lectures in the evening. Then they would have to catch up with their reading at night, before going out to work again the following morning. This was 1935, still the Depression years, and the university arranged classes in the evenings to make this arrangement possible, if exhausting, for working students. The Cutlers did not have much money and there were four other children to educate, so Roden got himself a job as a clerk in the Public Trust Office, as a very junior member of the New South Wales Public Service. Life looked as though it would be stringent but fulfilling for the young student, when his father was suddenly killed in a car accident. In Geoffrey Cutler's words:

> It was a tremendous shock, a great blow to everybody but especially to my mother. . . . She went away for several weeks to recuperate and when she came back she had to start all over again. It changed our financial position and of course the whole way of life for the family. I was at school at the time . . . I was only fifteen. I had been looking for a job but when she came back she said, 'Forget about jobs. Go back to school and finish your schooling.' She had definite ideas about what she wanted us to do.

For Roden the shock was also profound. His meagre salary from the Public Trust Office now had to stretch to cover most of the family's day-to-day expenses. There was some insurance money, but not enough to sustain the family, and Ruby Cutler did not believe in mothers going out to work. The family tightened their belts and the children stuck to their education.

One way of making a little extra money and having a good time into the bargain soon occurred to Roden. Sydney University had a flourishing militia, the University Regiment, which was a popular organisation for more than purely

military reasons. A provident government encouraged firms
to give paid leave to part-time students to train in the militia.
There were two annual camps and throughout their training
the part-time soldiers received the relatively handsome sum
of five shillings a day over and above their regular salaries.
Promotion was eagerly sought after by most of the cadets
because it meant extra pay and prestige, but it is clear that
to begin with Roden Cutler regarded the regiment more as a
source of amusement than a serious military training.

David Wood, one of his contemporaries in the regiment,
recalls:

> Cutler was an enigma, because he didn't take rank, not a
> commissioned rank, for three long years and because of that
> he was a little bit out of the ordinary. He used to drive around
> in a general service wagon in the small transport section, which
> was composed of rather individual people. . . . Cutler used to
> turn up at all sorts of places where the regiment was on
> manoeuvres, to give us our lunch. He seemed to glory in the
> fact that he was sitting in a wagon, driving along, while the
> rest of us chaps in the rifle companies had to march. So Cutler
> got to be known as someone who was a little bit different. . . .

Legends began to grow around him. There was a story, for
instance, associated with the small town of Liverpool which
was close to an area where the regiment was on manoeuvres.
According to David Wood, Cutler would wait until after the
pubs were shut, which was six-thirty in the old 'swilling' days
in New South Wales. He would then march into town with
two of his friends. The three young men in uniform, complete
with rifles and equipment, would hammer on the door of the
first pub they came to.

> Well, the poor devil of a publican would come down and see
> this huge figure in the dark and he'd open up pretty smartly.
> Cutler and his two chaps would go in and Cutler would say,
> 'Colonel Windeyer has instructed me to search your establish-
> ment for deserters.' Of course there were no deserters. We
> were all volunteers. However, he and his two men would
> march round the place, peering under tables and so forth and
> when he was through he would say, 'Well, Publican, I can
> report to Colonel Windeyer in the morning that your estab-
> lishment is in order. Now do the decent thing by my men.' In

effect, the publican had to give them free drinks. . . . Not many
of us would have had the nerve to do that.

In 1939 the University Regiment formed an artillery section. War was obviously coming and senior officers in Australia saw a need for trained artillery officers. Cutler stopped
fooling around in the transport section, became a gunner and
within six months had risen to the rank of sergeant. The
same year he completed his economics course at the university, choosing public administration as his speciality in his
last two years. Somehow he also found the time to win a
university 'blue' for shooting. But by September Britain was
at war and Cutler, together with most of his friends, recognised that they would be needed. The same autumn he
enrolled in an officers' training course, gained the rank of
lieutenant and resumed training in earnest with the artillery.
The gunners were transferred to the 18th Field Brigade where
they served for three months under the command of Lieutenant-Colonel C. G. Ingate, who had won a DCM in the First
World War. In April 1940 the Australian 7th Division was
formed and Colonel Ingate was given command of the 2/5th
Field Regiment, Royal Australian Artillery. He liked what he
had seen of the group from Sydney University and he chose
four young officers, Roden Cutler among them, to serve with
him. He also took on a small bunch of other ranks from the
university. So the new regiment had a distinct air of academic
excellence, though not, at this stage, much military experience.

In common with many other young men in Australia at
the time, Roden Cutler had no hesitation about joining up.
Most of them saw clearly that if Britain were to fall to Nazi
Germany they too would come under the jackboot sooner or
later. Older people, with terrible memories of Australian
losses in the First World War, may not have been quite so
eager. But Ruby Cutler seems to have had a clear idea of her
son's patriotic duty.

When I came back from the three months' camp my mother
said, 'There's no need to tell me. I know you'll be joining up.'
And I said, 'Yes', and that was it. . . . I got the impression
that she would have been quite disappointed in me if I hadn't

143

joined up. She knew me well enough to know I was going to.
She didn't become emotional, or give me her blessing or
anything like that. . . . She had a fairly determined personality
which I may have inherited.

There were no immediate partings because the 2/5th
Artillery, still training with First World War 18-pounders,
remained in Australia for most of 1940. On 20 October the
unit sailed on board the *Queen Mary* bound for the Middle
East as part of the 7th Division. The phoney war was at an
end; France had fallen and troops were urgently needed to
protect British oil supplies from the Persian Gulf. At this
stage, however, there was still a dismal shortage of modern
arms and material. The regiment was still equipped with its
obsolete 18-pounders and the first posting was to Deir Suneid
in Palestine, far from the action. Here they stayed for the
next three months until at last, in April 1941, they were
moved to Mersa Matruh in Egypt and issued with modern
25-pounders.

At this point, the British High Command decided to invade
Syria. Under the terms of their peace treaty with the Germans, the French government retained nominal control of
about two-thirds of metropolitan France and all of her
colonies overseas. Many French soldiers had followed De
Gaulle into exile in Britain and now served in the Allied
Armies as 'Free French' forces, but others, including most of
the colonial troops, remained loyal to the provisional government based at Vichy in France. Syria, which at that time
included the area now known as the Lebanon, was occupied
by Vichy troops (made up of elements of the Foreign Legion,
a small contingent from the regular French forces and units
from Morocco and Senegal). These forces were well trained
and equipped with modern weapons, including tanks. Since
Vichy France was now officially an ally of Germany, there
was a considerable danger that the Germans would be
tempted to move some of their troops into Syria and advance
on Cairo from the north-east. Rommel's newly formed 'Afrika
Corps' now offered a considerable menace from the west, and
there was a grave danger that the whole of the Allied Army
in the Middle East would be caught in a gigantic pincer
movement.

To forestall this, the High Command mounted a swift invasion of Syria. In addition to British units it was decided to use the Australian 7th Division, in the hope that Australians would prove more acceptable to the French as an invasion force than the British alone. A small contingent of Free French forces was attached to the Australians and these cheerfully informed their new comrades that the Vichy French would surrender without a battle. Accordingly, the Australians advanced across the frontier in May 1941 wearing their distinctive slouch hats. There were many bitter jokes about this within the next few days, when the bullets started whistling round their ears. Slouch hats came off and battle bowlers went on.

At first, the invasion force made swift progress. The Allied troops advanced in four columns, one along the coast road northwards towards Beirut, two well inland towards Damascus and the other along the central spine of Lebanon, through the fortress town of Merdjayoun. Fighting was brisk, but Roden Cutler admits that the Australians still had a lot to learn about warfare.

> I think our technical training was quite good, but there's a lot of difference between that and fighting. . . . I think we were all rather raw. When the shells and bullets begin to fly and when it comes to hand-to-hand fighting you grow up very quickly. And while I think the quality of mercy remained with the great majority of soldiers, nevertheless you can't afford to play second best when it's for keeps. . . .

Inexperience nearly led to disaster in the Syrian campaign. Merdjayoun was captured after a short and brisk battle in which the 2/5th Artillery played a part, and the British and Australian forces resumed their advance northward, leaving a small garrison to hold the town. But the French brought in an armoured column from Damascus, and the British garrison was too small and too dispersed to put up an effective resistance. Merdjayoun was retaken by the Vichy forces and one column of British and Australian forces were effectively cut off, their lines of communication blocked. There was nothing for it but to turn around and attack the place all over again.

The Second World War

Merdjayoun occupies a position of great natural strength. It is situated on a hill about 700 metres above sea level, overlooking the Litani River to the north and west. All routes through the mountains are commanded by the town, with one road passing through it and the other winding up the valley below. All approaches are steep and rocky and there is little in the way of natural cover. With a determined garrison, well dug in to defend all possible lines of attack, it is a formidable fortress.

It was decided to attack the town with two battalions of infantry, 2nd Pioneers and the 2/25th. The 2/25th was to advance up the slope to the west of the town and the Pioneers were to attack from the south, with the artillery supporting this attack by shelling enemy positions. Lieutenant Cutler and his troop commander, Captain Clark, went forward on 18 June to establish observation posts with a clear view of the enemy. The two officers took a small party of gunners with them to help carry the field telephone cable which was their only contact with their battery. Clark set up an observation post on the north-western slope below the town and called down artillery fire on two target areas – the Balate Ridge to their north and a clump of pine trees, known to them as the Copse, on the western edge of the town. This bombardment caused heavy casualties to the enemy, and Clark was later able to move his party into the Copse in order to cover the infantry attack the following day.

Early on the morning of 19 June the infantry began their advance. Almost immediately they came under heavy machine-gun fire from a rocky promontory which the gunners had named 'Castle Hill', just to the west of the town. Clark and Cutler were unable to see this feature clearly from the edge of the Copse, so they climbed still further up the hill, well in advance of their own troops, and set up a position in an abandoned hut overlooking the town. From here they were able to bring down artillery fire on to Castle Hill, but they were also extremely vulnerable to the enemy.

The party in the hut consisted of Clark, Cutler, three gunners from their own unit and three soldiers from the 2/25th Battalion. In Gunner Geoff Grayson's words:

The area over which we'd laid the line from our previous position was subject to mortar fire and when we got into the hut the first thing that happened was that we had no communications. So we had to go back and repair the line. . . . Cutler, although he was an officer, gave us a lot of assistance on the physical side of laying the line and when it was broken by mortar fire we both went out and repaired it. . . . I should say this happened five or six times.

They had not been in the hut for long when they were horrified to see two tanks patrolling the edge of the town. It soon became apparent that they had been spotted; the tanks and a group of enemy infantry started to advance towards them. Cutler and Private Pratt of the 2/25th were each armed with a Boyes anti-tank rifle. This clumsy weapon fired a small armour-piercing bullet of half-inch calibre, big enough to make a nasty hole in a tin can, but almost useless against tanks. Cutler later wrote in his official report:

We definitely registered hits low on the tanks, saw a small burst of smoke on each impact; we failed to stop them, but I am of the opinion that we troubled them, because they lurched about trying to get protection. About fifteen Legionnaires advanced behind them. Pratt and I exchanged our anti-tank rifles for a Bren and ·303 and fired on the infantry, who retreated behind a stone parapet and replied with exceedingly accurate small arms fire.

One of the tanks continued to advance, firing shells from its cannon as it did so. When it was about fifty yards away the gun scored a direct hit on the hut. The first shot showered the occupants with stones and masonry, and the second killed Private Pratt. The third mortally wounded Captain Clark, and Gunner Grayson was also hit.

The position of the group in the hut now looked hopeless. The tank continued to lumber towards them, firing as it came. In a few moments it seemed they must be overwhelmed, but instead of giving up or making a run for it Cutler calmly kept on shooting with the Boyes rifle. When the tank opened fire he shot at the turret in an effort to silence the gun, but he could see the bullets glancing off the armour, so he switched his fire to the tracks. So persistent and accurate was his shooting that after a bit more lurching about the leading

147

tank veered away and was unable to bring its gun to bear. Both vehicles then withdrew and the enemy infantry went with them.

Gunner Grayson was one of the wounded lying there in the hut. By this time Cutler was the only one of the party who was still shooting.

> Had it not been for Cutler I'm quite sure that tank would have annihilated the lot of us. . . . My last recollection is of him shooting, because he continued to engage the tank. . . . He was firing at the tracks and he managed to stop the tank, which slewed around and couldn't fire at us any more. He was cool, he was calm, his orders were quite clear and concise. There was not one element of panic and I think that did a lot to inspire those serving under him.

As the tanks withdrew, the front line of the 2/25th Infantry, who had been advancing slowly up the hill, came up close to the hut. Private Jack Tannock, who was in one of the leading sections, had witnessed the whole scene.

> There was a lot of firing coming from the hut and I think this must have worried the first tank. . . . It seemed to go away and there was mortaring going on and the next thing I saw was this tall-looking chap come out. . . . And we took cover and this chap walked around, no worries at all. . . . And he must have realised that we were, you know, a bit rattled. And he said, 'Righto lads, stay with us, we've got some wounded men here'. . . . And some of us went and carried these men out. And I don't know what it took to win a medal but I thought, now this cove deserves something. That was the impression I got.

Cutler got the wounded away, but as soon as he had seen them on their way to the dressing-station he went back up the hill to talk to the officers of the leading infantry companies. Lacking effective anti-tank weapons and faced with what seemed to be stiff resistance, the infantry officers wanted to withdraw. Cutler, who was junior to all of them in rank, pressed for an advance. He argued that the French could not be confident or they would not have withdrawn from their skirmish with him. He also pointed out that once the infantry were in the town they would have better cover from the buildings and the tanks would be at more of a disadvantage. Eventually the infantry officers agreed to consolidate on their present position and try to advance by stages into the town.

Cutler was convinced that a more aggressive approach was needed. He managed to persuade the most energetic of the infantry officers, Captain Marson, to give him five men to help him set up an even closer observation-post within the town itself. Together the two officers led a small group into the buildings on the northern outskirts of the town, but the infantry were forced to withdraw in the face of heavy machine-gun fire. Cutler was also urged to withdraw, but he insisted on setting up his observation-post. He left four of his party in a house on the edge of the built-up area and went forward himself with one lance-corporal into Merdjayoun cemetery. From here he could see the road which provided the only access to the town from the east. He was able to take bearings, register the target, and call down artillery fire within a few yards of his own position.

Late in the afternoon he and the lance-corporal were still there. To their consternation two enemy tanks lumbered into the cemetery and the crews got out and started a council of war with some infantrymen only a few yards from their hiding place. John Firth, the Australian artillery officer at the other end of the field telephone line, could hardly believe his ears.

> Ro was whispering. . . . It must have been an unusually good phone connection, because they didn't often work that well. . . . He instructed us in good Australian language not on any account to ring the buzzer on the phone because the enemy were about twenty yards away and he told me that he intended to try and walk out of that horrible position when it got dark.

Roden and his signaller, Lance-Corporal Williamson of the 2/25th Infantry, sat tight in their hiding place until the French seemed to have settled down for the night. Cutler recalls:

> We waited – with trepidation I must admit, a good deal of apprehension – until dark, when I said to the signaller, 'We take off our boots, put them around our necks and we'd better try and make our way back,' because we had received infor-

mation before the tanks arrived that the French were counter-attacking and I was worried, getting back in the darkness, that our own troops would fire on us.

The two men crept out without being detected. Cutler picked up the rest of his party from the house where they had been hiding and the little group of Australians picked their way slowly down the hill to where they guessed the front line of the 2/25th must be. By chance it happened that an old comrade of Roden's from university days, a young stockbroker turned soldier named Cam Robertson, was with a patrol of the 2/25th who had come up the hill in the darkness to organise the withdrawal of the battalion. As they approached the area where they thought they might find their own troops, Cam Robertson and his patrol peered ahead of them into the darkness.

> We saw this defile alongside a wall, and along that wall came three stooping forms. We didn't know whether they were ours or the French and we took up a position to shoot them and that's when I called out, 'Who goes there?' and a voice from the other side came out, 'Is that you, Cam?' Ro had remembered my voice from our being on the *Queen Mary* together . . . and he said, 'For God's sake don't fire!'

The two men met up, made contact with Captain Marson and eventually, after some hours of searching for stray groups of men, the whole battalion was safely evacuated from the hill.

The infantry did not renew their attack until reinforcements arrived, but the work that Cutler had done in pinpointing a bottle-neck on the one road out of the town meant that the French garrison could not be reinforced, nor could they escape. A few days later the French surrendered, and the 2/5th Artillery were ordered to move across country to the coast road in order to support the major advance on Beirut. The French had established heavily defended positions just north of the Damour River about twenty miles south of the city and it was here that Cutler was to complete the work which led to the award of the Victoria Cross.

On 5 July 1941 Cutler was sent forward to establish an observation-post in support of an attack by the Australian

2/16th Battalion. A shortage of trained signallers, an inadequate supply of maps and the incompetence of one of the
senior officers of the 2/5th Field Regiment (whom Cutler still
refuses to name) all combined to defeat his purpose. Through
no fault of his own Cutler eventually found himself, late in
the evening, at the headquarters of the 2/16th Infantry,
without a field telephone and without any clear orders as to
how to proceed. The infantry commander was incensed. He
needed artillery support and he was determined to get it.
Cutler takes up the story:

> I said to the 2/16th, 'I really can't do much without a field
> telephone. Your radios won't work in this hilly country.' There
> was a bit of grumbling, almost as if I was frightened to go, and
> I said, 'Well, I'll come, but I'm warning you there's not much
> I can do.' And I sent a message to the officer who was
> supporting me to run the telephone wire forward and meet me
> at the river the following morning at dawn. Of course, the
> unnamed officer countermanded that, so we found we were in
> a sticky situation.

Cutler made his way to the river before dawn, but no one
came forward with a field telephone. So, throwing caution to
the winds, he chose to join up with the infantry and make the
best use he could of their primitive radio to call down artillery
fire wherever it might be needed. When the infantry attacked
at first light, Cutler went with them. The first wave went
ahead and he was about fifty yards behind them with his
radio operator. The only weapon that either of them had was
Roden Cutler's service revolver, and whatever they could
borrow from the infantry around them.

> The next thing we knew we were being fired on from in
> between our own front rank and ourselves. The infantry had
> overrun three French machine-gun nests in the darkness. . . .
> I didn't see much point in having them firing either in front of
> us or behind us, so I called on the first position to surrender
> in what the CO called my bad French. The Frenchmen
> understood it all right and came out.

The second position was weaker in understanding, so
Cutler ran forward and jumped into the trench waving his
revolver. He was taking an almighty chance but it paid off,

and the enemy machine-gunners came out with their hands up. But the third group were less tractable. They kept firing. Calling on a Bren-gunner of the 2/16th to give him covering fire, Cutler again ran forward, but this time he hurled a hand grenade and followed it up by leaping into the trench. Several of the enemy were wounded and the rest surrendered. Cutler sent his party of prisoners back towards his own lines and then went forward to join the infantry commander. For any one man to capture three enemy machine-gun posts was no mean feat. For an artillery officer, whose main job was observation and not physical combat, it was even more remarkable and those who saw it marvelled at it.

By this time the 2/16th Infantry had overrun two lines of trenches, but it was now broad daylight, they still had no accurate artillery support and the attack had lost its momentum. A third line of enemy machine-guns had them pinned down on the hillside. Cutler volunteered to go back to the river in the hope that his field telephone had now arrived and he would be able to call down artillery fire on the enemy positions. As he ran down the rocky slope which he had just ascended, a burst of machine-gun fire caught him in the leg. He went down instantly. The main arteries were severed and the bones of his leg were smashed in several places.

Cutler could easily have died within a few minutes from loss of blood. Fortunately he had the presence of mind to fasten his revolver lanyard as a tourniquet around his thigh, thus arresting the flow of blood. The enemy soldiers who had shot him came out briefly from their hiding place to make sure they had got him, but they did not venture far and he was left alone. He lay there all that day, with the midsummer sun of the Lebanon blazing down on him. He had given most of the water in his canteen to the wounded French prisoners he had captured early that morning, and now had none left. He did not dare to allow himself to lose consciousness, because he knew that if he did not loosen the tourniquet from time to time, gangrene would set in; he would certainly lose his leg and almost certainly die. He had taken off his shirt to help staunch the flow of blood, and he lay there and burned in the sun.

As an additional irony, the area where he lay was pounded

with shell fire from time to time by the guns of the Royal
Navy firing offshore – he was even shelled by the guns of his
own regiment. When darkness eventually came he thought
relief had come with it. The 2/16th Infantry pulled back from
their exposed position on the hillside, and a party of Australian soldiers found him and carried him down towards the
river. They left him close to the bank, promising to send help,
and gave him a full water bottle. However, this was soon
gone and he was too weak to crawl to the water's edge. Again
he had to wait.

By this time the officers of his own regiment had realised
that he was missing. Dr Adrian Johnson, the medical officer,
and the signals sergeant, John Robinson, (both friends of
Roden's from university days), set out to look for him.
Unfortunately they had no clear idea where to look and of
course no notion whether they would find him dead or alive.
After stumbling around in the scrub for some hours they were
obliged to give up. But as dawn came up the following
morning they renewed the search and eventually, twenty-
seven hours after he was first hit, they found him. The
stretcher party that brought him in was made up of four
captured French soldiers (four of the same men whom Roden
himself had taken prisoner a little over a day before) who
recognised him. 'Doucement,' said the leading Frenchman as
they lifted him on to an improvised stretcher . . . 'Gently.' It
is not a word that is often heard on any battlefield. Adrian
Johnson takes up the story:

> He was in a very parlous condition . . . as near to death as
> anyone would ever wish to be. . . . At that stage all we could
> do for him in the open air was to give him morphiu and then
> we carried him back to a stone hut, which as far as I remember
> was all that was left of the village of Yerima. . . . When we
> picked him up there had been a lull in the proceedings, but
> when we got him back to the stone house enemy shelling began
> again.

As Dr Johnson was fitting a Thomas splint, a device which
makes it easier to move a patient without undue pain, a shell
landed in the doorway of the house, killed one of Johnson's
assistants and came close to killing them all. Another shell

153

hit their make-shift ambulance, but fortunately it remained functional. Somehow they got their patient out and, after a juddering journey over rutted roads, to the field hospital, but Cutler's life was still in danger. Despite the periodic loosening of the lanyard, gangrene had developed in his leg and amputation had to be swift. Then, when he should have been on the way to recovery he developed a condition known as empyema – a collection of pus in the pleural cavity. Again he was very close to death until a second operation drained away the corruption and he began to make a proper recovery. There was no doubt that Cutler had a tremendous determination to live, even though he had quite coolly placed his life in danger on many occasions over the previous few weeks. There was no doubt either, according to Adrian Johnson, about his courage.

> I'd liken it to what in surgical practice is called informed consent. . . . This is when a patient's about to have some dangerous or new operation. . . . All the things that can possibly go wrong are explained to him and in the light of that knowledge the patient decides to go ahead with the operation. Now I think this is the sort of courage he displayed at Merdjayoun. . . . On the other hand the adrenalin-produced courage that causes a man to rush a machine-gun post . . . some people call it 'battle mad' . . . I think he showed that kind of courage too in the infantry battle at Damour.

Despite the loss of his leg Cutler still wanted to play an active part in the war, but his pleas for a desk job close to the front were ignored and he was sent home to Australia on board the hospital ship *Oryana*. Whilst sitting reading in the lounge one day one of the ship's officers came up to him.

> He said, 'Are your Christian names Arthur Roden?' And I said, 'Yes'. 'Well,' he said, 'you've won a VC.' And of course I didn't believe it. I listened to the next news on the BBC and they repeated it and I still didn't believe it, but I thought, seeing that the ship had produced a little printed scroll signed by a representative from every ward . . . and seeing that the ship's surgeon had given me a prescription for champagne *ad libidinum* – and it was a dry ship – then it must be true. . . . I suppose that a VC to me was something that was well beyond the reach of most men. . . . It only happened to the very

exceptional individual. And here I was, alive, and I didn't think I'd done that much and here I was with a VC. . . .

When the *Oryana* docked at Sydney, Roden's sister Doone was there to welcome him.

It was joyous, absolutely joyous. . . . They gave the school children a holiday and the ferries all put up bunting and balloons. . . . And we came through the city and walked on to the ferry and they cock-a-doodle-dooed all the way down the harbour. . . . And when we got to Manly there were big crowds with lots of bunting and they had this official reception for him. . . .

It was Cutler's first taste of public life and he had to make a speech of thanks and, although he still felt tired and was still on crutches, he seems to have made a good job of it. The State Government had kept open his old job for him, but before long he was offered a new post as assistant secretary to the Returned Servicemen's League in New South Wales. This was a job which entailed a round of speeches and fund-raising activities which kept him very much in the public eye. The good-looking young officer with the dignified limp and the Victoria Cross was the hero of every ex-servicemen's gathering and the darling of every drawing-room. It was at one of these private parties that he met Helen, the girl who was to become his wife.

I had just joined the Australian Women's Army Service and when I took my first leave I arrived at my parents' home to be told that we were going to a party . . . and that Cutler VC, was to be there. And before leaving my course I had been told: whenever you see a VC always salute. So I didn't want to take my hat off until I'd had the opportunity to pay my respects. So I was taken into the room and there he was, on crutches, looking marvellous, terrific smile, surrounded by women . . . and I gave my salute. That was our first meeting.

Helen's military work soon took her to Melbourne, where she took over the job of running a transport depot for the Australian Women's Army Service. Cutler, meanwhile, had been appointed to a senior post in the Security Services in New South Wales, and the romance with the saluting lady soldier might have gone no further. But his career was

155

progressing by leaps and bounds. In 1945 he was given the post of Assistant Commissioner of Repatriation for Australia, and posted to Melbourne. There, quite by chance, Roden and Helen met again, and within a few months they were engaged to be married.

Before the marriage took place, Cutler was offered yet another job, this time for the Ministry of External Affairs as High Commissioner for New Zealand. He was not yet thirty. It was an astonishing appointment for one so young, and this post was the first of a long string of diplomatic appointments which took the Cutlers to Ceylon, Egypt, Pakistan and finally to New York.

Perhaps only in Egypt was there a need for the kind of qualities which had won the young diplomat the Victoria Cross. In 1956 the Suez Crisis was at its height, the British were *persona non grata* and the young Australian High Commissioner had to represent Britain's interest in Cairo at a crucial phase in negotiations. The Australian prime minister, Bob Menzies, flew in to chair a five-nation committee to try and negotiate a settlement without bloodshed. But with the Israelis waiting in the wings and the British and French poised for invasion there was little prospect of a peaceful solution. Most western diplomats were evacuated, fearing riot and confusion in the city. Helen Cutler, who was by this time the mother of three young boys with a fourth on the way, was obliged to leave her husband and fly home. When the Suez Committee packed up, Cutler was left in an almost empty chancery, with just three members of his staff.

> It was an alarming time, because the Egyptians are capable of emotional upsurges. . . . Eventually we were put under house arrest and not allowed out even into the garden. We destroyed all our records, our seal and everything, so all that was in order. . . . And then in the dead of night we were taken out and put on the train for Libya.

In those pre-Gaddafi days Libya was still moderately conciliatory towards the West, and the Australians found their way safely home. The crisis had called for coolness and deliberation, the unspectacular courage of the diplomat rather than the soldier. But it also illustrated another quality which

156

had contributed to Cutler's winning of the Victoria Cross – a strong sense of responsibility. Roden's younger brother Geoffrey puts it like this:

> Ro was never ostentatious. . . . But he had a lot of quiet determination and if he set his mind to do something he usually did it. I think in addition to that he has a high sense of duty. I don't want to make him sound too pompous but if he thought he should do something he did it. . . .

The Cutlers' third son, Richard, now married and with children of his own, still admits to idolising his father.

> He's very conscious of his duty to others and he's very strict on how he performs that duty. . . . He has a lot of time for his family, even though he has a very busy life. He's very cautious in what he does in the sense that he doesn't want to upset others. . . . But he's not afraid to stand up and be counted, to express his views, even though at times they may be thought controversial.

Cutler's career in the Diplomatic Service was eventually rewarded with a knighthood and in 1965, whilst serving as Australian ambassador to the Netherlands, he was offered the post of governor of New South Wales. At forty-nine, he was once again extremely young for the job. He took office in January 1966 and retired over fourteen years later in November 1980, the longest-serving governor in the history of the state.

Even today many ordinary Australians, perhaps especially in his home city of Sydney, think of Sir Roden as 'the Governor', and among men and women in the street he seems to be held in universally high regard. This is perhaps less because of his achievements – the office does not, in normal conditions, carry a great deal of political power – but because he managed to combine a great awareness of the dignity of office with a strong concern for the welfare of ordinary people. During the Vietnam war, for instance, the Australian government introduced a lottery system for young men eligible for military service. Sir Roden thought this unjust and said so, publicly and effectively. There was a noisy and acrimonious public debate and Sir Roden was castigated by some Australian politicians for interfering in matters which were felt to be outside his responsibility. Sir Roden is still unrepentant. 'In my view I was quite entitled to do it, because it was a national matter and there was a lot of feeling amongst the young people. But if I had wanted to be safe and careful, no, I shouldn't have said anything.'

The distinction between national and state affairs is important, because he never interfered overtly in the politics of his home state. He served under state premiers both of the left and the right and was able to talk as easily to communist trade unionists as he was to Sydney businessmen. This common touch has been one of his greatest assets in public life. In Helen Cutler's words:

> My husband really has a wonderful way with people, both young and old and those in between. People warm to him immediately. He has the gift of putting people quickly at their ease and he has a wonderful sense of humour which is so quick and yet won't hurt anyone, so he gets them smiling.

But there was at least one occasion when he was unable to bring his charm to bear. At the height of the Vietnam war he was called upon in his capacity as Visitor to Sydney University to preside over a degree ceremony. There was a noisy anti-war demonstration and the mood of some of the protestors may not have been soothed by the appearance on the scene of the Sydney University Regiment in full fig. While inspecting the regiment, of which he was also colonel-in-chief, Sir Roden himself was abused and pelted with tomatoes. He continued with his inspection while tomatoes spattered his robes, and appeared benignly unconcerned.

> I thought it was understandable. I resented being given the Heil Hitler salute and being called a fascist, but knowing the university and being closely in touch with it, I wasn't surprised and it didn't upset me. A little humour gets over these things sometimes.

Tolerant and humorous he certainly was, but he was also a stickler for protocol, a governor who insisted on due respect being given – if not to himself as a man – at least to the office he held.

Although he retired as governor in 1980, Sir Roden now

holds several directorships, takes an interest in a large number of charities and is chairman of the New South Wales Bank – as he himself observes, he probably still works as hard as ever. If not exactly rags to riches, his is the story of a man who rose from very modest beginnings to very high office. The Victoria Cross was a step along the way insofar as it brought him to public attention, but the courage he showed at Merdjayoun and Damour was also a reflection of the high sense of responsibility which has governed the whole of his life.

> The Victoria Cross brought me into the public limelight . . . but I think if I hadn't been able to back that up with other qualities it would have faded into the background and not influenced things so much. Unfortunately, many VC-winners have tended to become a bit too sociable . . . perhaps drink a bit too much. I've enjoyed people but I haven't let the VC rule my life.

10
Parkash Singh

The King has been graciously pleased to approve the award of the Victoria Cross to:

No. 14696 Havildar Parkash Singh, 8th Punjab Regiment, Indian Army.

On 6 January 1943 at Donbaik, Mayu Peninsula, Burma, when two carriers had been put out of action, Havildar Parkash Singh drove forward in his own carrier and rescued the two crews under very heavy fire. At the time, the crews of the disabled carriers had expended their ammunition and the enemy were rushing the two disabled carriers on foot. This NCO's timely and courageous action, entirely on his own initiative, saved the lives of the crews and their weapons.

On 19 January 1943 in the same area, three carriers were put out of action by an enemy anti-tank gun and lay on the open beach covered by enemy anti-tank and machine-gun fire. One of these carriers was carrying the survivors of another carrier in addition to its own crew. Havildar Parkash Singh, on seeing what had happened, went out from a safe position in his own carrier and, with complete disregard for his own personal safety, rescued the combined crews from one disabled carrier, together with the weapons from the carrier. Having brought the crews to safety he again went out on the open beach in his carrier, still under very heavy anti-tank and machine-gun fire, and with the utmost disregard to his personal safety dismounted and connected a towing chain on to a disabled carrier containing two wounded men. Still under fire, he directed the towing of the disabled carrier from under enemy fire to a place of safety.

Havildar Parkash Singh's very gallant actions, entirely on his own initiative, were an inspiration to all ranks, both British and Indian.

Parkash Singh

Every year in New Delhi there is a grand parade to celebrate Republic Day, 26 January. Picked troops from the famous regiments of India, resplendent in full dress – some marching impeccably in step, some mounted on handsome horses – move in ceremonial procession down the Rajpath, the wide avenue which leads from the former Viceregal Palace, Rashtrapati Bhavan, to the great arch at India Gate. In the van of this superb parade is a short procession of jeeps. Foremost of all are the holders of modern India's highest awards for courage. Next in order and next in honour throughout the nation are the holders of the Victoria Cross. Even though they became independent of British rule nearly forty years ago and have gladly turned their backs on most of the symbols of foreign rule, the Indian people do not forget that theirs was the largest volunteer army in two world wars and that the soldiers who fought then were fighting against a far worse tyranny than the British Empire. So the heroes still lead the parade and among them, standing erect in his jeep, is a tall Sikh – Major Parkash Singh vc.

Parkash looks exactly as a Sikh ought to look – big, broad-shouldered, always impeccably dressed with his immaculate turban and his full beard neatly tucked away. He is a handsome man with a clear, steady gaze and a slightly diffident smile, as though he believes that life is a fundamentally serious business and smiles are a bit of a luxury. His manner seems a little formal, almost brusque at first. He does not waste words and usually restricts himself to the minimum necessary to convey the business in hand, but in the evening, when he has a glass of whisky in his hand, when friends gather and the cards come out, the diffidence vanishes. He becomes broad, humorous, expansive, even voluble. He laughs and reminisces about the old days, and all the fundamental warmth of his character comes to the surface.

Parkash was born in Lyallpur, a town in the western part of the old province of Punjab in what is now Pakistan. His father was a small farmer, making just enough money to keep his wife and five children in modest comfort. Even though his father was what Parkash describes as a 'pukka Sikh', Parkash himself had his head shaved as a child, despite the usual religious prohibition against the cutting of hair. He only went

161

to the temple, the *gurdwara*, 'for fun' as he remembers it. He also seems to have been a bit of a rascal. Because he was able and strong-willed, his schoolmaster made him responsible for a group of younger boys in his home village. Parkash recalls what happened:

> The teacher told me to look after them. He said I could give them hell if they didn't obey me, so I used to give them hell every day . . . anybody disobeying my orders, because I was strong enough to control them and whatever I said they would have to obey. On Sundays we used to go out to some other village, have competition, football, hockey, anything . . . and it was a free for all! If there was a fruit tree in somebody's garden I would tell them 'All right, go ahead. Get everything, whatever you feel like.' Nobody could object to what I said.

Parkash seems to have got away with his bad behaviour because he was a clever student and an exceptional athlete. By the time he was seventeen his running ability, especially at 800 metres, was so marked that the headmaster of the government college at Lyallpur offered him a free scholarship if he would join the school and go on to higher education. But Parkash had already passed matriculation in the school certificate and he had other ambitions. One of his brothers was in the army and, like many younger boys in the same situation, the youth was impressed by the uniform and the confident bearing of his soldier brother. At first Parkash wanted to join the Viceroy's Police, an élite team of six-footers, but when he found there were no vacancies he decided on the army instead, and in 1936 he joined the 8th Punjab Regiment of the Indian Army.

It was in the regiment that Parkash first learned about the traditions of the Sikhs, about the teachings of their founder Guru Nanak, who strove to bring together the best of Hindu and Moslem ideas into a single unified faith. He also learned of the martial traditions which sprang up in response to religious persecution by the Moslem ruler Aurangzeb in the seventeenth century and the struggle to build an independent Sikh state in the Punjab. By the time the British began to dominate the sub-continent, the Sikhs were among the most powerful peoples in the north-west of India and one of the last to come under British rule. But once they had agreed to serve under the British flag they made soldiers of unmatched courage and loyalty.

Since the great Mutiny of 1857 the government in India usually preferred mixed regiments to those made up of a single religious or ethnic group. The 8th Punjab was composed of two companies of Moslems, one of Sikhs and one of Jat Hindus, all serving under a cadre of British officers. The theory was that if one group of men proved disloyal or mutinous the other groups would stand firm and any trouble would be contained. It was the old principle of divide and rule, but there was also a certain amount of friendly rivalry between the different religious groups, which made for a competitive spirit throughout the unit. Larger formations, like the 47th Brigade to which the 5th Battalion of the 8th Punjab Regiment was later assigned, were usually made up of one British unit (in this case the Royal Inniskilling Fusiliers) and two Indian battalions. The idea was for the British to 'stiffen' the Indian units, though in practice it was often the Indians who did the stiffening.

At the time that Parkash joined it, 5/8 Punjab was part of the force based on the north-west frontier of India, and most of his early service was in this area. Long before the war he saw action when part of his battalion was ambushed by Pathan tribesmen and sixty men, including the British commanding officer, were killed. Partly as a result of this, Parkash himself won early promotion and went up through the ranks as a lance-naik, then naik (or full corporal) and finally a havildar, or sergeant. His athletic prowess was also a help to him. In his early twenties he had already equalled the all-India record for the 800 metres, but the coming of the war put a stop to his ambitions in the sports arena.

In 1941, when Parkash was a havildar in the headquarter company of the 8th Punjab, Bert Causey joined his battalion as a second lieutenant. For Bert the whole experience of the war had already been bizarre. Called up as a conscript and shipped out to India, he had been selected for officer training, commissioned at Dehra Dun and now found himself, a plain Lancashire man, serving as a junior officer in one of the great infantry regiments of the Indian Army. He immediately liked and respected the young havildar and the two men – the short youth from Lancashire and the tall young Sikh – made friends. In 1942, when the 5th Battalion of the 8th Punjab became part of 47 Brigade, they moved to the headquarters of the 14th Division of the Indian Army at Comilla in Bengal, in order to help oppose the Japanese invasion.

In the wake of the Japanese advances of 1942, which had now reached the frontiers of India itself, one of the problems which most worried the senior Indian Army commanders was that of morale. To British and Indian units alike it had come to seem that the Japanese were invincible. The arms and equipment with which they were expected to defend India against the triumphant Japanese troops were often obsolete and always in short supply. The struggle against Germany was given priority in everything and the troops strung out through the eastern provinces of India – in Bengal, Manipur and Assam – had already begun to think of themselves as 'the forgotten army'. If they were to recover an offensive spirit they needed to believe that they could fight the Japanese and win, so the High Command decided on a limited offensive campaign.

It was known that the Arakan area in the north-west of Burma, close to the Indian frontier, was only lightly garrisoned by the Japanese, and if an eventual counter-offensive by the British was to succeed they would need to seize the town of Akyab, with its airfield and port facilities, which is situated on an island just south of the Mayu Peninsula. It was therefore planned to advance with the whole of the 14th Division, with its full complement of British and Indian troops, down the length of the Mayu Peninsula to seize Akyab, recover some of the ground lost to the Japanese and secure a base for further offensive operations.

On paper the plan looked feasible enough. The 14th Indian Division would have a clear numerical superiority over any enemy forces they were likely to encounter. A swift advance should encounter little opposition, and once they had secured the Peninsula and the island port of Akyab the division would be in a reasonable position to defend themselves against Japanese counter-attack. But even at the planning stage there does not seem to have been complete conviction in the likely

164

success of the operation. It would have been possible, as Lieutenant General William Slim (still a relatively junior figure in the hierarchy) pointed out, to use Orde Wingate's newly formed Chindit Brigade to work around through the jungle and take Akyab in the rear. At the same time a series of amphibious landings could be made down the coast to outflank the Japanese as they tried to counter the invasion. But Slim was not at that time in full control of the situation and both these measures were considered unnecessary. 14th Division must do the job for itself.

Of the many problems confronting the divisional commander, General Lloyd, the nature of the terrain itself was probably the worst. The Mayu Peninsula consists of a long ridge of precipitously steep hills, clothed from top to bottom in dense jungle, with a narrow strip of scrub and paddy fields on either side, sloping down to the Mayu River to the east and the Indian Ocean to the west. The division would have to advance on a very narrow front on either side of the hills. Since they were still almost completely untrained for manoeuvring through the jungle, the troops on the east would be almost completely out of contact with those on the west. To make matters worse, the strip of semi-cultivated land alongside the beach was intercepted by numerous streams, or *chaungs*, very few of which were bridged. So although the British and Indian troops were trained to be heavily reliant on wheeled transport, the division had to leave most of its vehicles behind. The only effective transport in the front line were the universal carriers. A carrier was little more than a metal box mounted on caterpillar tracks, capable of seating four men in reasonable comfort. The armour plate was just about thick enough to stop a rifle bullet, but the vehicle was completely uncovered and the only armament was a Bren light machine-gun and the rifles of the occupants.

Bert Causey was in command of the carrier platoon of 5/8 Punjab and Parkash Singh was his havildar. When the invasion of the Mayu Peninsula began, Bert Causey and his platoon of carriers were sent off in advance of the battalion to carry out a reconnaissance along the whole length of the beach. In the middle of December 1942 they set out, and travelled by stages along the coastal strip. The rest of the division followed up slowly behind them and, to begin with, the carriers were able to rendezvous with their own advance units by night. But early in January 5/8 Punjab were sent through one of the few passes over the hills to strengthen the eastern flank alongside the Mayu River, and their carrier platoon was attached to brigade headquarters, together with the carriers from the two other units in the formation, the Royal Inniskilling Fusiliers and 1/7 Rajput Rifles. So far, Parkash Singh and Bert Causey had seen no sign of enemy activity and had been able to reach Foul Point at the extreme tip of the peninsula and look across the narrow sea inlet, just a few miles away, to Akyab itself.

A rapid deployment of the division throughout the peninsula might at this stage have provided a springboard for a successful attack on Akyab, but General Lloyd was anxious to secure his lines of communication. Deprived of their transport it was difficult for the troops to make a rapid advance. The Japanese, however, did not seem to suffer from the same difficulties. Early in January Parkash Singh and Bert Causey saw footprints on the beach which might have been made by an enemy patrol. On 5 January, near Donbaik, Lieutenant George Semple, who commanded the Inniskilling's carrier platoon, had a fierce little battle with a group of men dressed in loincloths who opened fire on the British vehicles from the cover of the jungle. Later the same day it was learned that a party of the enemy had infiltrated into the area around the village of Donbaik itself. Early the following morning the Inniskillings put in an attack across the *chaung*, and the carriers were ordered to advance along the beach on the right flank to give what support they could.

Bert Causey set out, together with the other carriers in his platoon, with Parkash Singh following up in his own vehicle a few hundred yards to the rear. Bert took his carrier across the *chaung* and, stopping close to a patch of scrub on the edge of the beach, began to search the horizon with his binoculars. Unfortunately for him a group of Japanese had taken up a position in the scrub within a few yards of the place where he had stopped. Several of them crept through the undergrowth and, without warning, hurled a salvo of grenades at the carrier. Luckily, none of the grenades scored a direct hit, but several splinters hit Bert in the face. His driver immediately turned
166

the vehicle about and headed back the way they had come. Temporarily blinded by the blood from his wounds, Causey called out to Parkash to take over command, while he returned to the regimental aid post to have his wounds patched up.

Two of the other carriers, meanwhile, had become bogged down in the stream. Seeing their opportunity, the Japanese immediately opened fire and advanced towards the trapped vehicles. The frightened men inside hammered away at the enemy with their Bren-guns, but each time they stopped firing to change magazines a party of Japanese would rush a few yards closer. The men in the stranded vehicles started to cry out for help.

Parkash's own carrier was well back under cover and he could easily have withdrawn and left the others to their fate. Instead he drove forward to the rescue, crossed the *chaung* – shouting at the men inside the trapped carriers to make a run for it – and charged towards the Japanese with his own Bren-gunner firing by his side. As they careered towards the enemy the gunner was hit. Without pausing, Parkash wrested the gun from the wounded man and drove with one hand while he fired the Bren-gun with the other until all his ammunition was exhausted. Momentarily dumbfounded by the bravado of the attack, the Japanese ran for cover and Parkash circled his vehicle crazily in front of their positions, bluffing them into a headlong retreat. Then he charged back across the *chaung* to pick up the men from the stranded vehicles, who had gathered in a frantic huddle close to the bank. As he stopped to let them clamber on board, the leading Japanese troops broke cover and raced across the *chaung*, firing as they came. Eight terrified men tried desperately to get inside a vehicle designed for four, which was already crammed with men and equipment. As soon as the first of them were safely on board, they began to scream at Parkash to get going and leave the others to the Japs. 'I had to beat two of those fellows severely,' he recalls. 'I would not leave until they were all on the vehicle.' With the leading Japanese only a few yards away, the last man got a precarious hold on the carrier and Parkash let the vehicle into gear. Rocking wildly as they fled over the uneven ground, with a hail of Japanese bullets about their ears, they finally reached the safety of their own lines.

The Second World War

Parkash had thoroughly enjoyed himself: 'I would love to go and fight the enemy . . . I like it very much. I used to volunteer myself. . . . I don't know whether I was aggressive or not but I liked to go into action. I never got frightened of the enemy.'

Perhaps the same could not be said for all the troops concerned. Over the next twelve days there were a number of other brave attempts to dislodge the Japanese from Donbaik, but never in sufficient strength, and the enemy were able to bring in many more men through the jungle and consolidate their position to the north of the village. The Japanese adopted a system of defence with which the 14th Indian Division were to become all too familiar. They dug deep underground shelters in the banks of the *chaung* and lined the walls with timber; openings were dug overlooking one another on the forward slope of the bank in a complex network of interlocking fields of fire. The openings were then sealed up with heavy logs, and each bunker was carefully camouflaged to merge with the background. The Japanese soldiers inside were expected to live there for days if necessary, and they were armed with heavy and light machine-guns, plentifully supplied with ammunition. The bunkers themselves were proof against artillery and mortar fire – indeed against almost anything except a very heavy calibre weapon at point-blank range.

If the first wave of an assault managed to reach the bunkers, the British and Indian troops would find that the narrow openings were impossible to penetrate. The Japanese would then let loose a deluge of artillery and mortar fire on their own forward positions, and counter-attack with reserves that were held in the rear. These positions, fortified in depth, were therefore almost impossible to take without tanks or flame-throwers. The 14th Division had neither. Fearful of moving large bodies of troops through the jungle, General Lloyd made no large-scale attempt to outflank the enemy and decided to launch yet another frontal assault on Donbaik on 18 January. As a diversion to the frontal attack, 47 Brigade carriers were to advance along the beach and try and draw the enemy's fire.

The assembled carriers, under the command of Lieutenant George Semple of the Inniskillings, took cover in a patch of woodland close to the beach. From here they raced forward, three or four at a time, until they could bring their Bren-guns to bear in the approximate direction of the enemy. They could not see the Japanese bunkers, but the carriers themselves made a splendid target. Mortar bombs exploded in among them and machine-gun bullets rattled on their sides. Worse was to come. According to George Semple, 'We got a suspicion that they were in fact also firing solid shot, because some of us felt that something went whistling past us which was rather different from small-arms fire.'

Bert Causey, in one of the carriers out on the beach, was in no doubt what was firing at them.

> We saw these shells coming out of the jungle, ricocheting off the beach. . . . We knew immediately that it was an anti-tank gun. Well, a carrier is no proof at all against an anti-tank gun shell. It just goes straight through. So it was a bit scarey, knowing that if you got a hit, you'd had it.

More than a little alarmed, the carrier crews returned to their forward base. The infantry attack was repulsed with heavy losses and everyone waited anxiously to see what would happen the following day. It is easy to be wise after the event. Perhaps the brigadier had good reason to use the carriers in this rather pointless fashion, but they might have been better employed ferrying troops forward for a flanking attack, which would at least have provided the Japanese with something else to think about. The carrier crews themselves certainly believed that they were exposing themselves to needless danger without achieving anything.

But the following morning the orders were the same, another frontal attack while the carriers circled round on the beach and invited the enemy to shoot at them. George Semple was determined not to risk lives unnecessarily: 'I only put two men to a vehicle, instead of the three or four crew which was normal, and we ran a shuttle service; two carriers went out and patrolled up and down and did what they were supposed to do in the way of drawing fire and ran back again. They got out and two others took their place and so on.'

Parkash Singh made one of the first runs out on to the beach, zig-zagging his carrier to avoid the anti-tank gun shells and stopping from time to time to let off a burst of Bren-gun fire at the Japanese. His stint done, he returned to the cover of the clump of trees. When it came to Bert Causey's turn he and his driver duly set off up the beach. Knowing that it was pointless trying to bring fire to bear upon an invisible enemy, Bert did not even take his Bren-gun with him. They circled around a bit and were heading back towards their own base when they were hit. Bert remembers a terrific bang, then a shocked pause while he took stock of the situation.

> I looked at my driver and I saw that the shell had come in on his side. It had taken his right leg off below the knee and his left foot and passed out in front of me. When I looked down I saw that my shoes were all torn and I realised that I had been hit as well. We had come to a halt and there was nothing, absolutely nothing we could do about it.

Unknown to Causey, at least two other carriers had also been hit. One had caught fire and smoke was billowing along the beach. It was this blazing vehicle which first caught Parkash Singh's eye as he watched from the relative safety of the patch of woodland, half a mile to the north. Without telling anyone what he planned to do, he ordered his driver Mani Ram to go out on to the beach to see if they could help the stricken carrier. When they reached the blazing wreck, Parkash saw three British soldiers, all of them burned and scarred by exploding ammunition, lying in the shelter of the burning vehicle. They were too badly hurt to move of their own accord, so Parkash picked them up one by one as though they were children and put them on board his own carrier. Under heavy fire he and Mani Ram then returned to base and handed the wounded men over to the stretcher-bearers.

It was at this stage that Parkash realised that Bert Causey and his driver were missing. He asked the other officers and NCOs what had happened to them.

> They said not to worry myself about them. They said he must be dead by now . . . but I thought that I must go and help my colleagues – not particularly that Captain Causey was there. If somebody else was there I would still have volunteered myself. Nobody ordered me. In fact people stopped me going. 'Don't go there. You'll be killed. You'll be captured.' People told me so

much that Captain Causey must have been captured or killed, but I said, 'I must check up.'

Parkash replenished his ammunition and started looking round for his driver, Mani Ram. He found him hiding in the bottom of a trench. 'He was very much frightened to go there again,' says Parkash, 'so I had to drag him out of there.'

Meanwhile, out on the beach, Bert Causey had given up hope of rescue. With a great effort he hauled his horribly wounded driver over to the gunner's seat and levered himself painfully behind the wheel. But the clutch pedal had been blown off and it was impossible to restart the carrier. Another anti-tank gun shell tore through the carrier and rifle and machine-gun fire hammered against the thin armour-plate. Frightened and in great pain, Bert Causey crouched in a pool of blood in the front of the disintegrating vehicle. 'I can't remember what I felt,' says Bert Causey, 'except just a feeling of helplessness. Then suddenly I heard a voice shouting "Are you all right?" and I called back "No, we're not all right. We've both been wounded." A short while later Parkash Singh poked his head over the top of the carrier.'

Parkash and Mani Ram had been under continuous fire since the moment they left the shelter of the trees, half a mile to the north. Now he proposed to lift out Bert and his driver and get them back to safety, but they were too badly injured to pick up in safety and they would in any case be exposed to close-range machine-gun fire as he lifted them from one vehicle to the other. 'Go on, get out. Save yourself,' said Bert. Parkash ignored him. 'We will tow you out,' he said. Then he recalled that he did not have a pair of tow chains with him. 'There's one on the back of this carrier,' Bert told him. Parkash persuaded Mani Ram to manoeuvre his own vehicle alongside Causey's so that it would give him some cover from enemy fire. Then he crept round the back, got out the tow chain and made his way back to the front of Causey's carrier to attach the shackle. As he did so he saw a group of Japanese soldiers break cover from a clump of bushes a couple of hundred yards away and come racing across the sand towards them. There was no time for a getaway. Parkash seized his Bren-gun, rested it on top of the carrier and let rip at the advancing soldiers.

'Two or three I killed straight away,' he recalls with some satisfaction. 'The others were wounded or ran away.'

Quickly he fastened the other end of the tow chain to the rear of his own carrier and directed Mani Ram to start up. But their troubles had only just begun. The tracks spun wildly in the soft sand, Causey's carrier would not budge. 'It's in gear,' yelled Bert. 'Then get it in neutral,' Parkash shouted back. 'I can't,' Bert shouted back. 'I'm too weak to budge the lever.'

All this time the machine-gun and rifle fire was pelting both vehicles across the open beach. At any moment the Japanese might launch another attack, but having got so far Parkash decided that he would never give up. At great risk to himself he vaulted over the side of Bert's carrier, only to land heavily on the wretched driver as more bullets cracked overhead. Reaching across, he pulled at the jammed lever and freed it with a single tug. Then he had to expose his lanky frame to enemy fire once more as he hauled himself out of the vehicle. The risk was worth taking. This time both vehicles moved when Mani Ram started up, but they were still in great danger. Because there was only one tow chain the towed vehicle yawed wildly and tacked across the beach like a crippled crab. Parkash had to walk, crouched on the seaward side of Causey's carrier and stop every hundred yards or so to change the attachment point for the chain. Enraged at the possible loss of their prey, the Japanese anti-tank gunners kept firing and two more shells crashed through the thin armour, but fortunately the tracks kept turning.

At this point, the brigadier decided to put down an artillery smoke-screen to try and shelter his own attacking forces. The smoke billowed over the beach and partly hid the carriers from view. 'In one way it helped us,' says Parkash. 'But in another way it was dangerous. I could not see where I was going. One minute we would be heading into the sea. The next minute we would be almost on top of the Japanese.'

Forty minutes after they had set out, Parkash Singh and Mani Ram returned triumphantly to their clump of trees with the knocked-out carrier still in tow. For the last hundred yards Parkash mounted the front of his vehicle with Japanese bullets still whistling about his ears and sat there with his arms folded as Mani Ram headed for home. George Semple was watching.

Parkash Singh

There was a bit of bravado about it, particularly in the way he drove out . . . but it wasn't foolhardy . . . He felt this was something that he should do and he did it . . . in fact one of my men turned to me and said, 'There's a fellow winning a VC.' And he was right.

Parkash Singh lifted the wounded driver out of his puddle of blood in the front of the wrecked carrier. The driver was conscious and even managed to smile. He was usually a non-smoker, but he asked for a cigarette as the stretcher-bearers came up. Parkash gave him one. Ten minutes later the driver died.

Bert Causcy was hurried back to the regimental aid post, in great pain from the wounds in his feet but extremely relieved. 'If it hadn't been for Parkash,' he said, 'I would still be down there.'

Inspired by Parkash Singh's action, Corporal Scott and Private Newman of the Inniskillings made a similar rescue dash and succeeded in bringing in another wrecked carrier. The mood of the unit changed in the space of an hour or so from profound gloom to something close to celebration. One thing particularly struck George Semple.

We had a mixture in the unit of Sikhs, Hindus, Punjabi Mussulmen and of course Christians . . . and they'd all squat down and chat away together and they were all very good friends. But there was one place the line was drawn; we didn't eat together or drink tea together . . . the Sikhs and the Hindus could, but the Punjabi Mussulmen and the Christians, we were apart. And on this particular occasion the automatic reaction was, 'Let's brew up' . . . and immediately tea was made. And that was the first, and only, and last ever occasion that I saw mugs of tea passed round between Hindus, Mohammedans and Christians. And it was a salute.

Unlike most men who are recommended for a VC, Parkash Singh was not surprised when he won it. 'I was not surprised at all. I knew it. I was determined. The recommendation was made in such a way that it was the VC or nothing.'

The process whereby a Victoria Cross is awarded is always shrouded in mystery, and to avoid invidious lobbying it is just as well that this should be so. But on this occasion George

173

The Second World War

Semple recalls that he himself made the initial recommendation and put it to the brigadier. 'Very well,' said the brigadier. 'Get me six eye-witnesses who saw it happen and we'll see what we can do.' The eye-witnesses were quick to come forward. Parkash Singh got the VC, his driver Mani Ram the IDSM, traditionally one of the highest awards in the old Indian Army, and the two Inniskilling soldiers were also decorated. The investiture, which took place at the Red Fort in Delhi, was presided over by the Viceroy, Lord Linlithgow – a man of such exceptional height that even Parkash Singh looked small beside him. He was quickly promoted to the lowest commissioned rank of jemadar and soon afterwards to subedar, but he did not see action against the Japanese again.

Following the action of Donbaik, General Lloyd tried another series of frontal assaults, all as disastrous as the first. Eventually he was relieved of his command and another division, the 26th, was brought in to take over from the worn-out troops of the 14th. By this time the whole of 47 Brigade, apart from the carriers, had been sent across the Mayu Range to guard the eastern flank against Japanese attack. But the Japanese were still too good for them. In a brilliant series of flanking movements they scattered the whole brigade, and British and Indian troops fled in small groups over the jagged hills and through the jungle towards the road back to India. The Japanese kept up the momentum of their attack, flinging road blocks across the road to the rear of the division. The scattered elements of 47 Brigade only extricated themselves with great difficulty, having lost all of their transport and certainly all hope of taking Akyab.

5/8 Punjab, together with most of the other units which had taken part in this disastrous campaign, were pulled out of the line and sent as far away as possible from the front so that their low morale should not have too damaging an effect on other troops. After re-training, especially in the techniques of jungle warfare, some of the units returned to the front in time to take part in the triumphant advances of 1944 and 1945. 5/8 Punjab were given special training in amphibious warfare and were due to go into the assault in Malaya and Indonesia, when the Japanese surrendered in August 1945. In the event, the sea-borne actions never took

174

place, but the troops were engaged instead in tricky internal security duties, ultimately against Indonesian freedom-fighters in Java and Sumatra.

When Parkash came home on leave to Lyallpur in 1946 he was a famous man in his home town. The provincial government in the Punjab made a far more practical gesture towards the home-coming hero than any authority in Britain itself has ever seen fit to do. They rewarded Parkash with a grant of sixty-four acres of land near his home village. Men with daughters of marriageable age were anxious to have such a son-in-law, and a marriage was duly arranged with a girl of good family named Raminder, who had never seen her prospective husband. At the time she was at a college in Lyallpur, training to be a teacher. She remembers her friends coming in to see her and teasing her about her famous husband-to-be. 'They had all seen these posters with his picture on them and they said to me, "Oh we have seen his picture. He is very handsome." I was very excited.'

The couple were married later that year, and Independence Day in 1947 found them stationed in married quarters in the town of Thal on the north-west frontier, close to the Khyber Pass and a long way from home. The new state of Pakistan was formed overnight in the blood and misery of partition. Thousands of Hindus and Moslems were murdered on both sides of the new frontier and thousands more lost their homes, their land and all their possessions in the refugee trail from one side of the border to the other. It had been decided that the 8th Punjab should become a regiment of the new state of Pakistan, and the Sikhs were ordered to stay with them after partition, but a few days later when some of their Moslem colleagues reproached them for displaying a flag in the *gurdwara* the Sikhs decided that India was really their home. Even those who had been born and brought up on the Pakistan side of the border, like Parkash Singh himself, had to give up everything they owned and prepare for the long and difficult journey to India.

Parkash was made responsible for the safety of all the wives and children in his unit, and the Sikhs were joined by other groups as they boarded a train for the Indian frontier. The railway at that time was a line of death. Hordes of brigands would hold up the trains, intent on robbery, rape and murder.

The Second World War

Several trains had already arrived in Delhi full of dead men, women and children. The Sikhs had kept their rifles and although they were fired on several times they were able to keep the worst of the brigands at bay, but when they arrived at Kohat, where they were supposed to be air-lifted to India, they found the town in a shambles. The Sikhs and their families took refuge in a deserted military cantonment, and Parkash and his young wife moved into an empty hut. That night they decided to hold a funeral for several men who had been killed, and the darkness was lit up by the funeral pyres. Bands of Pathans, who did not dare to make an outright attack on the camp, kept firing at the blaze and Parkash had to go out to help ward off a possible attack, leaving Raminder to fend for herself. Solemnly the subedar took his bayonet from its scabbard and handed it to his wife. 'If anyone tries to molest you, kill him with this. If you cannot kill him then kill yourself.'

Dutifully, Raminder took the bayonet. She recalls the sleepless terror of that night, while her husband was away and the shooting of the Pathans seemed to echo all around her and the shouting came closer and closer in the deserted barracks. She laughs about it now, even teases Parkash a little, but he remains grave. 'A Sikh woman,' he says, 'must not be dishonoured. She must be as brave as a man.'

Eventually the couple reached the Indian town of Jalandhar without having to make use of the bayonet. As the new government began to sort out the chaos, Parkash Singh vc was not forgotten. A compensation board allotted him sixty-four acres of land close to Jalandhar to replace the land he had lost at Lyallpur. This farm was to be the foundation of the family's prosperity, but for the next twenty years Parkash served as an officer in one of the exclusive Sikh regiments of the new Indian Army. Raminder and he had four children, all of them girls, all of them clever and well educated. 'Father was very strict about education,' says Alep, one of the younger daughters. 'My clearest memory of him as a child is of sitting at the table in the evening while he made me do my mathematics.'

He was a stern and rather awe-inspiring father, always insistent upon good behaviour and hard work, but when the

176

family gathers together it is obvious how much affection and loyalty still exists between all of them. Such gatherings are rare, because the eldest daughter, Nimrita, is now married and living in Saudi Arabia, and the other three are at present in London. Nirlap's husband is a solicitor working in England, and her unmarried sisters, Alep and Jyoti, live with her in their north London home. None of them feel any sense of astonishment that their father should have been so brave in battle. Alep remembers a period during the Indo-Pakistan war in 1972 when air-raid warnings were a frequent occurrence in Jalandhar.

> We had some trenches dug in the garden and during the air raids my mother wanted all of us to go down and take shelter there, but my father would not leave his bed. 'If I survived the Second World War,' he would say, 'I will survive this.' So he went on sleeping.

Parkash retired from the army with the rank of major in 1968, and since then he has devoted most of his time to the efficient running of his farm. He has been obliged to sell off much of his land to conform to Indian law, but he still owns one tract of eighteen acres and manages another on behalf of his daughters. His agricultural methods are modern, efficient, and highly intensive. Crops of wheat alternate with potatoes and various pulses in a year-round cycle of continuous cultivation, with tube-well irrigation and a carefully controlled programme of fertilisers and pesticides. He employs several men, at least one of whom is a Hindu. Despite the high tension between Sikh and Hindu in the Punjab today, Parkash believes in toleration and is opposed to extremism in all its forms.

This is one of the reasons why he is a greatly respected figure in Jalandhar, and most especially in the village of Alowal, where one of his land holdings is situated. Here he is invited to sit on the village council, the Panchayat, and his advice is sought on all kinds of local matters, ranging from politics to marriage settlements. 'They know I have no axe to grind,' he observes. 'I am not involved, so they listen to me.' But there is another reason for the respect. The villagers call him 'Victoria' and even if they are not quite sure of the significance of this dignified appellation they know that

The Second World War

Parkash was a warrior famed for his courage. Despite the tolerance of his views today, he is still in no doubt about the value of courage when it comes to the point.

> We all pray that there should be no war, because war causes misery, destruction and poverty . . . but if the war is forced upon you, you must fight back with your full force and courageously, and you must give full incentive to your soldiers to do something extraordinary. That gives encouragement to the others also . . . otherwise you will be run over by the enemy. You must have courage.

11
Fred Tilston

The King has been graciously pleased to approve the award of the Victoria Cross to:

> *Major (acting) Frederick Albert Tilston, the Essex Scottish Regiment, Canadian Infantry Corps.*

The 2nd Canadian Division had been given the task of breaking through the strongly fortified Hochwald Forest defence line which covered Xanten, the last German bastion west of the Rhine protecting the vital Wesel Bridge escape route.

The Essex Scottish Regiment was ordered to breach the defence line north-east of Udem and to clear the northern half of the forest, through which the balance of the brigade would pass.

At 0715 hours on 1 March 1945 the attack was launched, but due to the softness of the ground it was found impossible to support the attack by tanks as had been planned.

Across approximately 500 yards of flat open country, in face of intense enemy fire, Major Tilston personally led his company in the attack, keeping dangerously close to our own bursting shells in order to get the maximum cover from the barrage. Though wounded in the head, he continued to lead his men forward through a belt of wire ten feet in depth to the enemy trenches, shouting orders and encouragement and using his sten gun with great effect. When the platoon on the left came under heavy fire from an enemy machine-gun post he dashed forward personally and silenced it with a grenade; he was first to reach the enemy position and took the first prisoner.

Determined to maintain the momentum of the attack he ordered the reserve platoon to mop up these positions and with outstanding gallantry, pressed on with his main force to the second line of enemy defences which were on the edge of the woods.

As he approached the woods he was severely wounded in the hip and

179

fell to the ground. Shouting to his men to carry on without him and urging them to get into the wood, he struggled to his feet and rejoined them as they reached the trenches on their objective. Here an elaborate system of underground dugouts and trenches was manned in considerable strength and vicious hand-to-hand fighting followed. Despite his wounds, Major Tilston's unyielding will to close with the enemy was a magnificent inspiration to his men as he led them in, systematically clearing the trenches of the fiercely resisting enemy. In this fighting two German Company Headquarters were over-run and many casualities were inflicted on the fanatical defenders.

Such had been the grimness of the fighting and so savage the enemy resistance that the company was now reduced to only twenty-six men, one quarter of its original strength. Before consolidation could be completed the enemy counter-attacked repeatedly, supported by a hail or mortar and machine-gun fire from the open flank. Major Tilston moved in the open from platoon to platoon, quickly organising their defence and directing fire against the advancing enemy. The enemy attacks penetrated so close to the position that grenades were thrown into the trenches held by the troops, but this officer by personal contact, unshakeable confidence and unquenchable enthusiasm so inspired his men that they held firm against great odds.

When the supply of ammunition became a serious problem he repeatedly crossed the bullet-swept ground to the company on his right flank to carry grenades, rifle and Bren ammunition to his troops and replace a damaged wireless set to re-establish communications with Battalion Headquarters. He made at least six of these hazardous trips, each time crossing a road which was dominated by intense fire from numerous well-sited enemy machine-gun posts.

On his last trip he was wounded for the third time, this time in the leg. He was found in a shell crater beside the road. Although very seriously wounded and barely conscious, he would not submit to medical attention until he had given complete instructions as to the defence plan, had emphasised the absolute necessity of holding the position, and had ordered his one remaining officer to take over.

By his calm courage, gallant conduct and total disregard for his own safety, he fired his men with grim determination and their firm stand enabled the regiment to accomplish its object of furnishing the brigade with a solid base through which to launch further successful attacks to clear the forest, thus enabling the division to accomplish its task.

9a *above left* Second Lieutenant Albert Ball, photographed before his rise to fame

9b *above right* Captain Freddie West

9c *below* The last fight of Albert Ball

10a Two Japanese tanks destroyed by Rifleman Ganju Lama
at Ningthoukong in Manipur, 1944

10b Ganju Lama in hospital with his father and two brothers

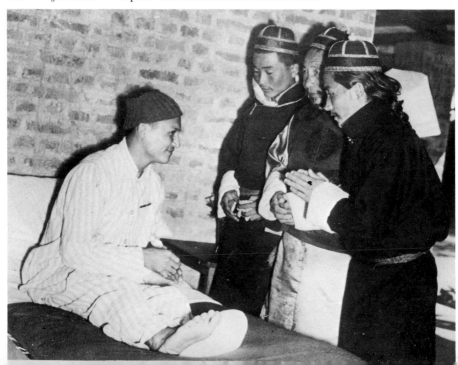

11a *above* Ganju Lama's
investiture at the Red
Fort in Delhi. He is
seated in a wheelchair

extreme left

11b *below left* Sergeant
Keith Elliott

11c *below right* General
Montgomery investing
Keith Elliott with the
Victoria Cross

12a Lieutenant Roden Cutler vc

12b Cutler being carried back to the dressing-station at Damour by four of the French prisoners he had captured himself the day before. The medical officer, Captain Adrian Johnson, is on the right

13a Havildar Parkash Singh in the driving seat of a universal carrier

13b Parkash Singh receiving the congratulations of General Auckinleck after his investiture

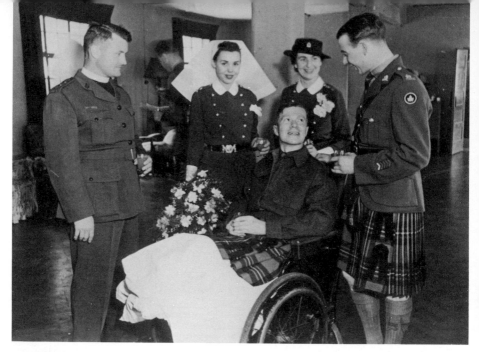

14a Major Fred Tilston receiving news of the award of the Victoria Cross

14b The scene outside Fred Tilston's home in Toronto at the time of his return

15a Wing-Commander
(later Group-Captain)
Leonard Cheshire

15b Leonard Cheshire
with the crew of the
Halifax bomber
Offenbach in 1942. Jock
Moncrieff is standing
next to Cheshire on the
right of the picture

16a Captain Charles Upham vc and Bar

16b Private Bill Speakman vc, Korea, 1951

Fred Tilston

The day I met Fred Tilston I had missed a turning on the road and arrived at his door very late and minus the other seven members of the film unit. 'I am very sorry, Colonel Tilston,' I apologised, 'but I am very late and I seem to have lost my troops.'

'Welcome to the Canadian Army,' he said with a grin.

This instant repartee is typical of him. So is the warmth of the greeting that followed, and the keen interest he showed in every aspect of the television team's business. Although he is now seventy-nine, he is far more active than many men twenty years his junior. But if his smile seems a little quizzical at times it may be because one of his eyes is made of glass. He lost an eye after an operation a few years ago, but the real damage was caused by a German mine in Normandy in 1944. If he moves a little stiffly it is not simply his age – Fred lost both legs just below the knee following the action in which he won the Victoria Cross. However, he takes a firm line on the problems of the double amputee.

> First thing you have to do is to make up your mind there's no use crying over spilt milk – crying isn't going to grow a new pair of legs. So I simply made up my mind that I'd live with it. All you need is good surgery and properly fitting prostheses, and if you have both these and you don't walk well it's because you don't want to. Because [he says, indicating his head and then his artificial legs] you walk up here, not down there.

Fred Tilston makes an immediate impression as a man of great charm and confidence, but without any of the overt aggression that one might expect in a military man. He is, however, many other things: a rather snappy dresser with a taste for turquoise belt-buckles and bow-ties, a great conversationalist, an inveterate traveller, a connoisseur of art and good living – with a dangerous reputation for drinking everyone else under the table. For all his modesty and mocking self-deprecation, Fred Tilston is still a formidable man.

He was born in Toronto, Canada, in 1906, the eldest of three children – the other two girls. When he was eight his parents moved to Chicago and the family lived in the United States for the next three years. Even as a small boy Fred was high-

181

spirited and adventurous and has many tales of youthful pranks. On family holidays in Northern Michigan he made a pastime of collecting snakes, and from time to time would take one of his harmless pets and lie in ambush in the shrubbery close to a group of weekend cottages on the lake shore. As unsuspecting holidaymakers made their way along the track, he would spring his ambush, hurling a snake adroitly into their path. There would be gratifying scenes as terrified ladies and gentlemen fled to safety while Fred and his little sisters giggled in the bushes. At school he developed a much more dangerous game, thrusting two small fingers into the electric power socket while a string of schoolfellows, some of them innocent to what was in store for them, linked hands in a long line. As Fred's fingers made contact with the electric current, one child at least would get the shock of his life. But despite these delinquent activities Fred had the redeeming feature of being nice to his little sisters, who adored him then as they do now.

Like a number of other men who have won the Victoria Cross, Fred had to face tragedy in his early life. When he was eleven his father was killed in a street accident in Chicago, and Estelle Tilston was obliged to bring her young family back to Toronto. Fred was sent to live with his grandparents while his sisters were boarded out with an aunt. Estelle showed characteristic Tilston determination by taking herself off to business school so she would be able to make a decent living for the family. In two years she had got herself a job and found rented accommodation in an old house close to the city centre, where the family were reunited – all four of them in a single room. Fred went out to work, doing a paper round before and after school every day in order to help out with the family finances.

The Tilstons were Roman Catholics. The family went regularly to Mass and when he was old enough Fred was sent to De La Salle High School, a Catholic foundation near St Michael's Cathedral, where he developed an enthusiasm for science and mathematics. Some of the Christian Brothers who taught at the school made a deep impression on Fred and reinforced in him a sense of responsibility both for his own destiny and for the welfare of others. At around the same time he graduated from doing a paper round to working in the evenings as delivery boy for a pharmacy in downtown Toronto. The job took him into every corner of the city and also introduced him to the profession which he was to follow for the rest of his working life.

When he left school Fred had no intention of devoting himself to pharmacy. He wanted to be a doctor, but as there was no possibility of finding the money for six more years of full-time study he opted instead to become a pharmaceutical apprentice, working during the day at a drugstore and studying during the evenings. After a three-year apprenticeship he spent two years alternating between the Ontario College of Pharmacy and the University of Toronto. In order to keep the money coming in he was obliged to do relief work at drugstores – either on night shifts or all day at weekends – but somehow he managed not only to get a degree but to graduate second out of a student class of 105. He was beaten by his friend Norman Hughes, later to become Dean of the Faculty of Pharmacy at Toronto University, who recalls:

> Fred was chairman of the graduation dance committee in the second year and he did such a superb job that it was worth recording in the journal . . . he was elected vice-president of the class, he played football and he was an excellent student academically. . . . In the year book I tried to find a suitable quotation for every member of the class and for him I chose, 'Greatness is as greatness does'.

Greatness did not do very much for Fred over the next few years. He worked first as a dispensing pharmacist in a drugstore and then went out on the road as a travelling representative for a big American firm – Sterling Drug. His stock-in-trade were the branded medicines manufactured by the company and widely advertised in the press and on radio. The job entailed travelling round the country by train or, where possible, by car, and peddling these wares to widely scattered drugstores and pharmacies. Although he must have been one of the most over-qualified salesmen in the field, the life of a commercial traveller appealed to Fred's warm and friendly nature. After a spell in his native Ontario he moved up to Quebec and then out west to Alberta and British

Columbia. Here he fell in love with the scenery of his native country – the great Canadian wilderness which consists, as he puts it, of 'miles and miles of bugger-all'.

When he was not selling his branded medicines Fred spent his time exploring the countryside, shooting duck during the autumn and winter and fishing during the summer. He also met a girl named Helen, who worked as a hairdresser in Edmonton, Alberta. There was a romance, but at the time Fred felt no compulsion to settle down, perhaps because he was enjoying himself too much. 'They were the best days of my life . . . you were your own boss. There were no such things as long-distance phone calls in those days. You were strictly on your own. You were on partial commission and if you worked hard you could make money, and good money.'

Eventually he settled down to a desk job and by the age of thirty-three, in 1939, Fred was sales manager at the Sterling Drug headquarters in Windsor, Ontario. But, with the world at his feet and under no compulsion to do anything he did not want to do, he decided to volunteer for the army. His local regiment was called the Essex Scottish, an unlikely conjunction of names which stems from the county in which the unit was formed and from an enthusiasm, on the part of its founding colonel, for the kilt. Fred's motives for joining up were solidly patriotic. He had no wish to see Britain overrun by Germany, because he felt that Canada's fate as a nation was inextricably bound up with that of the mother country.

He enlisted as a private soldier but was immediately commissioned as a second lieutenant, no doubt because of his age and professional qualifications. But although he was six foot two, well built, and to all appearances every inch a soldier, Fred had one or two early problems in the army. An incredulous sergeant-major faced the spectacle of a young officer who advanced across the parade ground with his right arm parallel to his right leg, his left arm in vague conjunction with his left leg – a physical dyslexic with no sense of rhythm and timing. On the drill square Second Lieutenant Fred Tilston was a mobile disaster.

Fortunately, a wartime army has little time for parade ground niceties. After a few despairing attempts to frog-march him between two stalwart NCOs in an effort to get him to swing his right arm with the left leg, the sergeant-major gave up and Fred went off to field training, for which he was far better equipped. Impatient to get overseas as quickly as possible, he transferred to another regiment and got himself shipped to England in 1941. It was eighteen months before he rejoined his old unit in July 1942 and he was kept back from taking part in the disastrous Dieppe raid in August of that year, during which the Canadians suffered terrible casualties and the Essex Scottish regiment was almost wiped out.

Shocked and disillusioned by the tragedy of Dieppe, the Canadian government was reluctant to risk antagonising its own French-speaking community and conscription was not enforced until late in the war. Most Canadian fighting men, like Fred, were volunteers. During the early years of the war, therefore, the number of Canadian soldiers serving abroad was relatively small and their government was unwilling to allow them to be used piece-meal to reinforce Allied forces in North Africa or the Far East. In July 1943 the First Division went into battle in Sicily, but the bulk of the Canadian forces were kept at home. Three divisions, rather grandly known as the Canadian First Army, were engaged in apparently endless training exercises in England, and it was during one of these that Fred Tilston met with an accident which almost finished his army career before it was properly begun. At the time he was in command of a rifle company of the Essex Scottish. That battalion was taking part in a mock battle, with live machine-gun bullets firing along fixed lines to add realism to the scene.

The commanding officer at the time was Bruce McDonald. 'There was a mix-up in the orders and a signal wasn't observed that should have been and the machine-gun fire continued, while Fred went ahead with the attack as if nothing was happening. This was his job and he did it, and he got a bullet in the back.'

According to eye-witnesses Fred went down like a log, but when his men rushed to help him he opened one eye and remarked dryly, 'Custers's last stand.' But the wound was no joking matter. A bullet had passed through his lung and entered the pericardium, the muscle tissue around the heart. It came within half an inch of killing him outright. Delicate and dangerous surgery followed, but Fred came through it cheerfully and was soon on his way to recovery. Some of his contemporaries insist, though he himself denies it, that he could have opted at this time to be shipped back to Canada and invalided out of the army. At all events, this did not happen and he rejoined his regiment shortly before they were transferred to France in July 1944.

For most of his time with the battalion Fred served as adjutant, the principle administrative officer and Bruce McDonald's right-hand man.

> He wasn't the flamboyant type . . . he was a very mild genial fellow. He was my adjutant for over a year and I relied on him enormously. He was the guy who kept things going with his good nature, good humour and as adjutant he got things done for me. He wanted very much to be sent to a rifle company, but he was too valuable to me and to the regiment to let him get away like that.

The Canadian Third Division were among the first Allied troops to hit the beach in the D-Day invasion of Normandy on 6 June 1944, but the Second Division – to which the Essex Scottish belonged – played no part in the landings. Instead they were designated 'break-out' troops, the intention being to send fresh formations leap-frogging over the units which had taken part in the initial invasion, once the bridge-head was secure. By 9 July the city of Caen had at last fallen to British and Canadian forces, and the fresh troops were launched in a drive south of Caen, designed to relieve pressure on General Bradley's American forces far to the west. On 20 July the Essex Scottish were in support of the South Saskatchewan Regiment in an attack on the Verrières Ridge, five miles south of Caen. Continuous downpours of heavy rain robbed the attacking troops of air cover, and their armoured support – battered the day before in heavy fighting – failed to move forward with them. So the Canadian infantry faced the tanks of the First SS Panzer Division alone. After a desperate stand, during which they lost a third of their men, the South Saskatchewans were driven back through the lines of the Essex Scottish.

Panic and confusion followed. The tactical headquarters

Fred Tilston

and one company of the Essex Scottish were overrun by the enemy and most of them taken prisoner. Poor communications, terrible weather and sheer lack of battle experience all played their part. The regiment was pulled out of the front line, the battalion was reinforced and re-organised and a new commanding officer was put in command, but it was not until Lieutenant-Colonel Peter Bennett took over, a few weeks later, that the Essex Scottish began to recover their morale.

> It was a partially broken battalion at that time, because it had lost a lot of its officers and Fred was very obviously a key figure. He was the person who knew most about what had happened to the battalion and he had that marvellous personality which breeds confidence . . . even the company commanders would come and ask Fred what to do. . . . He was an excellent adjutant.

Under Bennett's command, a few weeks later, the Essex Scottish fought its way into Falaise. They had advanced so far and so fast that they were out of contact with brigade headquarters, so Fred and a driver were dispatched in the CO's jeep to advise the brigadier of their position. The jeep made it to brigade HQ, but on the return run Fred chose to take the shortest route – the main Caen–Falaise road – without checking whether the road was still in enemy hands. It was. But, amazingly, they made it to within a mile or two of their destination before the jeep hit a German mine and blew up. Fortunately, the driver had put sandbags on the floor of the jeep or their legs would have been shattered, and in fact they were both able to pick themselves out of the wreckage and stagger back to their own HQ. Here Fred's main concern seems to have been the loss of the jeep, but he was more badly hurt than he realised. Colonel Peter Bennett recalls.

> Come dawn, when we all had to stand to and you could hear the German tanks milling about down below, there was always that business of getting the family out of bed in the morning. Well, I saw this big bottom sticking out from under a jeep, so I gave it a real whack and told it to stand to. Out came Fred and said, 'I'm terribly sorry, but I don't feel too well.'

It was a typical Tilston understatement. He was badly concussed, his eardrums were blown and he had shrapnel wounds in his right eye. Once again Fred was a casualty; he

187

was shipped back to England and spent the next two months in hospital, where he gradually recovered from the effects of the blast. (In fact for many years his eyesight remained relatively unaffected, until the minute pieces of shrapnel were dislodged in a minor accident and his right eye had to be removed.) At the time he appeared to be unaware of the extent of the damage and he rejoined his battalion the same autumn, during the difficult advance northward through Belgium and Holland. After heavy fighting the Essex Scottish found itself, as part of the Canadian Second Division, in forward defensive positions near the village of Groesbeek in Holland, close to the German border at Nijmegen. By this time the enemy had fallen back on the Siegfried Line, a long chain of heavily fortified strongpoints and trench systems following the frontier from Nijmegen southward through the Ardennes and the Saarland to the Rhine, and then due south again to the Swiss border. Behind the line were defences in depth, minefields, fortified villages and strongpoints guarding all possible approaches to the Rhine. Allied strategy called for an advance on a broad front along the length of the line in order to deny the enemy any opportunity to concentrate their forces.

The German reaction was the great winter offensive in the Ardennes in December 1944. By January the Allies had repelled this counter-attack and recovered the initiative. The main task assigned to the British and Canadian armies in the north was to break out of the Nijmegen salient and clear the area between the river Rhine and the Maas, while the Americans attacked further to the south across the river Roer. In the event, the American assault was delayed, but on 8 February 1945 the British 30th Corps, supported by the Canadian Second and Third Divisions, burst out of Nijmegen and began a series of bitter battles with troops of the German First Parachute Army in and around the great forest known as the Reichswald, south of the ancient town of Cleve. The German response was to flood huge areas of land in the river valleys and to contest each foot of ground in a series of bitter rearguard actions. The First Parachute Army of the Third Reich, though no longer airborne, were highly trained troops and were under orders not, under any circumstances, to retreat across the Rhine. They, and the remnants of many other

German formations who joined them, fought with stubborn ferocity.

Bad weather favoured the defenders, because the British and Canadians could make little use of their superior air power. When saturation bombing was used, as in the assault on the town of Goch, it killed few of the enemy, turned fragile homes into formidable heaps of rubble and made the roads impassable for the Allied tanks. The advance was slow – every house, every stream, every patch of woodland seemed to hold an ambush. Although the Germans were outnumbered, the tanks and anti-tank guns they still possessed were more than a match for Allied armour and they had the advantage of well-prepared bunkers and strong defensive positions. There was no question of surrender for the Germans. Every nest of the enemy had first to be destroyed.

At long last Fred had managed to get himself assigned as second-in-command of a rifle company ('C' Company), but much to his disgust he was left out of battle when the Essex Scottish went into the attack on the road between Goch and Calcar. The battle was vicious and bloody. When they reached their objective the Canadians were subjected to ferocious counter-attacks by strong German armoured units and many of them were killed or wounded, including the commander of Fred's company. So Fred at last had what he wanted, a command of his own.

The first attack which he commanded, early in the morning of 1 March 1945, was also to be his last. The Essex Scottish had been given the task of clearing the edge of the Hochwald, a thick coniferous forest several square miles in extent, which guarded the approach to the town of Xanten, close to the Rhine. The battalion was to attack with two companies forward – 'A' Company under Major Paul Cropp on the right, Fred Tilston's 'C' Company on the left. The start line was the edge of a group of farm buildings about five hundred yards from the forest, and between the farm and the first trees in front of 'C' Company was a stretch of flat, level farmland, which offered no cover of any kind. The attack was supposed to be supported by tanks, but they were unable to make progress where the going was soft and so were only able to use

189

the firmer ground on the right of the line of attack. On the left the flank was wide open.

The attack was planned for the half light of early morning, but the tanks were slow to get forward. At nine o'clock, later than originally intended, the first shells of the Canadian artillery barrage burst along the edge of the start line. Several shells exploded within the farmyard itself, causing some casualties. It was not a good omen. But as the barrage lifted and began to shatter the ground ahead of them, the Essex Scottish started to advance across the open field. Fred was in front of his men. He had disposed them according to the book, with two platoons forward and one following up in reserve, but he placed himself – together with his wireless operator – slightly ahead of the first two platoons instead of behind them. This move made him a prime target for any enemy machine-gunner, but Fred Tilston believed in leading from the front.

The forward platoon on the left was commanded by Lieutenant Charles Gatton. 'Of course we hadn't gone far when machine-gun fire started to come across, raking the field in two directions – one from the right and one from the left. People started to fall, but we kept moving. Major Tilston was hit in the head and he fell, picked himself up and kept going.' German mortars now opened up and the shells added to the Canadian casualties. With an exposed left flank and no tank support there was nothing that 'C' Company could do but keep walking stolidly forward across the open field as mortar shells and machine-guns blasted huge gaps in their ranks. Halfway across they hit the first line of German trenches.

Fred Tilston went running into the attack, fulfilling a private ambition (as he later admitted) by blowing up an enemy machine-gun nest with a hand grenade. In fierce fighting, the Canadians overwelmed the first line of defence and, urged on by their company commander, continued their advance towards the edge of the wood. It says a great deal both for the fighting spirit of the Essex Scottish and the leadership of their commander that they did keep going. Many of the men were raw recruits, newly drafted into battle, and half the company had already been killed or wounded. The Bren-gun carrier, which carried the company's reserve ammunition supplies, turned back to evacuate the worst of the casualties, while the leading platoons advanced towards the edge of the wood. Here they encountered another obstacle – a low-level barbed-wire entanglement, with diagonal strands of wire strung between short posts about ten or twelve inches off the ground. The wire was strung with anti-personnel mines and was designed to bring men crashing down, while a machine-gun on the flank shot them to pieces. Had they advanced in darkness this trip-wire might well have proved too much for them. Lieutenant Gatton described what happened:

> We sort of played hopscotch through the wire and of course some people tripped and fell. Then another fifty yards or so we hit the edge of the forest and I was really surprised to look up and see the barrel of an 88mm gun. Major Tilston ran forward and threw a grenade. I followed up and when we got to the 88 the crew were gone. There was another machine-gun off to the left which Major Tilston took out with grenades. . . . Our objective was about a hundred yards into the brush, so we carried on into this and there was a slight trail going across, so I positioned my men on this.

Charlie Gatton had only ten men left in his platoon to hold the position they had won. Two more of them died shortly after they reached their objective. The survivors of this terrible advance were still in great danger.

At the edge of the wood they had overrun a network of trenches and well prepared dug-outs. Before the Canadians reached their objective the Germans had ducked back into these bunkers but now they emerged and began to snipe at their enemies from the rear. Charlie Gatton had a private war of his own with one group of paratroopers whom he repelled by taking a pile of unattended German hand grenades and blasting them with their own bombs. He drew Fred's attention to the danger and the two officers pulled back the shattered remnants of the company and consolidated their position in a group of enemy trenches. Badly wounded men were propped up against the trench walls and set to cleaning and reloading weapons, while those still fit to fight had to repel repeated counter-attacks from the paratroopers. The Canadians now felt the loss of their Bren-gun carrier with its load of ammunition. They had run out of grenades, and rifle and Bren magazines were almost exhausted.

The Second World War

While 'C' Company were engaged in this desperate battle in the woods, 'A' Company had also reached their objective – a group of farm buildings on the edge of the forest. They had fared rather better than their comrades on the left and their carrier, with its precious load of ammunition, had reached the shelter of the farm. Between the two companies was a stretch of open ground which the Germans were now plastering with mortar bombs, and across the middle of this murderous wasteland was a track which served as a perfect target for machine-gun and mortar fire. Fred Tilston had been wounded again, this time in the hip, and most commanders in his position would have seen their job as more than fulfilled if they simply stayed with their troops and sent up a runner for ammunition. But this was not Fred's style. As he himself puts it, 'Never ask anyone to do anything you are not prepared to do yourself.' So, urging his men to stand firm, Fred set off himself to fetch ammunition from 'A' Company.

At the farm the other company commander, Paul Cropp, watched Fred as he came towards them.

> I saw him coming across, no worries, just a smile on his face . . . and in he sauntered, more or less, and said, 'We are short of ammunition, what can we have?' So we supplied him. He was of course bleeding from a number of wounds and we patched them up for him and sent him back. But the thing that really struck me about Fred was that this man was really enjoying the war. Here am I, terrified by what's going on most of the time, and here is a man who is totally enjoying what is happening.

Fred ran back through the gauntlet of fire separating the two companies' positions, this time encumbered with hundreds of rounds of ammunition and two boxes of grenades. He reached his own men just in time to help them repel the next German counter-attack.

> The Germans again appeared [recalls Charlie Gatton] and we fought them back again and this sort of attack and counter-attack went on all afternoon. Major Tilston encouraged us – he was a real inspiration to us. He had no regard for fire, enemy fire. He must have been beyond caring, I suppose, because he never got down into the trench. He just stood on the parapet or squatted beside it and just discussed our problems as if we were at a board meeting. He was absolutely cool. . . . Fred made

several trips across the road under fire and brought us grenades and boxes of ammunition . . . I can't remember how many boxes of grenades we used up. You wouldn't believe it – it was just like a snowball fight really.

Charlie Gatton himself collected one load of ammunition and two other men were sent across in the course of the afternoon, but Fred went six times – six times across three hundred yards of open ground, twelve journeys in all, and most of the way dodging a continuous hail of machine-gun bullets and mortar shells. Thanks to this constant supply of ammunition and the cheerful confidence of their commander, the handful of men remaining in 'C' Company held on to their objective. The rest of the battalion, including Captain Alf Hodges with 'B' Company, then advanced through their lines to push further into the wood.

We came under quite a bit of fire from that flank . . . mostly machine-gun fire, and I lost about half my company going across the same ground that Fred had crossed. . . . I saw Fred when I reached the woods and he greeted me with the cheerful words, 'Just keep going, Alf. They've got nothing but a few rifles and machine-guns.' And all the time the artillery and mortar shells were dropping around us in the woods. It was typical Fred.

Minimising danger was always typical of Fred. After the rest of the battalion had passed through, he made one more trip to get ammunition, just to make sure that his men could meet any emergency. 'Between our position and Paul Cropp's headquarters was a very large crater. I was just passing through it when a mortar shell landed and I was at the wrong place at the wrong time. It got me. So I never made that final trip.' One of his legs was blown off completely below the knee. The other was so badly shattered that any movement was impossible. 'I made myself as comfortable as possible under the circumstances. I simply undid my webbing, got into a reasonably comfortable position, gave myself a shot of morphine and waited. I think I became unconscious, you know, intermittently.'

When he was found by men of his own unit he refused to leave the battlefield until he was sure that the last of his gallant command could hold the ground they had won at so much cost. Out of 103 men who had left the start line in 'C' Company that morning, only 27 were still on their feet. Eventually Fred was picked up by stretcher-bearers and taken to the field dressing-station. From there he was shipped back to the Canadian Military Hospital at Horley in Sussex, and after a hard fight to save the damaged leg the surgeons were obliged to amputate this as well.

As the story of Fred's courage on that day became known, the machinery was set in motion for some kind of decoration to be given to him. As witness after witness recounted what they had seen and heard it became obvious to the Canadian commander, General Crerar, that only one decoration was appropriate – the Victoria Cross. On the day after the battle, Major Paul Cropp had tried to put into words what he felt about Fred's actions at the Hochwald. 'It was partly his attitude to the whole thing, his obvious willingness to face any kind of danger with a smile on his face . . . making light of any wounds he had, going back and forth when the danger was so obvious that most of us would be hiding our heads as much as we could.'

But perhaps the most remarkable thing about Fred's behaviour on that day was his consistent good humour, and this humour stayed with him. When his Victoria Cross was gazetted, an inquisitive reporter asked Fred what quality was most important in winning a Victoria Cross. 'Inexperience,' was Fred's reply. When both legs had been removed and he was lying in bed on board a hospital ship, an over-zealous Red Cross lady came fussing down the ward, enquiring of each man what was wrong with him. When it came to Fred's turn he eyed her cryptically and said, 'A bad case of athlete's foot, madam, both feet.' When film of his investiture was seen by his anxious sisters back home in Canada they both agreed: 'When we saw he still had that twinkle in his eye we knew he was going to be all right.'

Compassion and good humour carried Fred through the long ordeal of operations, physiotherapy and convalescence in hospital in England. His main concern seems to have been not for the loss of his limbs, but for the loss of so many lives in his own company. When he was not grieving over those who had died he turned his attention to those around him. There was no room in his philosophy for self-pity.

> In a hospital where there are war injuries the atmosphere is good. You're not in there because of a kidney infection or because you are a diabetic or something. You've been caught some place and you need a little servicing, otherwise you're in pretty good health. And no matter how bad you are there is always somebody worse than you and that in itself is a boost. I know I had a friend come in shortly after I was in – he'd lost two legs, but he had lost one above the knee. Well, I'm better than he is. I feel sorry for him. And a few days after that, we had another chap come in from a British unit, who was paralysed from just below the neck down. My friend immediately felt, 'Gee, I'm lucky, he's a lot worse than me.' And if you ever feel at the bottom of the ladder, just go down to the burns unit and then you'll know how lucky you are.

As he says this, forty years after the event, there are tears in Fred Tilston's eyes.

In July 1945 Fred went home to Toronto to a grand parade and civic reception. Unhappily, his mother had died during his absence at the front, but his sisters were overjoyed to see him. As soon as the ceremonies were over he got down to business, and in short order he had himself fitted with artificial legs. Told that he might have to settle for a few inches' loss of height, he insisted, 'I have to be six foot two with size thirteen boots.' Fitted up to his satisfaction, he then went through the long and often painful business of learning to walk on artificial legs. His friend Keith Norris tells a story which illustrates Fred's determination. 'On one occasion, after he had learnt to walk with a cane, he sort of stumbled on the sidewalk and I put my hand out to grab his shoulder and he said, "Just keep your hands off me. If I'm going to fall I'll fall on my own. I don't want you pushing me."'

Within a few months Fred had learned to walk without crutches, had got his old job back with Sterling Drug and had courted and won the girlfriend, Helen, whom he had met in Edmonton before the war. When they were married, in 1946, he walked proudly down the aisle with his bride. In due course Helen and Fred had a son, Michael, and when father and son were both at home, they became virtually inseparable. 'There are all these old pictures,' says Michael, 'showing Dad doing something about the yard and me just tagging along with him wherever he went.' Fred taught his son how to fish, and the two of them would go off on expeditions together. In the mid-1950s the family took to going on holiday on a dude ranch in Arizona, where Michael learnt to ride and where Fred one day decided to take up riding himself. No one was very impressed. Even those who know Fred well say that they often have difficulty remembering that he has lost his legs. His sister Josephine tells a story about Fred watering the garden and getting his feet wet. 'Oh my goodness,' cried Josephine, 'you'll catch your death of cold.' She had clean forgotten that he had no feet.

At Sterling Drug, Fred worked his way steadily up through the hierarchy of the sales department, becoming vice-president in charge of sales, then head of the buying department and finally, in 1956, president of the Canadian Division. He supervised the moving of the manufacturing plant from its old home in Windsor, Ontario, to big new premises at Aurora, tirelessly keeping abreast of new developments in the drug industry. As a senior executive he decided that he needed a refresher course from time to time. One of these involved an expedition to the Canadian Arctic, canoeing down fast-flowing rivers to explore sites for new hydro-electric plants. On another occasion he decided that he should qualify as a pharmacist in British Columbia, the one state in Canada which did not recognise his qualifications. He passed the examinations with good grades, heedless of the possible embarrassment which might have resulted from failure. 'Failure,' observes his friend, Keith Norris, 'is not a word in Fred's vocabulary.'

Throughout his active career he never allowed the loss of his legs to prevent him from doing anything he wanted to do. Even when he retired, Fred retained a lively interest in many different fields. He did voluntary work for the Order of St John – work which was eventually recognised with the award of a Knighthood of the Order. He also became honorary colonel of the Essex Scottish regiment, keeping a fatherly eye on the voluntary militia who still train regularly at the old regimental armoury in Windsor. He is a tireless traveller, touring widely in the Far East, always interested in the lives of ordinary people and taking great pains to learn as much as possible about their way of life. Companions who have travelled with him complain that he often turns his back on the tourist itinerary of temples and palaces, preferring to spend hours getting to know a market trader or a village craftsman. In a more sombre mood he has also spent many weeks touring battlefields of both world wars, always visiting the cemeteries and paying homage to the young men who died.

After his wife Helen died ten years ago, Fred moved from the family house in Aurora and rented a trailer-home over-looking a pleasant valley in the countryside near Kettleby, Ontario. It is a modest dwelling, but enough for his own needs, and he has a spare room for the occasional visitor. Here, when he is not on one of his frequent trips away from home, he lives quietly by himself. A cleaning service helps with the house-work, but he cooks and caters for himself and for his guests, driving himself around the country to visit his friends and keep up with his interests. A few years ago he felt that his French needed brushing up, so he went back to college for a two-year course. Then he decided to catch up on new developments in mathematics and happily joined a class of eighteen-year-olds grappling with the new maths. At the age of seventy-nine he is still active, still alive to new experiences.

Looking back over the years it seems apparent that Fred Tilston's behaviour on the battlefield at the Hochwald was of a piece with his life. On that day he took appalling risks in order to prevent disaster from overwhelming the men remaining in his command. The fact that so many had already been killed or wounded, while he himself was still comparatively able-bodied, certainly prompted him to do his utmost to save those who had survived. Like most men who win the Victoria Cross, Fred had a powerfully developed sense of responsibility, perhaps enhanced by the early loss of his father and the need to support his mother and younger sisters even as a child. As for the danger, he cannot have been unaware of the risks he was running – having been wounded twice on that day and twice on previous occasions, he must have known that he was just as vulnerable as anyone else. But the stubborn tenacity and lack of self-pity which were later to take him through the ordeal of learning to walk again after the amputation also took him through the gauntlet of fire at the Hochwald. The rather wicked sense of humour that prompted a small boy to throw snakes at peaceful visitors to Lake Michigan may well have played a part in powering the arm that hurled grenades at German machine-gunners. The daring, the excitement, kept that smile on his face, but the most powerful force in Fred Tilston on that day and throughout his life was not aggression but compassion – the desire to protect those weaker than himself. Brigadier Joe Cardy who was, in 1945, chaplain for the Essex Scottish, puts it like this.

> I think in many ways he was a very ordinary kind of guy. He wasn't removed from people; he was a people person. But I also think of him as a leader who led by his own example. I always said Freddie Tilston had big feet – when he got on a piece of ground nobody was ever going to move him off it. But he was a caring person . . . in the best sense of the word he loved his men and cared for them very deeply.

12
Leonard Cheshire

The King has been graciously pleased to confer the Victoria Cross on the under-mentioned officer in recognition of most conspicuous bravery:

Wing-Commander Geoffrey Leonard Cheshire DSO, DFC *(72021), Royal Air Force Volunteer Reserve, 617 Squadron.*

This officer began his operational career in June 1940. Against strongly defended targets he soon displayed the courage and determination of an exceptional leader. He was always ready to accept extra risks to ensure success. Defying the formidable Ruhr defences, he frequently released his bombs from below 2,000 feet. Over Cologne in November 1940, a shell burst inside his aircraft, blowing out one side and starting a fire; undeterred, he went on to bomb his target. About this time, he carried out a number of convoy patrols in addition to his bombing missions.

At the end of his first tour of operational duty in January 1941, he immediately volunteered for a second. Again, he pressed home his attacks with the utmost gallantry. Berlin, Bremen, Cologne, Duisberg, Essen and Kiel were among the heavily-defended targets which he attacked. When he was posted for instructional duties in January 1942, he undertook four more operational missions.

He started a third operational tour in August 1942, when he was given command of a squadron. He led the squadron with outstanding skill on a number of missions before being appointed in March 1943 as a station commander.

In October 1943, he undertook a fourth operational tour, relinquishing the rank of group captain at his own request so that he could again take part in operations. He immediately set to work as the pioneer of a new method of marking enemy targets involving very low flying. In June 1944, when marking a target in the harbour at Le Havre in broad daylight and without cloud cover, he dived well below the range of the light batteries before releasing his marker-bombs, and he came very near to being destroyed by the strong barrage which concentrated on him.

During his fourth tour which ended in July 1944, Wing-Commander Cheshire led his squadron personally on every occasion, always undertaking the most dangerous and difficult task of marking the target from a low level in the face of strong defences.

Wing-Commander Cheshire's cold and calculated acceptance of risks is exemplified by his conduct in an attack on Munich in April 1944. This was an experimental attack to test out the new method of target-marking at low level against a heavily defended target situated deep in Reich territory. Munich was selected, at Wing-Commander Cheshire's request, because of the formidable nature of its light anti-aircraft and search-light defences. He was obliged to follow, in bad weather, a direct route which took him over the defences of Augsburg and thereafter he was continuously under fire. As he reached the target, flares were being released by our high-flying aircraft. He was illuminated from above and below. All guns within range opened fire on him. Diving to 700 feet he dropped his markers with great precision and began to climb away. So blinding were the searchlights that he almost lost control. He then flew over the city at 1,000 feet to assess the accuracy of his work and direct other aircraft. His own was badly hit by shell fragments but he continued to fly over the target area until he was satisfied that he had done all in his power to ensure success. Eventually, when he set course for base, the task of disengaging himself from the defences proved even more hazardous than the approach. For a full twelve minutes after leaving the target area he was under withering fire, but he came safely through.

Wing-Commander Cheshire has now completed a total of 100 missions. In four years of fighting against the bitterest opposition he has maintained a record of outstanding personal achievement, placing himself invariably in the forefront of the battle. What he did in the Munich operation was typical of the careful planning, brilliant execution and contempt for danger which has established for Wing-Commander Cheshire a reputation second to none in Bomber Command.

A great wooden cross hangs on the wall of Leonard Cheshire's sparsely furnished London office. Sitting beneath it he seems perfectly cast for the role of a twentieth-century saint. His body is thin, painfully thin, and his face is long and lean with deep-set brown eyes and a very intense, slightly disquieting gaze. When he listens, which he does with total attention, he appears to absorb everything, both the spoken and the unspoken word. When he speaks his voice is quiet and only very slightly modulated, as though it is a weapon he has learned to keep under careful control. He talks with great clarity of thought and expression, sometimes shading his eyes with his left hand the better to concentrate on what he is saying. Most of the time he seems diffident, almost shy; but occasionally, without appearing to break the mood, his voice takes on a turn of gentle irony – so gentle that it is not immediately obvious that he is making fun of his visitor. Then suddenly it is obvious. What he has just been suggesting is absurd, outrageous. His face splits into a wide smile and he laughs delightedly at his own joke, then, suddenly contrite, he reaches out a hand in apology. It is difficult not to like him, difficult not to feel the persuasive power of this gentle, quiet, perceptive man.

Some people say that Leonard Cheshire is very like his father, not so much in physical appearance as in manner. Geoffrey Cheshire was a distinguished academic lawyer at Exeter College, Oxford, author of one of the seminal works of his generation of lawyers and greatly admired by all who knew him. His wife Primrose was a beautiful and sensitive woman, a protective and affectionate mother. Leonard was born in 1917, his brother Christopher two years later. The Cheshires were not rich, but they were what used to be called comfortably off and for many years they had a large and pleasant home in the countryside outside Oxford. The boys were sent to the Dragon School, a well-known prep school in the city, and then to Stowe, where Leonard just managed to get a scholarship.

His brother Christopher recalls Leonard's schooldays:

> He was quite a figure. People talked about him. . . . I suppose it must be said that he was very much an above-average performer both scholastically and on the games field. Now he wasn't a natural ball-hitter, or a natural athlete, except if you saw him play tennis you'd think he was, because he's a very good tennis player. But he had tremendous determination. For instance, at the school mile at Stowe, he just forced himself into

the race and he nearly won it against all the odds, on the principle that 'if that man's legs can move fast, mine can move as fast as his and I can keep up with him', which was sheer determination because he wasn't a natural runner at all. In fact on the occasion of the school mile, the headmaster, when he announced the prizes, remarked that his was a very courageous effort. Of course it was just the same in the cross-country; he just forced himself to keep behind the man in front of him. . . . I think he was definitely happy at school, because he had many interests both on the playing field and scholastically. He was the editor of the school magazine and in his final year he was made head of house.

Leonard himself remembers his schooldays as happy, but from an early age he wanted to be different, to be exceptional in some way. As a boy he greatly admired a number of people who had been spectacularly successful in their own field. Fred Astaire was one hero; the racing driver, Raymond Mays, another.

It is not surprising, therefore, that when he went up to Oxford in 1935 he bought himself an Alfa Romeo, which he could not afford, and drove it with terrifying skill, covering the fifty miles from London to Oxford on several occasions in rather less than fifty minutes. Freed from the irksome discipline of school life he went a little wild at Oxford.

I used to challenge people to see how late they could leave running across the road in front of an on-coming car. We used to do that up the Iffley Road. . . . It was sort of a compulsion to try it, till one day a car knocked my shoe off and the driver got out and said, 'I think I'm going to thump you.' I thought I'd better slow down after that. . . . I used to go to the dog track and I enjoyed that kind of world . . . I went and helped make a book at Ascot . . . there was an irresponsible side to me and I think Father and Mother knew that.

There were other adventures. He would stay out late, going to dances in London, and have to climb in over the college wall. Still in evening dress he would sign on for the college roll-call in the morning, daring the don in charge to reprimand him for wearing white tie and tails at breakfast-time. He liked to be sensational. On one occasion at the end of his university career he made a bet of a pint of beer with the landlord of the pub that he could take himself to Paris on fifteen shillings, won the bet and managed to get the story into the newspapers. On another, he contrived to get himself stranded on top of Merton college tower with the door mysteriously locked behind him. A newspaper photographer just happened to be in the neighbourhood and took pictures of the rescue. These were harmless pranks, but they earned him a certain notoriety – and notoriety was what he seemed to crave. At the time, on his own admission, he wanted nothing better than to be rich and famous.

More unusual, and perhaps more attractive, was the capacity that Leonard had to make friends in surprising places. He formed a friendship at Merton college with Bert Gardiner, his 'scout' (or college servant), and Fred Hulbert, the man who tended the boilers. These friendships stood him in good stead when he discovered a coal chute into the cellars which offered an easy entry into college after the gates were closed at night. Foresight, combined with daring and the careful cultivation of people whose knowledge might be useful to him, was a habit which stayed with him in his later career.

Cheshire joined the university air squadron within six months of his arrival in Oxford.

> At that time you were expected to join one of the university cadet corps. I thought, I don't want to be an infantryman. I want something different from the usual. So I decided to join the cavalry. But then I discovered you had to turn up at seven a.m. at a dreadful drill hall to be shouted at by a sergeant major. . . . He made you run at the horse and jump on to it; he made you somersault backwards off it, and it was just horrible. So I thought, I'll go to the other extreme and find a more comfortable way of serving. . . . So I went to the Oxford Air Squadron and I just took to it. I just sort of felt at home there. Then that began to take a lot of my time because I really enjoyed it. I wasn't particularly good, but I liked the sound of the air because there were open cockpits then. I liked my instructor – he was a lovely man and a great character. I was being brought in touch with another generation that I didn't know, the serving Air Force. It made me feel a bit, you know, important.

In just seven hours and twenty minutes of flying time

The Second World War

Leonard Cheshire flew his first solo on an Avro Tutor bi-plane. Although it may not have seemed so at the time, this event marked one of the turning-points in his life. He joined the volunteer reserve of the Royal Air Force, and the next year, in 1938, he came to see that war with Germany was inevitable. He did not find the idea altogether unpalatable. For one thing, he knew that he was completely unprepared for his final examinations in law.

> In 1938 we had Munich, and obviously as an undergraduate you don't know much – you don't really understand the details of it – but I remember clearly a deep sense of betrayal. I felt that something was wrong. I felt that we, although I didn't quite understand it, had done the wrong thing. I was convinced that that meant that war was coming. So I went to my father and I said, 'I'd like to join the Air Force.' Of course I also thought that that would get me off my finals – joining the Air Force, I would never do my exams. Father said, 'No, you can't.' Of course in those days you obeyed your father. But the Air Force would allow you to apply for a permanent commission and if they accepted you you took it up when you finished your finals.

By diligent last-minute cramming Leonard managed to get a second in law in the summer of 1939, which went some way towards pacifying his father, and he applied for a permanent commission in the RAF. Hitherto he had always imagined himself in the glamorous role of a fighter pilot, but the air force did not give him the opportunity. After flight-training at Hullavington and Abingdon he reported to 102 Squadron at Driffield in Yorkshire in June 1940. Driffield was a Bomber Command base. Leonard had already distinguished himself as a trainee pilot of exceptional ability, but at this stage he did not know how well or how badly he would stand up to the test of operational flying.

> I was a frightened man . . . I was a worried man. How am I going to behave? I'm not used to being under gunfire. And I got inside the station and everything at first was completely normal and nobody was acting any differently from what I'd seen at the flight-training school. And you felt you could begin to feel that you were part of a tradition – you were, as it were, carried along. You realised that you weren't there just in your own right, you were occupying a place in the squadron that others

in past years and in past battles and wars had occupied. You felt that you owed them a duty.

Within a couple of days of his arrival at Driffield he flew his first sortie on a Whitley bomber under the guidance of an experienced New Zealand pilot-officer named 'Lofty' Long, who was generous as well as level-headed. He allowed Leonard to take the controls over enemy territory and ensured that he became absolutely familiar with the aircraft; within a few weeks he was flying with his own crew. His early assignments included a spell in Northern Ireland, submarine-spotting for Atlantic convoys. One of these missions nearly ended in disaster when a combination of bad weather and lack of advance preparation resulted in Leonard and his crew becoming lost in thick cloud, unable to fix a bearing on their home base. Disregarding orders to use an advance landing-strip he eventually landed at base with only ten minutes' fuel left in his tanks.

In the autumn of 1940 102 Squadron returned to Driffield, and Leonard flew a number of missions over Germany. It is difficult at this distance in time to imagine what those early raids over Germany must have been like. The discomfort in itself must have been unpleasant: the noisy unpressurised aircraft, bumping violently through the up-draughts; the cramped uncomfortable seats, the smell of fuel oil, the biting cold. Add to that the knowledge that at any moment a German night-fighter might come screaming into the attack out of the darkness, unseen until it was too late to do anything to avoid it. Then, once over enemy territory, the searchlights stabbing upwards through the gloom, the streams of tracer from light anti-aircraft guns, the bursting shells of the heavies – rocking the plane when they came too close. On one occasion Leonard brought back his Whitley with more than a hundred holes in it. Simply to follow orders on a bombing mission must have demanded courage of a high order, but even at this early stage in the war Leonard was convinced that he should go in to the attack at well below the prescribed height. Bombing in those days was notoriously inaccurate – according to one estimate only 16 per cent of RAF bombs landed within three miles of the target. Leonard believed that a low-level bombing run would be both more accurate and safer, but on the night of 12 November, running in for an attack on Cologne, he flew at the officially planned height of 8,000 feet.

> We were going in to the target and by this time, of course, defences were heavy. We were right in the middle of the defences now, but on this evening everything was completely silent. There wasn't a move, there wasn't a gun and it was a very eerie feeling. I felt much more uncomfortable than under the normal attack when there was gun-fire, because it felt wrong and I somehow felt I was flying into a trap, but I could do nothing about it. I had to go to my target and suddenly about six guns fired. I was actually going in to the target so I couldn't take evasive action and one shell, two shells hit us; one came through the cockpit but didn't explode, fortunately, and the other went into the fuselage and hit the photoflash which exploded in the face of the wireless operator who was about to drop it. Of course it blinded him completely, burnt his face very badly and set fire to the aircraft. But the shell that had come through the cockpit, I think it must have slightly concussed me because the engine stopped. I had lost control of the aircraft. The cockpit was full of smoke and we were going down, more or less vertically down. . . . And up to that moment I had always thought, well, the last thing I ever want to do is to jump in my parachute, but when the moment comes I won't mind, anything to get out of the aircraft. But somehow I couldn't bring myself to jump. I don't know why, I just couldn't bring myself to jump or give the order to jump. And then I began to hear something and I thought, those are engines. I looked at my instruments and they seemed to be working and I gently pulled the stick back and it responded and I realised that we weren't out of control and that the engines were running. So by the grace of God we got the aeroplane right. We dropped our bomb on some sort of a target and slowly made our way home with a large, very large, ten-foot hole in the fuselage.

The wireless operator, eighteen-year-old Henry Davidson, stuck to his post despite hideous burns and was awarded the DFC for his courage. Leonard Cheshire, who by his coolness in the face of danger had managed to save both aircraft and crew from further injury, was awarded the DSO.

In January 1941 Leonard completed his first tour of operations and immediately volunteered for a second. This time he was assigned to 35 Squadron at Lynton-on-Ouse, which was equipped with the new Halifax bombers. After several sorties against German ports and oil installations, Leonard's squadron was ordered to attack the harbour at Kiel on 15 April. High cloud blanketed the target, so instead of going in to the attack at 10,000 feet he brought his aircraft down to 6,000 and had the satisfaction of seeing his bombs fall on the target area. In March his skill and courage as a pilot was further recognised with the award of the DFC and in April with a Bar to his DSO.

For several weeks in the spring and summer of 1941 the Halifax bombers were withdrawn from service for modifications. Rather than face inactivity Leonard volunteered to go to the United States on a mission to ferry American Hudson bombers across the Atlantic. Delays in the programme gave him the opportunity to take several weeks' leave in New York where, as a highly decorated RAF pilot, he was given a hero's welcome and fêted by his American hosts. In New York he met Constance Binney, a twice-married, twice-divorced ex-film starlet, who was then forty-three – old enough to be his mother – but she was witty, entertaining and wealthy. Her friends and her glamorous life style impressed him. In the unreal atmosphere of the time, with no certainty that he would survive the next few weeks, let alone the rest of the war, Leonard raised no objections when she suggested that they should get married. He returned to England late in July, a married man.

He went back to operational flying with 35 Squadron. In August, on a raid over Berlin, Leonard's brother Christopher was shot down and taken prisoner. Not knowing whether Christopher was alive or dead, Leonard was deeply depressed and may not have been as confident as usual when he took his aircraft in to the attack on Magdeburg a couple of nights later. A senior officer had suggested that the German defences were alerted by sound-detection equipment. Accordingly, Leonard decided to experiment by 'feathering' his engines, switching off the power and gliding in to the attack, but when he tried to re-start the engines he forgot the correct procedures and the aircraft began rapidly to lose height. His wireless operator on this and on many other flights was a pugnacious Scot named Jock Moncrieff.

> I was in the wireless operator's cabin and he was up in the cockpit. Now, being wartime aircraft, they didn't have any false ceilings or anything, you know, and I had a clear view of his feet on the rudder pedals and I could see that his movements were getting more and more frantic and excited. . . . And then we seemed to be in a sort of strange attitude and he suddenly shouted, 'Bail out.' So I thought, 'Oh, for God's sake!' It wasn't as though the Germans had shot us and we'd had to bail out. This was rather like getting run out at cricket or something, you know, or hitting your own wicket. I thought, this is crazy. And so I said to him, I said, 'For God's sake, Chesh, pull your bloody finger out, you can do better than this!' There was a pause and he said, 'Yes, Jock, I think I can. I think I can.' So I started shouting to Paddy – he was the flight engineer – I said, 'Paddy, for God's sake come up here.' So Paddy came rushing up and nursed him through it. Fortunately, to my relief, by which time we were down to about six or seven thousand feet, the starboard and then one of the port engines picked up (the fourth one never picked up – we came back on three) and then from then on things got under control and we came home.

It was perhaps the nearest that Leonard Cheshire ever came to panic. Characteristically, rather than keep quiet about his mistake, Leonard himself reported what had happened to the station commander and accepted what he judged to be a well-deserved reprimand. But the fact that his superiors thought very highly of his abilities was made plain a few weeks later when he was officially confirmed in the rank of squadron-leader. Much to his disgust, he was removed from operational flying at the end of his second tour and in January 1942 was posted to Marston Moor as an instructor to 1652 Heavy Conversion Unit, training young pilots to fly Halifax bombers. Although he took his duties seriously and even managed to fit three operational flights into his six months as an instructor, he longed to return to active service. And after six months he was back on operations as commander of his brother's old unit, Number 76 Squadron.

Leonard now flew with the acting rank of wing-commander and had no regular air crew of his own. This gave him the opportunity to fly with each different crew in turn and assess their capabilities. It also gave them an opportunity to assess him.

> I recall one day somebody coming to me and saying that the navigator who had been on one of these trips had said, 'I'm pleased to see that the CO was just as scared as I was going in to the target.' And it came as quite a shock to me because I thought, 'I don't remember being afraid.' I thought, well either he's imagining it or I was afraid and was showing signs of which I was unaware. So I think that any subjective judgement on yourself is suspect – I just honestly don't know whether I was afraid or not. All I can say, as somebody who used to brief crews going into action on many nights, I could see some who were really afraid, some for whom the thought of the flak and the opposition dominated, and others who were concerned only with how to get there. Clearly those who were afraid were the braver men because you can't maintain that there is courage unless it's overcome fear. You may do what appears to be a very brave action, but through ignorance of the danger. So I don't really know what true criterion there is for courage, but I do know that if you have a dangerous job to do you can't really afford to let the thought of the danger enter your mind. Once it's inside your mind it's very difficult to cast out. So somehow you've got to guard your mind and you've got to prevent the thoughts of fear and danger and so on, distractions, from getting into your mind. I think some people have perhaps an easier gift in this than others, and undoubtedly one thing that helps is concentration on your job. The more you concentrate on your job the less freedom of mind you have for fear and the more you concentrate on your job the better you're going to handle whatever it is that you're doing and the greater chance it's going to give you of overcoming any obstacle

It is not likely that many of the aircrew in Bomber Command in wartime would have stopped to analyse courage in the way that Leonard himself did, but most of those that flew with him would probably agree with Jock Moncrieff's assessment.

> His tenacity and purpose over the target were quite incredible. . . . Whereas previous pilots I've flown with were, well, they'd think, 'My conscience is salved, I've done all my duty. I've got to get home now even if I can't find the target. . . .' But Leonard would watch his fuel gauge. He would run until he

209

was perfectly sure he'd done everything possible to bomb that target. He would not give in, you know. He was marvellous really, looking back on it. . . . I liked flying with Leonard, yes. I liked him. He never showed any signs of panic, never. Now you may wonder how a pilot shows signs of panic. Well, just a rise in his voice, a sort of shrill note comes into his voice, impatience with the navigator or he keeps constantly saying to the rear-gunners you know, keep a good look-out. You could tell, and that kind of panic could spread through a crew. It wasn't good for crew morale. Leonard was never like that. I had absolute confidence in him.

Leonard completed another twenty operational flights with 76 Squadron without any serious mishap at a time when the life expectancy of most Bomber Command air crews was horribly short. He himself believes he was lucky, but luck does not account for the skill with which he captained his own plane and the high reputation he built for his squadron as a whole. This reputation depended on the care and preparation that went on before a raid, almost as much as on the skill and courage which Leonard showed when actually flying. Other pilots marvelled at the length of time that he spent with his ground crew. Always at the end of a mission he would stop and talk with the men whose job it was to service the plane and patch it up ready for the next operation. He knew how vital their job was to his own effectiveness as a bomber pilot and he took care to make them feel part of the team. As far as possible he made sure that all the pilots in his squadron did the same.

When he was grounded again at the end of his third tour he felt bitterly frustrated. Promotion to group-captain as station commander at Marston Moor, and even the announcement of a second Bar to his DSO, were no consolation. But he kept his discontent to himself. He ran the Heavy Conversion Unit with his usual close attention to detail and apparently unfailing enthusiasm until the opportunity arose for him to return once again to operations as Commander of 617 Squadron.

This was the unit which had earned glory for Wing-Commander Guy Gibson vc in the costly but successful raid on the Eder and Mohne dams. Guy Gibson had since been killed, but the memory of him was still very much alive in his old squadron, and Gibson's was a hard act to follow. There were other reasons why the veterans of 617 Squadron felt there was reason to be dubious about the qualities of their new commander. During the long hours of relative inactivity during his first spell at Marston Moor, Leonard had written a book called *Bomber Pilot*, which told in rather racy prose the story of his own war in the air. The book was vividly written and gave due credit to others, but to a critical eye there were traces of vanity – and any hint of self-glorification was totally contrary to the ethos of all the armed services at the time, and of the RAF perhaps most of all. To the great relief of the air crew of 617 Squadron the famous Leonard Cheshire was much more modest and unassuming than they had imagined he would be. One of the veterans of 617 Squadron, Dave Shannon, recalls:

> Leonard was a first-class pilot. There's no doubt about that. . . . He was a very good leader in a very different fashion, I think, from Guy Gibson. Guy Gibson was very much one of the boys, although Leonard of course was one of the boys as well, but Gibson on duty was very much the disciplinarian; he could be a bit of a small martinet in a way and specifically so once airborne. Leonard, I think, led by example and led by persuasion and led by the air of calmness that he gave off in knowing that things could be done; and persuasion that if everybody went along with him any raid would be a success. He had a tremendous knack of persuading people to his way of thinking, and the wry sense of humour that was always coming through from Leonard meant, I think, that in a very short space of time the squadron really took to him as a first-class leader.

The first thing that Leonard had to learn with 617 Squadron was how to fly a Lancaster and how to fly it low, for low-level attacks had been the speciality of the squadron. This technique already greatly appealed to him because of his awareness of the inaccuracy of high-level bombing with Whitleys and Halifaxes, but low-level attacks had proved extremely costly in lives and machines and the squadron were now equipped with a new bomb-sight which greatly improved the accuracy of the high-level attack. For many weeks after he first took over, therefore, Leonard had to rehearse his Lancasters, dropping dummy bombs on targets at Wainfleet Sands from 20,000 feet.

The Second World War

Although the chief of Bomber Command, Air-Marshal Harris, was dedicated to the idea that Hitler could be smashed into submission by the indiscriminate flattening of towns and cities, the forthcoming D-Day invasion of France called for much more precise and accurate techniques. The RAF could not afford to antagonise their allies by wiping out unduly large numbers of innocent French civilians. Yet somehow roads, bridges and railways, often in densely occupied areas, must be bombed in order to hamper movements of German troops opposing the Allied bridge-head in France. There were other, almost equally vital targets for precision bombing: the small and well-camouflaged launch sites for the V1 and V2 secret weapons with which Hitler was determined to counter the Allied bombing of German cities. So while the rest of Bomber Command continued with the policy of saturation bombing, 617 Squadron were reserved for special duties, the accurate bombing of small but important targets.

This meant fewer operations and more practice and the squadron spent many weeks over the markers on the ranges, but accuracy in itself was not enough. In order for the bombs to hit the right point in a night attack the target must first be marked with a flare in exactly the right place. On the few occasions that 617 Squadron were allowed to practise their new skills on real enemy targets, Leonard found to his disgust that the markers placed by the RAF Pathfinder squadrons were rarely in the right place. The result of this was, of course, that any bombs dropped by the squadron would be wide of the target, however accurate their aim might be. Pathfinder techniques had been developed in imitation of the Germans, using the most sophisticated techniques available at the time, but these were unfortunately fallible. Equally unfortunately, Air-Marshal Bennet, chief of the Pathfinder squadrons, was determined to ensure that the business of target-marking remained his exclusive preserve. Leonard was certain that he could do better if he was given the opportunity. Mick Martin, one of the pilots in 617 Squadron, had demonstrated, in illicit experiments, that it was possible to put a Lancaster into a steep dive and release the marker flares precisely on target, virtually from tree-top height. Leonard was convinced that this was a more effective technique than the elaborate methods used by the Pathfinders. Eventually he persuaded the commander of 5 Group, Air-Marshal Cochrane, to let him place his own markers, using his own eyes to find the target and drop his flares exactly where he wanted them. His first two missions using this technique were successful. Then came Limoges.

The Gnome Aero Engine factory in the city was surrounded by civilian housing, and the workers on the assembly lines were almost all French women who had been conscripted by the Germans. The factory had to be knocked out and as far as possible civilian casualties had to be avoided. Leonard was so confident that he could do the job that he willingly allowed an RAF film unit to turn his Lancaster into an airborne studio to record the results. On the night of 8 February 1944 he brought his plane in over Limoges at less than a hundred feet and circled the town three times, zooming low over the factory in order to give the civilian workers time to get out. On the fourth run, with the girls safely in the shelters, Leonard dropped his markers right on the factory roof. Dave Shannon and the rest of the pilots in 617 Squadron were able to use their precision bomb sights and drop their massive 12,000-pound bombs bang on target. The factory was destroyed and not a single French civilian died.

The success of this raid and the filmed record of the damage which a handful of bombers had been able to inflict enabled Leonard to press for what he really wanted. He believed passionately in the value of low-level marking, but the heavy Lancaster was not the right plane for the job. Limoges had not been defended, but in the face of opposition from well placed anti-aircraft guns a low-level approach with Lancasters could only result in heavy casualties. The dangers of the technique were underlined for 617 Squadron when they attacked a crucial viaduct at Antheor, on the railway line between Marseilles and Genoa. The viaduct was heavily defended, and Leonard's own plane was hit in an attempt to land a flare on the target from fifty feet. The second Lancaster to go in, flown by Leonard's number two, Mick Martin, was also hit and the bomb-aimer killed. None of the markers landed close enough to the viaduct and the raid was a failure. Leonard realised that the ideal machine for the job of marking was the light twin-engined Mosquito fighter-bomber with its much greater speed and manoeuvrability. Unfortunately, Mosquitoes were still in short supply and Air-Marshal Bennett of the Pathfinders was still resolutely opposed to experiments in marking by other squadrons.

But the high reputation of 617 under Leonard's command was in his favour. In 300 sorties they had lost only one plane. Then a series of brilliant raids which hit pin-point targets on munitions factories helped Leonard to carry his point. Early in April 1944 he got his Mosquitoes and, using the high speed and flexibility of the aircraft, he and his colleagues in 617 Squadron were able to mark crucial targets in France for the whole of 5 Group. The destruction of a number of arms factories was virtually complete, and the loss of civilian lives minimal, but the low-level marking technique still had to be proved against heavily defended targets in Germany itself.

At Leonard's own suggestion the target for 24 April was Munich, a city revered in Germany at the time as the birthplace of the Nazi party. The city was not only well-equipped with anti-aircraft batteries, it was so far from the nearest bomber base that the Mosquitoes, without the extra fuel tanks which Leonard requested but did not receive, had only fifteen minutes' fuel reserve for the journey there and back. The risks were enormous but Leonard accepted them. It was this raid that was to be singled out from the many in the citation for his Victoria Cross. At first, everything went according to plan. Leonard put his Mosquito into a dive from 5,000 feet, and dropped his flares exactly on target. Dave Shannon put the next batch of markers so close to his leader's that it was impossible to separate them. Then Cheshire called in the heavy bombers and the Lancasters released their loads on the markers. But as the original flares died down, new ones were dropped accidently on the outskirts of the town. Leonard circled in his Mosquito, flying beneath the Lancasters as they dropped their bombs, signalling frantically to try and correct the error. A fresh batch of markers was dropped in the right place but, as always, Leonard would not leave the target until he was sure that the raid was successful.

Of course under those circumstances you stay on target longer than you're meant to because everything's happening and you feel you can't leave. . . . We stayed for about ten minutes, set course for home, got outside Munich and I turned to Pat Kelly, my navigator, and said, 'Okay,' and then suddenly a searchlight caught us. We were being hit by heavy flak at 2,000 feet, and heavy flak wasn't supposed to be able to hit you that low, and both Pat and I almost completely lost control. He swore; he just did nothing but swear for about five minutes and I was all shaking and no matter what I did I couldn't throw this flak and the searchlights off and it taught me something that I hope I've never forgotten; you must never say 'I'm home' in your mind until you actually are home and on the ground. The trouble was I'd thought to myself, okay, we're out, we're safe, and so my guard was down and Pat's guard was down; so when we were caught by flak we weren't ready for it. We weren't psychologically prepared for it. I think this was the worst moment of my flying career, those ten – well perhaps it was only five or six – minutes till we got out.

Munich did not simply demonstrate Leonard's courage and steadfastness under enemy fire – he had proved that dozens of times already. The VC was awarded for the culminating act in a long series of acts, not only of courageous leadership but of brilliant tactical thinking and meticulous preparation; for the slow and careful building-up of the confidence and expertise of an entire squadron; and for then passing on those skills to much larger numbers of airmen in the whole of 5 Group, and to some extent throughout Bomber Command. In the fullest sense, Leonard Cheshire's courage and skill was an inspiration to others. All those who served with him gained from that inspiration and Leonard in turn is very conscious of the debt that he owes to them.

I was CO of 617 Squadron and that turned out to be a highly successful special-duties squadron. Undoubtedly a large part of my getting the VC was the fact that I was representing 617. If I hadn't gone to them and had just done another ordinary tour I certainly wouldn't have got a Victoria Cross, and yet the work that I would have done as a member of an ordinary squadron could well have been more dangerous. . . . Anybody who served through the war knows that there are so many squadron members, or members of any unit, who deserved an award and never got it. There are many people who weren't seen. One unit can only put in so many recommendations – there are all sorts of factors that come into it. I am very conscious that in 617 Squadron there were a number of people who should have been decorated, but never were, merely because the complement was made up.

617 Squadron's part in the Normandy invasion was unglamorous but extremely demanding. In order to deceive the German radar defences into believing that an additional invasion fleet was heading for the Pas de Calais, the squadron flew slowly backwards and forwards on meticulously prepared flight paths, dropping 'window' aluminium foil. The slow advance of the blips on their radar screens convinced German Intelligence that Normandy was only a diversion and that the real invasion was in the north. This meant that vital Panzer divisions were not sent south until after the Normandy bridgehead was secured. The operation, known as 'Taxable', demanded skill and discipline of a high order and was a complete success.

Leonard went on to lead 617 Squadron in a number of brilliant and extremely hazardous raids against the Saumur railway tunnel, the 'E'-boat pens in Le Havre and Boulogne, and the so-called V3 sites in Northern France. All these targets, but especially the last, were massive structures of concrete, dug deep into the earth. A special weapon was devised to deal with them – the 'tallboy' bomb devised by the scientist Dr Barnes Wallis. This streamlined 1200-pounder was designed to penetrate deep into the earth and destroy buried concrete structures by creating a minor earthquake, which literally shook the concrete to pieces, but in order for it to work it had to be dropped within a few feet of the target. 617 Squadron did exactly what was required of them and within a few weeks the last of the V3 sites had been reduced to rubble.

In these later missions Leonard marked the target using a North American Mustang, an even more flexible and speedy plane than the Mosquito. He created a sensation by taking over the machine from his ground crew virtually untested and taking off immediately on an operational flight. This flamboyant gesture was typical of him, but it was also one of his last with 617 Squadron. On 6 July 1944, with a hundred missions behind him, Leonard Cheshire was grounded – officially for the last time.

The announcement of the Victoria Cross followed. In Dave Shannon's words:

> I think a lot of other people also deserved Victoria Crosses who perhaps didn't get them. It's a very difficult assessment to make, but without a doubt Leonard's part in the war – with prolonged effort and bearing in mind the number of operations that he carried out against the enemy – far surpassed, I should say, many other awards that were given for one particular act of bravery: because the award of a VC to a man like Cheshire was given for continual acts of bravery, virtually non-stop through-out a long period, while Germany was being bombed by the Allied forces. And I don't think anybody in their right mind could think that the award given to Leonard was not well-deserved. It certainly was. . . .

Restored to his former rank of group-captain, Leonard flew to India as an RAF staff officer with Headquarters Far Eastern Command. He hoped to be able to bring some of his expertise in low-level marking to bombing operations against the Japanese, and to some extent he was successful, but he was not permitted to fly himself. Disregarding orders, he borrowed a Hurricane one day in November 1944 and flew down the Arakan peninsula to the Burmese port of Akyab. According to Intelligence reports it was still supposed to be occupied by the Japanese, but Leonard doubted the accuracy of the reports and was curious to find out if his surmise was true. He buzzed the town at tree-top height and no one fired at him. When he returned to base and announced his findings he was depressed to find that nobody believed him.

A few days later he heard that his wife Constance had been taken ill in New York and obtained compassionate leave to visit her. Constance was suffering a complete breakdown and Leonard was reluctant to leave her; instead of returning to India he succeeded in securing a new post with the Joint Staff Mission in Washington. When the Americans decided to drop atomic bombs on Japan, Leonard was sent as one of the two official RAF representatives to witness the effects of the weapon. The only other British national permitted to accompany the mission was the scientist William Penny, and on 9

217

The Second World War

August 1945, on board a B29 bomber forty miles from Nagasaki, they witnessed the explosion of the second atomic bomb. Leonard made sketches of the mushroom cloud, assessing the damage done and the likely effects on the outcome of the war with Japan.

> The part I'd played in the planning of the invasion had made me realise what the price of victory over Japan was going to be. McArthur estimated three million lives. Everybody knew from the experience of frontal attacks on Japanese-occupied islands in the Pacific what the cost of a landing was going to be. So that was one thing that dominated my thinking before I went on the trip. I had already begun to realise that whatever happened the world could not afford another world war, so I was beginning to think of ways and means of playing a part in helping to prevent that. So perhaps my first reaction over the bomb was one of immense relief. It's over. As we flew around and saw that dreadful-looking cloud over Nagasaki (it must have been sixty thousand feet high – two miles across in diameter), that ball of smoke balanced on this column of yellowy revolving smoke, it made me realise what a future war would mean to the human family. So I have to say that was my principal reaction: relief, followed by realisation of what the world now faced should we go to war. Then, as we circled round and saw the base of the column which spread out like a pyramid – it was black at the very bottom because of the intense heat of the explosion which was drawing up particles of dust and ash – well, inevitably I began to think of the people under it. To drop a bomb of any kind on a city is a terrible thing and it's something that nobody wants to do. But World War Two had already cost over fifty million lives. The conventional bombing raids on Japan, some of them – Tokyo on 10 March – had taken more bombs and more lives than had been lost in Hiroshima. So of course you not only think of the people that have suffered, but you think of the people who are not now going to die as a result of the end of the war.

Leonard obtained a medical discharge from the RAF on the grounds that he was suffering from psycho-neurosis, a vague term that covers many ills. Certainly he was depressed and searching for a purpose in life. Equally certainly, he had no wish to stay in the peacetime Royal Air Force. His marriage with Constance had broken up and, apart from a fortnightly column in the *Graphic*, he had no job when he first left the services. His mind was filled with schemes – some brilliant and far-sighted, others hare-brained – all of them more or less impractical, but two ideas obsessed him. One was the need to make some contribution, however small, to the cause of world peace. The other was to preserve somehow the companionship and collective endeavour towards a common goal that he had found so worthwhile in the RAF. At the same time he was beginning to try to come to terms with the Christian faith. During the war his beliefs had been unformed. He might have described himself as an agnostic, perhaps even as an atheist. Now he wanted to believe in God.

His first attempt to put his ideas into practice was a scheme to form collectives of ex-servicemen and women who would pool their skills for the common good. With his customary energy he set about finding volunteers and premises for the project (now known as VIP), but within a few months VIP had foundered on the rocks of financial mismanagement and everyday human selfishness. Leonard was left with a pile of debts and a Victorian mansion in Hampshire named Le Court, privately mortgaged to him by a kindly aunt. He had no money and was obliged to sell off the assets of the estate piecemeal in order to pay his creditors, until only the big empty old house and a few acres were left. But at this point a curious act of providence gave him an immediate purpose, though not at all the kind of purpose that he might have imagined for himself.

The telephone went one morning to say that Arthur Dykes, who used to be a member of the VIP community (he used to look after the pigs), was dying of cancer in hospital and the hospital could not afford to keep him because there was no more medical treatment for him and they needed his bed for others. I thought I could place him elsewhere, but nobody would take him although he was an ex-serviceman. So I ended, again impulsively, by asking if he'd like to come back to Le Court. Well, of course I didn't think he would, but I thought I must offer him something. I couldn't just leave him, and he rather startled me by saying, 'Yes, Len, I'd love to.' So he came to Le Court, which was now virtually an empty house, and as there was nobody else to do it I looked after him. I nursed him, I suppose, as best as I could, till he died. The hospital was pretending to him that he was going to live and he was building plans that I knew would never materialise, so I felt I must tell him the truth – although that wasn't easy. He was a lapsed Catholic and from the moment I told him that he wasn't going to live I watched him regain his faith. He made a deep impression on me because he was uneducated, but he could answer complicated questions in a simple way, with a certain serenity. Anyhow, the night that he died, when I had to sort of sit watch over him alone in this large empty house, I picked up a book to while away the time and this was Monsignor Vernon Johnson's reason for his becoming a Catholic, and as I read it I said this is what I'm looking for. . . . I can give logical reasons for it, but they aren't the real reasons. I just knew. I knew it with the same certainty that you have when you've met somebody and know that you've met somebody. It was, so to speak, an encounter – a personal encounter. I just knew, deep in myself, now at last everything fits.

He followed up his enquiries into the Catholic Church in conversation with friends, in reading and in prayer. He decided to take instruction and a few days before Christmas 1947 he was received into the Church. At the same time the community at Le Court was growing. Even before Arthur died Leonard had received another appeal for help and had taken an old lady of ninety-one, who was homeless and bedridden. The infant National Health Service of those days was even more inadequate than it has become today and there were thousands of incurably ill patients who were taking up hospital beds without any hope of improvement. Leonard opened the doors of Le Court to them and the hospitals were only too pleased to find somewhere to send them. The old lady was followed by a patient terminally ill with tuberculosis. And so it went on.

To begin with there was no formal apparatus for dealing with the patients, and Leonard himself had no experience in caring for the sick. Somehow, as always in Leonard Cheshire's life, people felt drawn to help him; some gave small amounts of money, others their time. One of the early volunteers at Le Court was a trained hospital almoner, a girl named Frances Jeram.

It wasn't organised at all . . . it was just hand-to-mouth. . . .

The day I arrived to help him he had gone to Switzerland to fetch a patient and somebody came up to me and said, 'Well, you're in charge now; the group-captain's away. What shall we have for supper?' So I said, 'Well, what have we got in the larder? Let's go and look.' And there was one tin of spaghetti . . . It was always understood that it was the group-captain's faith which kept things going, you see. It was GC's faith, which you sometimes talked about rather reverently and sometimes not so reverently . . . but it certainly worked for him, though it didn't always work for the rest of us. But something always turned up, somebody came, something happened and you had what you absolutely needed. . . . I suppose he prayed about it and would say, 'Please God, we must have at least a hundred pounds tomorrow.' And it would come in the post. I've seen it happen heaps and heaps of times. . . .

Despite the apparent chaos, Le Court impressed many visitors with its atmosphere of quiet happiness. The fact that the patients were encouraged to do as much as possible to help run the place enabled most of them to keep their self-respect. In fact they were not regarded as patients at all, simply as residents. But many of them were close to death and it was in the care of the dying that Leonard most inspired those who worked with him. Frances Jeram remembers:

He was absolutely wonderful. The care of the dying I think was his real God-given task. When somebody was very ill, probably dying of advanced TB, he would move into their room and put a mattress on the floor and he wouldn't leave them day or night until they died. And the rest of the house had to be quiet. . . . We had to, as it were, help this person over, you see. He did this quite wonderfully. Sometimes he'd put his head out and . . . this man would perhaps ask for some quite incredible thing, some dying wish and Leonard would somehow see that he had it. But most of the time he was there nursing the man himself, you know, and some of them were pretty infectious and very ill. And when it was all over, when the person had died, he would come out triumphant and then we could all talk and laugh again. . . . Some of the other patients found this difficult to get used to, but of course we ended up with the most wonderful philosophy about death. And then we'd have wonderful funerals down at the church and give them all a jolly good send-off.

The Second World War

The close exposure to tuberculosis was to take its toll on Leonard later on. But even at this stage his health was poor and he had still not decided that the care of the sick was his true vocation. For the next two years he seems to have been unable to commit himself, and for a while he considered leading the life of a religious contemplative. He came close to marrying again and then broke off the engagement a few weeks before the wedding. He handed over the running of Le Court to the staff, backed by a committee which included Lord Denning and his own father, Geoffrey Cheshire. Then he went to work again as a test pilot on a secret government project for Dr Barnes Wallis. But while working at the airfield at Predannak in Cornwall he still found time to visit Le Court every weekend, and gave up such spare time as he had to converting an old Air Force Nissen hut into another home for the incurably ill. Then he himself at last succumbed to TB.

For over two years Leonard was gravely ill. One lung had to be removed almost entirely and for many months he was himself close to death, but he used this experience as he used all his experiences to develop his ideas. He decided that he must delegate the work of running his homes to the local committees he had formed. He himself would devote his own energies first to spreading the Gospel, using loud-speaker vans to tour urban areas, and to founding new homes. The evangelical vans did not last long, but even before he left the Midhurst Sanatorium he was founding new homes – one at Bromley and another near Worthing and a third in a beautiful old house at Staunton Harold in Worcestershire. It was Leonard's energy and inspiration that got the homes going; it was others who ran them.

The constant challenge of looking for areas of need and responding to them, of finding and encouraging people who would take on the responsibilities of caring for others, suited his restless and energetic nature. Friends and colleagues speak of his compassion, of his capacity to give of himself to others. They also speak of his impulsiveness. As long as he confined his energies to his homes for the chronically ill, his work seemed to prosper. It was when he turned aside to take up some new enthusiasm that things sometimes tended to go wrong. In Leonard's own words:

Things have prospered for me against the odds. If you ask whether I trust in luck I can only answer that I find that if I'm doing what is put before me, then I think it succeeds. If I decide I'd like to go off and do something that strikes me as a good idea, it doesn't succeed. My view is that each one of us is given a place in life. We've each got our particular work to do, whatever that might be, but God all the time is calling us to different things and if he calls us to something and we accept and follow, then I know that we will receive the help we need, even if it's not in the form we want and even if it's after you think the last possible moment has gone. Quite why I was given the opportunity of doing this work I don't know. I don't think I'm really the most likely person to have succeeded in it. But I recognise that as long as I keep within my terms of reference I can expect to get help. Unfortunately, we tend to step outside our terms of reference and get carried away by something that's nothing to do with us. Success can go to your head.

New homes seemed to spring up wherever Leonard went. He spread his work abroad and was delighted to be able to start the first of several Cheshire Homes in India in 1953. Eventually, others were begun, either at his instigation or because people had heard of his work and wished to emulate it, in Canada, Australia, France – all over the world.

In 1959 Leonard married Sue Ryder, a woman of his own generation who had worked for SOE during the war and had been moved by the desperate need of some of the Nazis' victims to start her own foundation. The two organisations did not merge because each had its own separate administration and one foundation tended to complement the work of the other. With Sue, now Lady Ryder, Leonard found happiness as a family man. They had two children – a son and a daughter – and were also able to share a common sense of purpose which helped to enrich their lives. Their work often drew them apart, but it has also brought them together in mutual understanding. Together they established a community which has become important to both of them – a settlement for lepers at Dehra Dun in India known as 'Raphael' – which incorporates many of the ideas they share about helping the chronically ill to live their own lives in security and dignity.

At first sight it might not appear that this magnificent work for the sick could in any way be related to the heroics of World

223

The Second World War

War Two. But it was the RAF at war which first taught Leonard Cheshire what could be achieved by a group of people working towards a common goal. It was war which first awakened him to his own capacity to lead and inspire others and it was war which demonstrated to him the need to work for international peace. The Cheshire Homes are small but important paving-stones along that long and difficult road.

As for courage, who can doubt that he needed courage and a high degree of confidence in his own judgement to take the many risks involved in setting up the early Cheshire Homes? If at times he seemed foolhardy, erratic and impulsive, so was the bomber pilot of the Second World War. But the Victoria Cross was not awarded to Leonard Cheshire for one act of gallantry. It was offered for sustained courage over four years of extremely dangerous operations, for inspired tactical thinking and for qualities of leadership which made others willing to follow him wherever he led. In Jock Moncrieff's words:

> He was a natural leader. He was compassionate, he took care of everyone, he appealed to people and he knew what was going on in his squadron. . . . He had a terrific sort of power over other people, a kind of, what do you call it – magnetism, charisma? Heaven knows what it was but he certainly had it.

Not everyone is complimentary about Leonard Cheshire. Many people find it difficult to reconcile the image of the saintly ascetic today with the pleasure-loving self-publicist they remember. According to some he now 'backs shyly into the limelight' instead of grabbing fame and fortune with both hands. But if a man achieves as much, aims as high as he is aiming and shows as much courage as Leonard Cheshire has shown throughout his life, does it behove any of us to criticise? He is himself more than willing to accept criticism where he thinks it valid. Where he does not, he is just as stubborn and determined to do things his own way as the young group-captain of the war years. Whatever else they may feel about him, no one doubts Leonard Cheshire's ability to get things done.

Frances Jeram has the last word.

> As long as he was there you had the feeling that anything would be possible. . . . Somehow or other it was his faith, or whatever

it was, that the job he wanted to do could be done. And of course patients would have followed him anywhere too, so they put up with any amount of deprivation. It really was deprivation too – no heating, indifferent food, not much comfort and this sort of thing. But he provided them with this home and this chance to live and provided us with a chance to have a hand in this marvellous thing, and so you do follow someone like that, don't you, you must have belief in them. . . . I should think if he came in in that quiet way of his and said, 'Hello, Frances, I've got a new job for you to do,' I expect I should go like a lamb. But it wouldn't be exactly for him – it would be for what he wanted me to do.

Part IV
The Victoria Cross
Today and Tomorrow

Today and Tomorrow

In the forty or more years since the end of the Second World War the Victoria Cross has been awarded only eleven times. This is partly because of a shortage of campaigns available in which to win it, and partly because the Cross itself grows more difficult to win with every year that passes. In the years since the award was first created, many lesser decorations have been instituted, such as the Distinguished Service Order, the Military Cross and the Military Medal, to name but a few. As time has gone by there has been an increasing tendency to reward acts of courage with one of these, rather than the VC itself. The Korean War of the early fifties only yielded four VCs, Vietnam also four – all to the Australian contingent which fought for some years alongside the Americans; and there was one VC awarded to Lance-Corporal Rambahadur Limbu of the 10th Gurkha Rifles in 1965, for an exceptional display of courage during a border incident against Indonesian forces in Sarawak. Lance-Corporal Limbu, later promoted to Captain, was until recently the last serving VC in the British Army.

Prior to the Falklands campaign the most famous of the post-war VCs was undoubtedly that awarded to Private Bill Speakman of the Black Watch, in the legendary 'beer bottle incident' in Korea. At the time Speakman was serving with 'B' Company of the King's Own Scottish Borderers, when their defensive position came under heavy attack from charging masses of Chinese troops. As the enemy advanced, Speakman could see that they had killed or wounded almost every man in one of the forward sections and the position was about to be overrun. Entirely on his own initiative he gathered up as many grenades as he could find, called upon half a dozen other men to follow him and charged down the hillside hurling grenades at the astonished Chinese. Speakman is a very large man and he must have looked a daunting sight. His grenades effectively disposed of the leading enemy troops and severely discouraged the rest. When the enemy returned to the attack he returned to the charge and, despite a severe wound to the leg, he carried on with his bombing runs until the rest of the company had managed to retire and re-organise. The story goes that when the supply of grenades ran out, Speakman seized a pile of beer bottles which happened to be lying around in the bottom of his trench, and hurled these instead, to the even greater terror of the Chinese. Perhaps they were not stupid – in the huge Bill Speakman's hands beer bottles would probably have been almost as lethal as grenades.

That incident took place nearly half a lifetime ago. It was the Falklands War of 1982 which revived interest in the Victoria Cross, just as it revived interest, at least as far as the British public was concerned, in the pursuit of war itself – something which terror of a nuclear holocaust and the effects of humiliating rearguard actions in colonies approaching independence had rendered unfashionable. But the sheer dash and determination of the British assault on the Argentinians revived memories of earlier conflicts. A small and highly professional body of troops from Britain, fighting far from home, had taken on the superior numbers of the enemy and won. In the popular acclaim surrounding this feat the ethics of the conflict were quickly lost to sight and even if there were dissenting voices, that too is part of the British tradition.

The two Victoria Crosses that were awarded during the Falklands conflict illustrate several of the criteria that have become important to the award over the years, in practice if not necessarily in theory. Both of the actions for which the VC was won involved extreme risk – indeed they involved the ultimate risk, since both men died winning it – and both materially affected the outcome of the battle in the areas where they were won. Both actions were also undertaken in the hope of saving the lives of others. There was that element of self-sacrifice, present very strongly in some of the stories told earlier in this book, of Fred Tilston at the Hochwald for instance, of Major Harvey at Jutland, or of Arthur Martin-Leake in South Africa and Belgium. Again and again the same words appear in the written notice in the *London Gazette*: 'with total disregard for his own safety'.

The phrase crops up yet again in the citation for Lieutenant-Colonel 'H' Jones, Commander of the 2nd Battalion of the Parachute Regiment in the battle for Goose Green. This action will go down in military history books as an example of what can be achieved by a determined and well-trained unit against a much larger body of enemy soldiers in strongly fortified positions. On paper everything favoured the Argentinians at Goose Green. Nearly 1600 well-equipped and well-armed men, with close tactical air support, medium and light artillery and mortars, in strong defensive positions, were opposed by only 450 lightly armed men in 2 Para. The British had lost the element of surprise: their intentions and their approximate position had been broadcast to the world on the BBC the night before the attack, following an astonishing lapse in security on the part of the Ministry of Defence in London. And an attacking force is almost always at a disadvantage against an entrenched enemy with plenty of ammunition at his disposal. Most commanders seek a numerical superiority of three to one before even venturing into the attack. If the British Commander of Land Forces, Brigadier Thompson, had known that the boot was on the other foot and that it was the Argentinians who outnumbered the British by three to one it does not seem credible that he would have agreed to send one under-strength battalion into the attack at Goose Green. The Paras relied on their own high morale and fighting skills to defeat the enemy, but hardly a man in the battalion had ever been in action before, not even 'H' Jones himself.

Knowing that he had lost the element of surprise, Jones decided on a night attack, hoping to salvage what advantage he could from superior British training. Goose Green is a small settlement on the far side of a narrow isthmus which connects the two parts of East Falkland. This neck of land is commanded by ridges of higher ground to the north-west around Boca Hill, and to the south-east above the settlement of Darwin. As 2 Para advanced along the isthmus with 'A' and 'B' Companies forward, the leading troops came under heavy fire from Argentinians well entrenched in both positions, and the two companies were brought to a standstill. Colonel Jones did not

231

have enough artillery in support to make any effective impact on the Argentinian positions, and air strikes by RAF Harriers were impossible because of bad weather at sea. The enemy on the other hand were able to use their own ground-attack Purcara planes against 2 Para. The leading companies, pinned down in the open with only gorse and grass hummocks for cover, were beginning to take heavy casualties from Argentinian small-arms and artillery fire.

Jones knew he had to restore the momentum of the attack. He called up the support company with its heavier weapons which included 'Milan' anti-tank missiles, and he himself crawled forward with his tactical headquarters group until he was alongside 'A' Company below Darwin Hill. Piecemeal attempts by small groups of Paras to storm the slopes were repulsed, but Jones knew that if he could get his men moving forward with their customary verve and aggression they would overwhelm the enemy positions and seize the hill. Carefully surveying the hillside in front of him, he spotted an enemy machine-gun nest which was holding up every move forward with well-aimed fire. If he and the men in the tactical headquarters group could take it out, the company should be able to move forward and storm the hill.

Colonel 'H' divided his little group into two. One party would attack straight up the hill while he took another handful of men around the flank. Once on the move they went fast, and the two groups of Paras converged on the enemy position at less than thirty yards' range. But the Argentinians were better soldiers than first reports had suggested. The machine-gun nest was covered by other concealed positions further up the hill. As they charged their objective the Paras came under accurate fire from the concealed machine-guns. Jones himself was hit and rolled down the hillside, but he picked himself up and returned to the attack. As he charged home, firing his own sub-machine-gun from the hip, he was hit again in the back of the neck just a few feet short of his objective and fell again. This time he did not get up.

The citation for his Victoria Cross makes the claim that Jones's attack led directly to the collapse of the Argentinian resistance: 'the devastating display of courage by Colonel Jones had completely undermined their will to fight further'.

Without in any way wishing to diminish the courage of the commanding officer of 2 Para, it does not seem altogether probable that a single action by any one man could have such an extraordinary effect on a well-entrenched enemy. What is certain is that 'A' Company recovered their morale very shortly after Jones's death and made a successful assault on the hill. In that one attack a single company of the Paras, perhaps 80 soldiers in all, killed 30 of the enemy and took 76 prisoners. For an attacking force, short of ammunition and lacking effective artillery support, this was in itself a remarkable achievement. But 2 Para went on to storm the other defensive position on Boca Hill, before overrunning the airstrip, shooting down two of the enemy planes that attacked them, and closing in on Goose Green with such ferocity that the demoralised garrison surrendered the following day. The total losses to 2 Para were 17 dead and 35 wounded, but the enemy dead numbered 250, about 150 more scattered into the hills, and 1200 prisoners went into the bag. By any standards it was a remarkable feat of arms, rendered all the more remarkable by the fact that the Ministry of Defence in London had advance information about the strength of the enemy forces, but had neglected to pass the details on to the troops on the ground. Throughout history British soldiers must often have wondered which side their High Command was fighting on.

'H' Jones's valiant action came in for some criticism, not just from the strategists sitting safely at home but from officers on the ground. A commander's job, the critics said, is to stay alive, not to place his own life at unnecessary risk. But if that rule were to be observed by every commander, many more attacks would have failed. There will always be some officers who believe, like 'H' Jones or Fred Tilston or Roden Cutler at Merdjayoun, that it is their job to lead from the front. In the words of his second-in-command, Major Keeble, who successfully completed the job which 'H' Jones had started: 'He was only doing what he wanted the rest of his battalion to do.'

In the closing phase of the Falklands campaign, as the British converged on Port Stanley, they came up against strong Argentinian positions in the hills overlooking the town. The other airborne battalion, 3 Para, was assigned to Mount

233

The Victoria Cross

Longdon, a rocky ridge rising 600 feet to the north-west of Stanley. The plan called for a pincer movement by 'A' and 'B' Companies to take two enemy positions on either side of the summit. Once the Paras had taken Mount Longdon in a silent night attack, the other British battalions were to move against other positions in the second phase of the battle. But almost as soon as 3 Para crossed their start line they ran into trouble. A corporal stepped on a mine and was badly wounded. Immediately the night sky erupted as the defenders opened up with everything they had. The enemy artillery was poorly directed, but the rifle and machine-gun fire was not. It later turned out that the Argentinians were plentifully equipped with superb night-vision binoculars and rifle-sights. Their shooting was extremely accurate and 3 Para soon began to take casualties.

With the help of an exceptionally well-aimed British artillery barrage, 'A' Company struggled up to their objective on the north side of the hill and then found themselves pinned down by heavy enemy fire. 'B' Company were aiming for the summit itself, but the set-piece attack had by now fragmented into a series of separate little actions by groups of men operating more or less independently. The officer in command of No. 4 Platoon took a party of men forward to reconnoitre the enemy positions, but he was hit in the leg and his platoon sergeant, Ian McKay, took over. The position occupied by the little group of Paras was exposed to heavy enemy fire and McKay realised that if they stayed where they were many of them would be hit and the whole attack would disintegrate. Some of those with him, including the wounded and the dying, were boys whom he himself had looked after throughout their basic training. McKay decided that the best hope of protecting them lay not in trying to hide among the rocks, but in attacking and destroying the enemy positions. Leaving one group to give him covering fire, he led three men in a death-or-glory charge on the enemy bunkers. One of the Paras was killed almost immediately and the other two were wounded, but McKay himself, as the citation once again puts it, 'with complete disregard for his own safety' charged on alone, reached the bunker and hurled a grenade into it before he too dropped dead. The rest of his platoon were able to follow up his lead and the company eventually gained the summit.

234

The fact that the assault was eventually successful demonstrates yet again the importance of courage in action. The military historian John Keegan argues that courage is like a chemical reaction, which in turn causes a chain reaction among those who witness it. The momentum of an attack or the resolution of a defence are strengthened – if only in that one area – by a single act of courage. In warfare there can be no doubt that the kind of actions for which the VC is awarded are an essential component to success.

Unfortunately it seems increasingly to be the case that a man has to die in order to win the Victoria Cross. Of the 1350 or so men who have won the award, 300 died before they could receive the Cross and the proportion of posthumous VCs to those awarded to survivors increased sharply in the Second World War. Two of four Korean VCs were posthumous – a bleak 50 per cent – and for the Falklands the figure was an even bleaker 100 per cent.

To ask whether those that died had the kind of courage which would have stayed with them throughout their lives is academic, if not in outright bad taste. But of those who survived, especially in the early days of the award, it docs seem that a large number of men found it difficult to settle down when their fighting days were done. Some of those whose stories have been chronicled here, like Thomas Flinn of Cawnpore, or James Colliss of Afghanistan, lived more or less miserable lives and died in obscure poverty. No fewer than eighteen recipients of the Cross committed suicide, like the unhappy Valentine Bambrick who was imprisoned for theft, had his VC confiscated, hanged himself in Pentonville Jail and now lies in an unmarked common grave in Islington Cemetery.

In less extreme forms many of the more recent VCs have experienced great difficulties in later life. James Hollis, the only man to win a Cross on D-Day, became deeply depressed after the war and was embittered by the long delay in allowing him a disability pension. He is said to have tried to burn the telegram carrying the news of his award. Bill Speakman's marriage broke up; he sold his VC and left the country in disgust after he quitted the army. James Magennis, whose tenacity and courage as an X-craft submariner won him a VC

235

in the Johore Straights in 1945, was reduced to selling the medal when he fell on hard times. Many others have been driven to take the same course.

Less dramatically, there are men like the Australian VC, Edward Kenna, who saved his entire company from near annihilation by shooting the crews of two Japanese machine-guns in New Guinea in 1945. When the war was over Kenna returned to his home town of Hamilton in Australia, exchanged his rifle for a mop and bucket and served as a caretaker at the town hall for the remainder of his working life. It was an honourable task and he remains a respected figure in the community, but it could not be said that the Victoria Cross had set him on the road to success.

Others had the chance of glory in civilian life and chose to ignore the opportunities that might have opened up for them. Perhaps the most remarkable of these is Charles Upham. He is the only man alive, and one of only three men in the history of the award, to have won the VC and Bar. Unlike Arthur Martin-Leake and Noel Chavasse, he did not win distinction by calmly rescuing wounded comrades under fire, though he certainly performed that service among others. Upham's awards were for extraordinarily aggressive and tenacious leadership in battle, once at Maleme in Crete in 1941 and again at the El Ruweisat Ridge in Egypt in 1942. Asked by King George VI whether the VC and Bar were really appropriate, the New Zealand General, Howard Kippenberger, is said to have replied that 'Captain Upham has won the VC not just twice but many times over'.

When the war was over Upham returned to New Zealand and was immediately approached by influential men who wanted him to go into politics. He is a highly intelligent and thoughtful man and there is no doubt that he could have gone a long way, but he always wanted to be a farmer and when the government resettlement scheme offered him the chance of a farm of his own he was quick to accept it. He turned his back on the city and rejoiced in the peace and relative solitude of the hills of North Canterbury, where he still lives today. But Charles Upham knows that some people expected more of him, that he was under a kind of moral obligation to take part in public life. The resulting pressure has made it difficult for

236

him to recover his peace of mind in the relatively simple life of the New Zealand farmer. He would have much preferred to live in independent anonymity.

That other redoubtable New Zealander, Keith Elliott, experienced the same kind of pressure and responded to it by giving up his farm and becoming an embattled clergyman. The Australian, Sir Roden Cutler, was able to turn the same opportunity to his advantage in embracing a career in public life, and there are many others, especially among the officers who remained in the armed services, who were able to take advantage of the renown of the Victoria Cross and go on to achieve high rank. Most of these men would in all probability have succeeded in their chosen careers whether or not they had ever been singled out for an award on the battlefield. The VC is awarded to men from all classes and backgrounds and is not selective on any basis other than that of courage; and despite the difficulties of those who have found the exposure to glory too much for them, there are many more VCs who have made a success of their lives than one would expect from most other arbitrary cross-sections of the population.

So what does it take to win a VC? Rear-Admiral Godfrey Place ought to know. He won a VC himself, steering an X-craft midget submarine through the hazards of a Norwegian fjord in a daring attack on the German battle-ship *Tirpitz*. Now he is Chairman of the Victoria Cross and George Cross Association and knows all the surviving VCs personally. 'They just happened to catch the selector's eye,' he says. Most of the members of his Association agree, and the answers soon become a familiar refrain: 'Why me? I just happened to be singled out . . . there were hundreds of others who did just as much. I just happened to be the one who was picked out . . . I was just doing my job.' In some cases this may be true; in others it suggests becoming modesty; in others again it is plainly not true, at least to people other than the man in question. No one doubts that there are many brave men who perform courageous actions and happen not to be seen by the selectors. Equally, few people doubt that the men who do win the Victoria Cross have something to be proud of.

If there is one quality, however, that stands out above all others to their friends and relations it is not that VCs are outstandingly brave. It is that they are a stubborn lot. Men like Keith Elliott or Fred Tilston are described as 'pig-headed' by their friends. Admirers of Leonard Cheshire and Sir Roden Cutler use more restrained language and talk of 'determination' and 'single-mindedness'. 'Yes, he was stubborn,' says Freda McKay of her son Ian. 'Once he had made up his mind there was no changing it,' says Sarah Jones of her late husband Colonel 'H'. Ganju Lama is seen as 'inflexible'. Parkash Singh is 'resolute'. All of them are men with a very strong sense of purpose.

The other quality most often remarked upon is an equally strong sense of responsibility for other people. It is most obvious in men like Leonard Cheshire who have devoted their lives to helping those weaker than themselves. It is evident in Ganju Lama's concern for the schoolchildren of Sangmo, in Fred Tilston's grief for the boys who died, in Roden Cutler's work for a hundred different charities, in Keith Elliott's constant support for those in need. In the case of most of these men, and very many others who have won the Cross, the sense of responsibility developed early in their lives and has remained with them ever since. In this connection it is remarkable how many VCs – like Sir Roden Cutler, Ganju Lama, Fred Tilston and Freddy West – lost one or other of their parents when they themselves were children. Others, like Keith Elliott, had fathers who were often away or unable, for one reason or another, fully to support their wives and children. Either way, the embryonic VCs had to accept a measure of responsibility for their brothers and sisters at a very early age. Even when both parents were present throughout childhood, as with Ian McKay's mother and father, there were often younger children who had to be cared for and protected by their big brother.

Stubbornness and a sense of responsibility are one thing, courage another. Or is it? 'Courage,' says Freda McKay, with rare insight, 'is caring more for other people than you do for yourself.' She saw that quality in her own son when he looked after his younger brothers, who were both smitten with that cruel disease, cystic fibrosis. She saw it again when he rushed forward on Mount Longdon – attacking the Argentinians, certainly, but also protecting the boys in his platoon in the best way he knew, by sacrificing his own life for theirs. Those

238

telling words 'complete disregard for his own safety' are almost invariably coupled with a reference to the way in which this one man's action enabled the rest of his unit to press on with the battle unhindered by further casualties. The same implicit message runs right back through the history of the award to the first ever VC, Lucas's action on the deck of the *Hecla* in the Straits of Bomarsund, when he hurled the live shell overboard. He too risked his own life to save others.

In peace-time the opportunities for the highest degree of heroism are less frequent and usually less dramatic. Where they occur they are of course honoured with the award of the George Cross rather than the VC. But the combination of dogged determination and a regard for others also finds expression in quite undramatic aspects of life. Who will ever know just how much routine pain is endured by a man like Fred Tilston in forcing himself to walk on his artificial legs? To complain of pain is to inflict discomfort on others. To be in constant need of assistance or support is to burden others. Amputees like Fred or Sir Roden or Freddy West have kept quiet about their pain and learned to walk by themselves as well as they possibly could. We talk of people who overcome their disabilities in this way as having a lot of guts. We know that this means determination, but we also know that they are sparing our own feelings by keeping theirs to themselves.

There is one more characteristic shared by many of those who have won the VC, and that is the element of daring – the calculated risk of the gambler who works out the odds and the possible gains and is prepared to take the chance, knowing very well that it may not come off. 'Who dares, wins.' The well-known motto of the SAS would also serve as a motto for many VCs. Leonard Cheshire demonstrated the art of the calculated risk in a hundred bombing missions and went on to take hundreds more when he began his post-war career as a philanthropist. Very stupid and very insensitive men may not be aware of fear, but they rarely see an opportunity even when it is presented to them. Almost all of the men whose stories are told here will admit, under pressure, that there were times when they felt fear, but they will also explain that by one means or another they found a way to overcome it. To do that

The Victoria Cross

and at the same time be able to see a chance and take it demands the cool head of the gambler.

Plainly, not all recipients of the VC are stubborn, coolheaded gamblers with a high degree of social responsibility. But some or all of these characteristics do seem to crop up in a high proportion of them just as a high proportion go on to lead useful lives as peaceful citizens of the Commonwealth. Since they are all now more or less advanced in years they will not be able to do so for very much longer. By definition the award of a Victoria Cross demands a war and, even given the remarkable enthusiasm for bellicose activity which Britain and her Allies have shown over the past 125 years, there are unlikely to be a great many of them in the future. The Falklands' police action and its aftermath are estimated by some sources to have cost more than £4 billion pounds so far. Even little wars these days are extremely expensive, and it does not seem probable that we could afford many more like it, even if we had the inclination. If of course war becomes general and the nuclear missiles start flying it seems even less likely that there will be any need for heroes. So the Victoria Cross may one day become extinct.

Every two years or so an ever-diminishing band of old heroes assembles in London for a meeting of the Victoria Cross and George Cross Association. The Association enjoys the patronage of Her Majesty the Queen, and the President is Queen Elizabeth, the Queen Mother, but despite the honour in which members of the Association are held, the material rewards of winning a VC are still negligible. The pension which was worth something in 1857 when it was fixed at £10 is worth far less today at £100, and Admiral Place believes that this is as it should be. The award was always intended to be without cash value and it is only the sad vagaries of fashion that have made the Cross so valuable in the auction room. No one can buy courage, and the purpose of the Association is to ensure that courage is not forgotten. Admiral Place explains it like this:

> Once in your lifetime you're first to meet the Monarch. You head the queue right in front of all the KCBs and that sort of thing, and the main purpose of our Association is to ensure that

those who have won the award should not feel that they never get to the front line of things again; when they come to our reunions they are important people and I think that does them good.

The Victoria Cross is still at the head of the queue. It still takes precedence over all other awards, including distinctions as notable as the Order of Merit, but there are fewer than seventy men still alive who can put the coveted letters VC after their name. As the late Brigadier Jacky Smyth, founding Chairman of the Association, once put it: 'We would not have it otherwise, because any increase in our membership would mean another war, an occurrence utterly abhorrent to the holders of this decoration.'

I have said that it seems unlikely that there will be another war of the kind that brings a large crop of VCs, but it is not impossible, and it may be that the nature of war does not change – however much it might appear to do so. Many of the Russians who died when the British stormed the Heights of the Alma at the outset of the Crimean War were killed at the point of a bayonet. Many of the Argentinians who died defending Mount Longdon in the Falklands Campaign also fell to British bayonets. War has changed apparently out of all recognition with supersonic aircraft, missiles, and the threat of nuclear extermination, but every war that was ever fought and every war that ever will be, depends in the end on the individual quality of the men who fight it. War is appalling and may never achieve anything, but it has a sad habit of recurring all over the world with fearful regularity. If war ever does come to us again in any guise other than instant obliteration for all, we will once again be in need of individual courage in battle, the kind of courage which has won for a few the award which King Edward VIII once called 'the most democratic and at the same time the most exclusive of all orders of chivalry – the most enviable Order of the Victoria Cross'.

Bibliography

Abbott, P. E. and Tamplin, J. M. A., *British Gallantry Awards*
(Guinness Superlatives, London, 1971)
Blackmore, H. L., *The Armouries of the Tower of London*
(Volume I, *Ordnance*) (HMSO, 1976)
Bowyer, Chaz, *For Valour – The Air VCs* (William Kimber,
London, 1978)
Boyle, Andrew, *No Passing Glory* (Collins, London, 1955)
Braddon, Russell, *Cheshire VC – A Study of War and Peace*
(Evans Brothers, London, 1954)
Cheshire, Group-Captain Leonard vc, om, *Bomber Pilot*
(Hutchinson, London, 1955)
——, *Face of Victory* (Hutchinson, London, 1961)
Crook, M. J., *The Evolution of the Victoria Cross* (Midas Books,
Tunbridge Wells, 1975)
Cruttwell, C. R. M. F., *History of the Great War 1914–18*
(Paladin, London, 1982)
Dorling, H. Taprell, (revised by Alec A. Purves), *Ribbons and
Medals* (Osprey Publishing, London, 1983)
Elliott, The Rev. Keith vc and Adshead, Rona, *From Cowshed
to Dog Collar* (A. H. & A. W. Reed, Auckland, 1967)
Farrar-Hockley, General Sir Anthony mc, *The Somme*
(Batsford, London, 1964)
Farwell, Byron, *The Gurkhas* (Allen Lane, London, 1984)
Flower, Desmond and Reeves, James, *The War 1939–45* (two
vols.) (Cassell, London, 1960)
Foxley-Norris, Air Chief Marshal Sir Christopher (ed.),
Royal Air Force At War (Ian Allan, London, 1983)
Fraser, Ian, vc, *Frogman VC* (Angus and Robertson, London,
1957)

Bibliography

Fuller, Major-General J. F. C., *The Second World War* (Eyre and Spottiswoode, London, 1948)

Granatstein, J. L. & Morton, Desmond, *Bloody Victory* (Lester and Orpen Dennis, Toronto, 1984)

Hastings, Max and Jenkins, Simon, *The Battle for the Falklands* (Michael Joseph, London, 1983)

Keegan, John, *The Face of Battle* (Jonathan Cape, London, 1976)

——, *Six Armies in Normandy* (Jonathan Cape, London, 1982)

Liddell-Hart, Captain, B. H., *History of the First World War* (Cassell, London, 1930)

——, *History of the Second World War* (Cassell, London, 1960)

Lucas-Phillips, Brigadier C. E., *Victoria Cross Battles of the Second World War* (Heinemann, London, 1973)

——, *Springboard to Victory* (Heinemann, London, 1966)

Macdonald, Lyn, *They Called It Passchendaele* (Macmillan, London, 1978)

——, *The Somme* (Michael Joseph, London, 1983)

Mason, Philip, *A Matter of Honour – An Account of the Indian Army and Its Men* (Jonathan Cape, London, 1974)

Moran, Lord, *The Anatomy of Courage* (Constable, London, 1966 – first pub. 1945)

Mundell, Frank, *Stories of the Victoria Cross* (The Sunday School Union, London, 1895)

Owen, Lieutenant-Colonel Frank, OBE, *The Campaign in Burma* (Published for HMSO by the Whitefriars Press, London, 1946)

Parry, D. H., *Britain's Roll of Glory* (Cassell, London, 1898)

Roe, F. Gordon, *The Bronze Cross* (P. R. Gawthorn, London, 1945)

Slim, Field-Marshal, the Viscount William, *Defeat Into Victory* (Cassell, London, 1962 – first pub. 1956)

Smyth, Sir John VC, *The Story of the Victoria Cross* (Frederick Muller, London, 1962)

——, *Great Stories of the Victoria Cross* (Arthur Baker, London, 1977)

243

Bibliography

Sunday Times Insight Team, *The Falklands War* (Sphere Books, London, 1982)

Taylor, A. J. P., *The First World War* (Hamish Hamilton, London, 1963)

Thompson, R. W., *The Battle for the Rhineland* (Hutchinson, London, 1958)

Williams, Alister, *The VCs of Wales and the Welsh Regiments* (Bridge Books, Wrexham, 1984)

Wilkins, F. A., *The History of the Victoria Cross* (Constable, London 1904)

Winton, John, *The Victoria Cross At Sea* (Michael Joseph, London, 1978)

Index

Index

246

Index

247

Index

Index

Index

251

Index

Index

Index

Index